# Azure Cookbook
*Recipes to Create and Maintain*
*Cloud Solutions in Azure*

*Reza Salehi*

Beijing · Boston · Farnham · Sebastopol · Tokyo

**Azure Cookbook**

by Reza Salehi

Copyright © 2023 Reza Salehi. All rights reserved.

Published by O'Reilly Media, Inc., 1005 Gravenstein Highway North, Sebastopol, CA 95472.

O'Reilly books may be purchased for educational, business, or sales promotional use. Online editions are also available for most titles (*http://oreilly.com*). For more information, contact our corporate/institutional sales department: 800-998-9938 or *corporate@oreilly.com*.

**Acquisitions Editor:** Jennifer Pollock
**Development Editor:** Jeff Bleiel
**Production Editor:** Beth Kelly
**Copyeditor:** Penelope Perkins
**Proofreader:** Amnet Systems, LLC

**Indexer:** Potomac Indexing, LLC
**Interior Designer:** David Futato
**Cover Designer:** Karen Montgomery
**Illustrator:** Kate Dullea

July 2023:            First Edition

**Revision History for the First Edition**
2023-06-22:    First Release

See *http://oreilly.com/catalog/errata.csp?isbn=9781098135799* for release details.

978-1-098-13579-9

[LSI]

*Dedicated to my mother, Farideh, who gave me life and unconditional support.*

# Table of Contents

# Preface

As an IT professional, I have always been fascinated by the world of cloud computing and the endless possibilities it presents. Azure, in particular, stood out to me as a platform that offered a comprehensive range of services and tools for businesses of all sizes. With its ability to simplify the development, deployment, management, and scaling of applications, it has a significant potential to revolutionize the way organizations operate.

Global end-user spending on public cloud services is expected to reach $591.8 billion in 2023 (*https://oreil.ly/1as4t*), up from $490.3 billion in 2022, a 20.7% growth. This creates a huge demand for cloud professionals to fill in the job market talent gap. I had the opportunity to work on a wide range of Azure solutions for businesses of all sizes in the past few years, giving me a perspective on challenges that companies can face in a cloud journey. As a Microsoft Certified Trainer (MCT), I had the privilege of sharing this perspective with thousands of IT professionals. This book aims to enable you to quickly acquire hands-on expertise with the key Azure services and concepts. I hope you use this book as a reference to solve common, yet fundamental, challenges in your Azure cloud projects.

## Who Should Read This Book

This book is for cloud architects, developers, and engineers at all experience levels. Beginners will use the recipes in this book to familiarize themselves with the fundamental Azure services and gain hands-on experience with them. Expert cloud professionals will use this book to enhance their Azure projects, solve common architecture problems, and gain further perspectives. The recipes in this book showcase how multiple Azure services can be combined to deliver immediate value for you, regardless of your Azure expertise level. This book is for you, if you like to learn about a diverse set of Azure services for security, networking, big data, storage, databases, AI, containers, serverless, and web apps.

# Why I Wrote This Book

Writing this book was my way of contributing to the cloud revolution by sharing my experience with other professionals and enthusiasts. I wanted to create a resource that would not only provide an overview of a wide variety of Azure platform services but also guide readers through practical, hands-on scenarios and use cases. My aim was to equip professionals with the necessary skills to leverage Azure's capabilities and help organizations drive their digital transformation. By writing this book, I hope to inspire others to fully embrace the power of Azure and the future of cloud computing.

# Navigating This Book

The hands-on recipes in this book are organized into the following chapters:

- Chapter 1, "Security", provides methods to improve the security of Azure resources through *RBAC*, role-based access control, and network firewalls.
- Chapter 2, "Networking", reviews *Azure Virtual Network (VNet)* security, routing, and monitoring.
- Chapter 3, "Storage", provides recipes for *Azure storage accounts*, enabling you to optimize cost, secure your data, and protect it against accidental deletion.
- Chapter 4, "Persisting Data", provides guidelines to configure and protect the main Azure relational and NoSQL databases, Azure SQL and Azure Cosmos DB.
- Chapter 5, "Messaging and Events", enables you to set up reliable messaging between your services and solutions using Azure's messaging suite of services.
- Chapter 6, "Big Data", introduces Azure services, including *Azure Stream Analytics*, *Azure Synapse Analytics*, *Azure Databricks*, and *Azure Data Factory*, designed to mine insights from your big data.
- Chapter 7, "Azure Functions and Serverless Services", provides recipes to implement microservices using *Azure Function Apps*.
- Chapter 8, "Azure App Service", provides recipes to configure autoscaling, secure network access, and deploy App Services using several methods.
- Chapter 9, "Containers", introduces Azure services designed to host and run containerized applications in Azure.
- Chapter 10, "Azure Cognitive Services", helps you develop smart applications by using *Azure Cognitive Services*. Recipes in this chapter enable you to gain insights from images, audio, and text content using AI-backed services.
- Chapter 11, "Management and Monitoring", introduces tools to monitor and control Azure service costs and then reviews *Azure Monitor* platform logs.

# What You Will Need

Here are the resources and tools you need to get the most out of this book:

- Azure account (subscription):
  - See the Azure documentation (*https://oreil.ly/RgQz8*) for setup instructions. You'll need a user with Owner (administrative) access (*https://oreil.ly/-erDG*) over your subscription.
- Personal computer with Windows, macOS, or Linux OS
- Software:
  - A supported web browser (*https://oreil.ly/wW145*) (e.g., Microsoft Edge or Google Chrome).
  - Terminal with Bash or Z shell (Zsh).
  - Git (see the installation instructions (*https://oreil.ly/YRPog*)).
  - A code editor (e.g., VS Code, VSCodium). You can access the bash terminal from VS Code.
  - Azure CLI version 2.42 or later (see the installation instructions (*https://oreil.ly/EY5R9*)).
- The book repository (*https://oreil.ly/qqVmJ*):
  - Clone it (*https://oreil.ly/892Vc*) to a local folder on your machine.

# Getting Started

The recipes in this book use Azure CLI to provision and manage Azure resources. This section provides details to help you run Azure CLI commands on your workstation. Feel free to skip this section if you are already comfortable with Azure CLI.

 Although many Microsoft Azure services offer free tiers (*https://oreil.ly/yiLiQ*), Azure is a paid cloud service and you will be charged for any services that you create in the paid pricing tiers. To avoid getting charged, clean up (delete) any provisioned resource after completing a recipe. See the recipe cleanup section in the book repository (*https://oreil.ly/XgNH0*) for details.

## Azure Account Setup

You need a user with the subscription administrator (Owner) permissions. This user account enables you to create resources and identities as well as configure the permissions that are needed to complete the recipes in this book. Your Azure subscription comes with a default administrator account, which can be used. You can also create a Co-Administrator (*https://oreil.ly/EGikF*) user if preferred.

## General Workstation Setup Instructions

1. The CLI scripts used in this book can be found in the book repository (*https://oreil.ly/XgNH0*). Create a folder called *AzureCookbook* in any directory you prefer and set it as the current folder:

   ```
   mkdir ~/AzureCookbook
   cd ~/AzureCookbook
   ```

2. Now, let's clone the book repository into your current folder:

   ```
   git clone https://github.com/zaalion/AzureCookbook.git
   ```

3. Microsoft Azure provides several regions (locations). We use "eastus" in this book, but you can choose any region you like. Run the following command to get a list of all Azure regions:

   ```
   az account list-locations --output table
   ```

4. Store your desired region name in the following variable:

   ```
   region="eastus"
   ```

5. Set a default location for Azure CLI commands. This location will be used if no location is passed to the CLI command:

   ```
   az config set defaults.location=eastus
   ```

6. Log in to Azure CLI using your Azure subscription administrator username and password. Replace *<username>* and *<password>* with your admin account credentials:

   ```
   az login -u "<username>" -p "<password>"
   ```

    Running az login without passing account credentials will open a browser window where you can enter your username/password.

7. You should create your Azure resources in a parent container called a *resource group* (*https://oreil.ly/2tTdO*). Before starting each recipe, you have to create a new resource group. Replace *<resource-group-name>* with the desired name (*https://oreil.ly/irohg*). Store the resource group name in the rgName variable as shown in the following command. You will use rgName in every recipe:

```
rgName="<resource-group-name>"

az group create \
  --location $region \
  --name $rgName
```

You can alternatively run your commands in the Azure Cloud Shell (*https:// oreil.ly/Zzo_X*), as shown in Figure P-1.

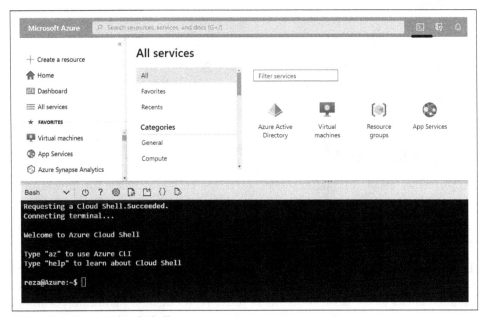

*Figure P-1. Azure Cloud Shell*

# Conventions Used in This Book

The following typographical conventions are used in this book:

*Italic*
> Indicates new terms, URLs, email addresses, filenames, and file extensions.

`Constant width`
> Used for program listings, as well as within paragraphs to refer to program elements such as variable or function names, databases, data types, environment variables, statements, and keywords.

`Constant width italic`
> Shows text that should be replaced with user-supplied values or by values determined by context.

This element signifies a tip or suggestion.

This element signifies a general note.

This element indicates a warning or caution.

# Using Code Examples

Supplemental material (code examples, exercises, etc.) is available for download at *https://github.com/zaalion/AzureCookbook*.

If you have a technical question or a problem using the code examples, please send email to *support@oreilly.com*.

This book is here to help you get your job done. In general, if example code is offered with this book, you may use it in your programs and documentation. You do not need to contact us for permission unless you're reproducing a significant portion of the code. For example, writing a program that uses several chunks of code from this book does not require permission. Selling or distributing examples from O'Reilly books does require permission. Answering a question by citing this book and quoting example code does not require permission. Incorporating a significant amount of example code from this book into your product's documentation does require permission.

We appreciate, but generally do not require, attribution. An attribution usually includes the title, author, publisher, and ISBN. For example: "*Azure Cookbook* by Reza Salehi (O'Reilly). Copyright 2023 Reza Salehi, 978-1-098-13579-9."

If you feel your use of code examples falls outside fair use or the permission given above, feel free to contact us at *permissions@oreilly.com*.

# O'Reilly Online Learning

 For more than 40 years, *O'Reilly Media* has provided technology and business training, knowledge, and insight to help companies succeed.

Our unique network of experts and innovators share their knowledge and expertise through books, articles, and our online learning platform. O'Reilly's online learning platform gives you on-demand access to live training courses, in-depth learning paths, interactive coding environments, and a vast collection of text and video from O'Reilly and 200+ other publishers. For more information, visit *https://oreilly.com*.

# How to Contact Us

Please address comments and questions concerning this book to the publisher:

O'Reilly Media, Inc.
1005 Gravenstein Highway North
Sebastopol, CA 95472
800-889-8969 (in the United States or Canada)
707-829-7019 (international or local)
707-829-0104 (fax)
*support@oreilly.com*
*https://www.oreilly.com/about/contact.html*

We have a web page for this book, where we list errata, examples, and any additional information. You can access this page at *https://oreil.ly/azure-cookbook*.

For news and information about our books and courses, visit *https://oreilly.com*.

Find us on LinkedIn: *https://linkedin.com/company/oreilly-media*

Follow us on Twitter: *https://twitter.com/oreillymedia*

Watch us on YouTube: *https://youtube.com/oreillymedia*

# Acknowledgments

Thank you to Jennifer Pollock for giving me the opportunity to showcase my technical writing skills and bring my book to life. I am grateful for your support.

I appreciate the O'Reilly Media team. Thank you to the development editor, Jeff Bleiel. Your guidance, suggestions, and insights enabled me to refine my work and bring this book to life. Thank you also to the production editor, Elizabeth Kelly, for getting this book in the best shape for release.

Thank you to the book reviewers for taking the time to share your thoughts and opinions on my work: Dipal Choski, George Mount, Hakan Silfvernagel, and Peter De Tender. Your feedback is greatly appreciated.

## CHAPTER 1

# Security

Data breaches happen frequently these days. Hacker and malicious users target IT systems in small, mid-sized, and big organizations. These attacks cost millions of dollars every year, but cost is not the only damage. Targeted companies will be on the news for days, weeks, or even years, and they may suffer permanent damage to their reputation and customer base. In most cases, lawsuits will follow.

You might be under the impression that public cloud services are very secure. After all, companies such as Microsoft spend millions of dollars improving their platform security. But applications and data systems hosted in Microsoft's public cloud (as well as clouds of other providers) are not immune to cyberattacks. In fact, they are more prone to data breaches because of the public nature of the cloud.

It is critical to understand that cloud security is a common responsibility shared between Microsoft Azure and you. Azure provides data center physical security, guidelines, documentation, and powerful tools and services to help you protect your workloads. It is your responsibility to correctly configure resource security. For example, Azure Cosmos DB can be configured to accept traffic from only a specific network, but the default behavior allows all clients, even from the public internet.

 Cloud security is an evolving subject. Microsoft Azure continues to introduce new security features to protect your workloads against new threats. Microsoft maintains the Azure security best practices and patterns documentation (*https://oreil.ly/HGgKo*), which you can consult for the most up-to-date security best practices.

We chose security as the topic for the first chapter of this book to deliver this important message: Security must come first! You should have security in mind while designing, implementing, and supporting your cloud projects. In this chapter, we'll share useful recipes showing how to secure key Azure services and then use these recipes' outcomes throughout the book.

 We cover important Azure security topics in this chapter. However, it is not possible to cover all topics related to Azure security. Azure services and capabilities continue to evolve on a daily basis. You must consult the Microsoft documentation (*https://oreil.ly/Lzn6M*) for a complete and updated list.

## Workstation Configuration

You will need to prepare your workstation before starting on the recipes in this chapter. Follow "What You Will Need" on page xi to set up your machine to run Azure CLI commands. Clone the book's GitHub repository using the following command:

```
git clone https://github.com/zaalion/AzureCookbook.git
```

# 1.1 Creating a New User in Your Azure Account

## Problem

The *Owner* (administrator) account has far more permissions than are needed for everyday development tasks. You need to create a new user account for a developer with just enough permissions to complete assigned tasks.

## Solution

First, create a new user in your *Azure Active Directory* (*Azure AD*). Then assign the *Contributor* role-based access control (RBAC) role to that user, so enough permissions are assigned without granting this user the same permission level as the Owner. An architecture solution diagram is shown in Figure 1-1.

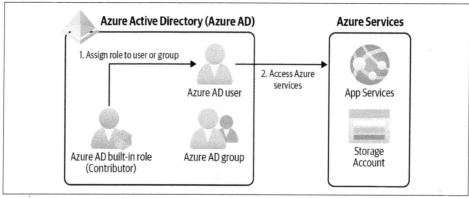

*Figure 1-1. Assigning a built-in role to Azure AD users/groups*

## Steps

1. Log in to your Azure subscription in the Owner role. See "General Workstation Setup Instructions" on page xii for details.

2. Visit the Default Directory | Overview page (*https://oreil.ly/sG2rN*) in the Azure portal to find your primary Azure Active Directory tenant domain name, as shown in Figure 1-2.

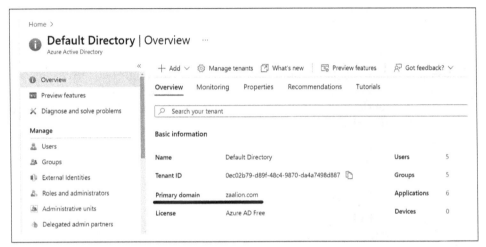

*Figure 1-2. Finding your Azure AD tenant primary domain*

3. Create a new user in Azure AD. Replace *<password>* with the desired password and *<aad-tenant-name>* with your Azure AD tenant domain name. This could be the default domain name ending with *onmicrosoft.com*, or a custom domain registered in your Azure Active Directory (e.g., *zaalion.com*):

```
password="<password>"

az ad user create \
  --display-name developer \
  --password $password \
  --user-principal-name developer@<aad-tenant-name>
```

 Use a strong password with lowercase and uppercase letters, numbers, and special characters. Choosing a strong password is the first, and the most important, step to protect your Azure subscription.

4. The user account you created does not have any permissions. You can fix that by assigning an Azure RBAC role (*https://oreil.ly/J8vj2*) to it. In this recipe, we go

---

with the Contributor built-in role, but you can choose any role that matches your needs. The Contributor RBAC role (*https://oreil.ly/og8SP*) grants full access to resources but does not allow assigning roles in Azure RBAC or managing Azure Blueprints assignments. You assign an RBAC role to an assignee, over a scope. In our case, the assignee is the user you just created, the role name is Contributor, and the scope is the current Azure subscription. First, store your subscription ID in a variable:

```
subscriptionId=$(az account show \
  --query "id" --output tsv)

subscriptionScope="/subscriptions/"$subscriptionId
```

5. Use the following CLI command to assign the Contributor role to the *developer@<aad-tenant-name>* user account. If you're prompted to install the Account extension, answer Y. You can now use the new *developer* account to complete this book's recipes:

```
MSYS_NO_PATHCONV=1 az role assignment create \
  --assignee "developer@<aad-tenant-name>" \
  --role "Contributor" \
  --scope $subscriptionScope
```

Git Bash automatically translates resource IDs to Windows paths, which causes this command to fail. Simply add MSYS_NO_PATH CONV=1 in front of the command to temporarily disable this behavior. See the Bash documentation (*https://oreil.ly/V4Zti*) for more details.

6. Run the following command to check the new role assignment. In the output, look for the roleDefinitionId field. Its value should end with /role Definitions/b24988ac-6180-42a0-ab88-20f7382dd24c, which is the Contributor role definition ID:

```
az role assignment list \
  --assignee developer@<aad-tenant-name>
```

## Discussion

It is not a security best practice to use a high-privileged account, such as the Owner (administrator), to perform day-to-day development, monitoring, and testing tasks. For example, a developer tasked only with reading a Cosmos DB container data does not need permission over other resources in the subscription.

Azure has several built-in RBAC roles for general and specific services. The Contributor RBAC role gives access to all Azure services. You could use service-specific roles if your user only needs to work with a single service. For example, the Cosmos DB

Operator role only allows managing a Cosmos DB database. Check the Microsoft documentation for a complete list of built-in roles (*https://oreil.ly/D21a_*).

> Granting a higher access level than needed to a user is a recipe for disaster. You have to identify which tasks a user needs to perform, and only grant the required access to their account. This is referred to as the *principle of least privilege* (*https://oreil.ly/9reIA*).

In this recipe, we assigned the Contributor role to our developer user account. This enables our user to manage all Azure services except RBAC roles and assigning Blueprints. See the Contributor RBAC role documentation (*https://oreil.ly/2J_hz*) for more details. If the Azure built-in RBAC roles do not exactly align with your needs, you can create custom RBAC roles and assign them to users. We will look at this in the next recipe.

# 1.2 Creating a New Custom Role for Our User

## Problem

You need to grant a limited set of permissions to a user, group, or Azure AD principal. There is no built-in Azure RBAC role that offers these exact permissions.

## Solution

First create a custom Azure role, then assign the role to the users, groups, or principals (see Figure 1-3).

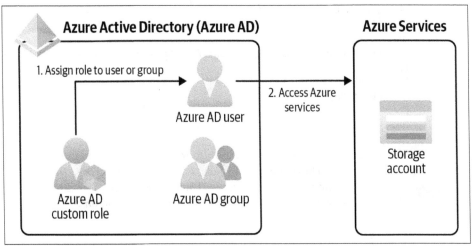

*Figure 1-3. Assigning a custom role to an Azure AD user/group*

## Steps

1. Log in to your Azure subscription in the Owner role. See "General Workstation Setup Instructions" on page xii for details.

2. Take note of the user account you created in Recipe 1.1. Later in this recipe, we will assign our custom role to this user.

3. When defining a custom role, you need to specify a *scope*. The new role will only be available in the passed scopes. A scope can be one or more Azure subscriptions or management groups. Run the following command to find your current subscription ID:

   ```
   subscriptionId=$(az account show \
     --query "id" --output tsv)

   subscriptionScope="/subscriptions/"$subscriptionId

   echo $subscriptionScope
   ```

4. We need a custom Azure role that enables users to read data blobs in Azure storage accounts. Create a JSON file with the following content, name the file *CustomStorageDataReader.json,* and save it on your machine. Next, replace *<subscription-scope>* with the value of the $subscriptionScope variable from the previous step. Since we only need to read blobs, the only action we need to add is Microsoft.Storage/storageAccounts/blobServices/containers/blobs/read. Check the Microsoft documentation (*https://oreil.ly/sEKj0*) for the complete list of Actions and DataActions you can use in your custom roles:

   ```
   {
     "Name": "Custom Storage Data Reader",
     "IsCustom": true,
     "Description": "Read access to Azure storage accounts",
     "DataActions": [
       "Microsoft.Storage/storageAccounts/blobServices/containers/blobs/read"
     ],
     "AssignableScopes": [
       "<subscription-scope>"
     ]
   }
   ```

    Make sure that the Actions are added to the correct section in the JSON file. These sections include Actions, DataActions, Not Actions, and NotDataActions. See "Understand Azure role definitions" (*https://oreil.ly/Kc1RK*) for more detail on role sections.

5. We have the custom role definition ready, so now we can create the custom role:

---

```
az role definition create \
  --role-definition CustomStorageDataReader.json
```

6. Your custom RBAC role is now created and can be assigned to users or groups the same way the built-in roles are assigned. In our case, the assignee is the user you previously created, the role name is Custom Storage Data Reader, and the scope is the current Azure subscription. In addition to users and groups, you can assign Azure roles to other Azure AD principals, such as managed identities and app registrations.

7. Use the following CLI command to assign the Custom Storage Data Reader role to the developer user account:

```
MSYS_NO_PATHCONV=1 az role assignment create \
  --assignee "developer@<aad-tenant-name>" \
  --role "Custom Storage Data Reader" \
  --scope $subscriptionScope
```

The developer user now has read access to all Azure Storage Account blobs within your subscription.

## Discussion

Custom roles are perfect for situations in which you need to assign exactly the right amount of permissions to a user. Access to multiple services can also be granted using custom roles. The role definition JSON files can be stored in a source control system and deployed using Azure CLI, Azure PowerShell, or even ARM templates. You can assign multiple RBAC roles to a user or group. Our test user has both Contributor and Custom Storage Data Reader assigned. In real-world scenarios, you will need to remove the Contributor role from your user, because it gives many more permissions compared to the custom role.

There might be an existing built-in role that satisfies the user needs and does not give more permissions than needed. Make sure to check the Microsoft documentation for built-in roles (*https://oreil.ly/1LdlJ*) before investing time in creating a custom role.

# 1.3 Assigning Allowed Azure Resource Types in a Subscription

## Problem

You need to limit the Azure resource types that subscription users can create.

## Solution

Assign the "Allowed resource type" Azure policy to the management group, subscription, or resource group scopes, with the list of allowed resource types as the policy parameter. An architecture diagram of this solution is shown in Figure 1-4.

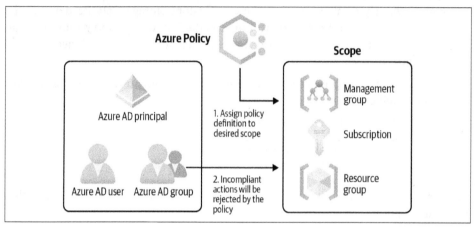

*Figure 1-4. Assigning an Azure policy to a scope*

### Steps

1. Log in to your Azure subscription in the Owner role. See "General Workstation Setup Instructions" on page xii for details.

2. First you need to find the Azure policy ID for "Allowed resource types." Use the following command to get this ID:

```
policyName=$(az policy definition list \
    --query "[?displayName == 'Allowed resource types'].name" --output tsv)
```

3. Use the following command to get the list of available policy IDs and names:

```
az policy definition list \
    --query "[].{Name: name, DisplayName: displayName}"
```

4. If your policy definition has parameters, you need to provide them at assignment time. In our case, we need to tell the policy which resources we intend to allow in our subscription. Create a JSON file with the following content and name it *allowedResourcesParams.json*:

```
{
  "listOfResourceTypesAllowed": {
    "value": [
        "Microsoft.Storage/storageAccounts"
    ]
  }
}
```

5. Now we have all we need to create the *policy assignment*. Use the following command to assign the policy definition to your subscription. For simplicity, we are only allowing the creation of Azure storage accounts in this subscription. In most cases, you need to allow multiple resources for your projects:

```
az policy assignment create \
   --name 'Allowed resource types in my subscription' \
   --enforcement-mode Default \
   --policy $policyName \
   --params allowedResourcesParams.json
```

We set the policy --enforcement-mode to Default. This prevents new resources from being created if they are not in the allowed list. You can also set the enforcement mode to DoNotEnforce, which allows the resources to be created, and only reports policy noncompliance in the logs and policy overview page.

6. If you leave this policy assignment in place, only Azure storage accounts can be deployed to your subscription. We need to deploy several other resource types in this cookbook, so let's delete this policy assignment now:

```
az policy assignment delete \
   --name 'Allowed resource types in my subscription'
```

## Discussion

Use Azure policy to govern your Azure resources and enforce compliance. Say you only want to allow your team to deploy Azure storage accounts and Cosmos DB to the *development* subscription. You could rely on your team to follow these guidelines, and hope that they comply, or you could use policies to enforce them. The latter is a safer approach.

There are numerous built-in policies, which you can assign to desired scopes. You can use these policies to allow or deny provisioning certain resource types, or to limit the regions that resources can be deployed to.

If you need enforcement, make sure the --enforcement-mode value is set to Default, not DoNotEnforce.

Several built-in policies are designed to improve your Azure subscription security. You can find the built-in policy definitions and names in the Azure portal, or by using tools such as Azure CLI. Azure also offers policies targeting specific Azure resource types; for instance, the "Storage account keys should not be expired" policy, when assigned, makes sure the Storage Account keys don't expire. Take a look at the Microsoft documentation (*https://oreil.ly/tfBHe*) for more details on policies.

# 1.4 Assigning Allowed Locations for Azure Resources

## Problem

You need to limit the locations (regions) Azure resource can be provisioned in.

## Solution

Assign the "Allowed locations" policy to the management group, subscription, or resource group, with the list of allowed Azure regions as the policy parameter.

### Steps

1. Log in to your Azure subscription in the Owner role. See "General Workstation Setup Instructions" on page xii for details.

2. First you need to find the ID of the "Allowed locations" Azure policy. Use the following command to get this ID:

   ```
   policyName=$(az policy definition list \
       --query "[?displayName == 'Allowed locations'].name" --output tsv)
   ```

3. If your policy definition has parameters, you need to provide them at assignment time. In our case, we need to tell the policy which Azure regions we intend to allow in our subscription. Create a JSON file with the following content and name it *allowedLocationParams.json*:

   ```
   {
     "listOfAllowedLocations": {
       "value": [
           "eastus",
           "westus"
       ]
     }
   }
   ```

4. Use the following command to assign the policy definition to the active subscription:

   ```
   az policy assignment create \
       --name 'Allowed regions for my resources' \
       --enforcement-mode Default \
       --policy $policyName \
       --params allowedLocationParams.json
   ```

5. You can modify the *allowedLocationsParams.json* parameter file to pass your desired locations to the policy assignment. Use the following CLI command to get the list of available locations:

```
az account list-locations --query "[].name"
```

 Use the --scope parameter with az policy assignment create command to define the scope for the policy assignment. The scope can be one or more management groups, subscriptions, resource groups, or a combination of these. If not mentioned, the default scope will be the current active subscription.

6. You can use the following command to delete this policy assignment:

```
az policy assignment delete \
   --name 'Allowed regions for my resources'
```

You successfully assigned the "Allowed locations" policy definition to our subscription. From now on, the resources can only be deployed to the eastus and westus Azure regions.

## Discussion

Many countries and regions have *data residency laws* in effect. This means the user data should not leave its geographical jurisdiction. The EU's General Data Protection Regulation (GDPR), which prohibits EU residents' data leaving EU boundaries, is an example of such a law. The "Allowed locations" Azure policy is the perfect tool to enforce compliance to standards such as GDPR.

# 1.5 Connecting to a Private Azure Virtual Machine Using Azure Bastion

## Problem

You need to connect to an Azure virtual machine using RDP or SSH. Your Azure virtual machine (VM) is a *private VM*, meaning it does not have a public IP address.

## Solution

Deploy an *Azure Bastion host* resource to the same virtual network (VNet) as your Azure VM. Then, you can use SSH or RDP to access your Azure VM. A private Azure VM has no public IP address, making it invisible to the public internet. See the solution architecture diagram in Figure 1-5.

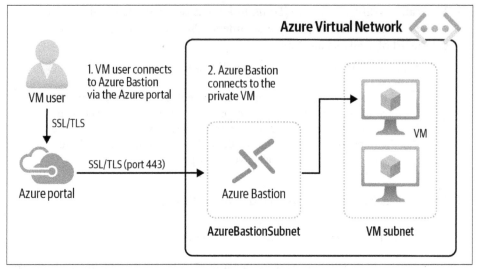

*Figure 1-5. Using Azure Bastion to connect to a private Azure VM*

## Steps

1. Log in to your Azure subscription in the Owner role and create a new resource group for this recipe. See "General Workstation Setup Instructions" on page xii for details.

2. Now, let's create a new Azure VM. Every Azure VM is deployed to an Azure VNet. The following command provisions a new Azure VM and places it into a new VNet with the *10.0.0.0/16* address space. By passing an empty string for `--public-ip-address`, you create a private Azure VM, with no public IP address. The `--nsg-rule SSH` parameter configures SSH connectivity for your new VM:

```
az vm create --name MyLinuxVM01 \
    --resource-group $rgName \
    --image UbuntuLTS \
    --vnet-address-prefix 10.0.0.0/16 \
    --admin-username linuxadmin \
    --generate-ssh-keys \
    --authentication-type ssh \
    --public-ip-address "" \
    --nsg-rule SSH \
    --nsg "MyLinuxVM01-NSG"
```

It is recommended to use SSH keys to authenticate into Linux VMs. You can also use a username/password combination. By passing `--authentication-type ssh`, you configured this VM to only allow authentication using SSH keys. See the CLI documentation (*https://oreil.ly/ybfFh*) and "Connect to a Linux VM" (*https://oreil.ly/eoT-a*) for details.

3. The previous command generated a new SSH key pair (both private and public keys) and saved them on your machine. The path to the private key can be found in the command output, for example */home/reza/.ssh/id_rsa*, as shown in Figure 1-6. Make a note of the private key filepath. You will need to upload this key to the Bastion service to log in to your new VM.

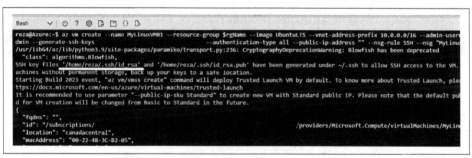

*Figure 1-6. Saving the SSH key on your local machine*

4. Use the following command to get the details of the new virtual network created as part of your VM provisioning. You will need this name to configure your new Azure Bastion host in the next steps:

```
vnetName=$(az network vnet list \
    --resource-group $rgName \
    --query "[].name" --output tsv)
```

5. For security reasons, the Azure VM we created does not have a public IP address. One option you have for connecting to this VM is to use Azure Bastion. This service allows both SSH and RDP connections. Before creating an Azure Bastion host, you need to create a *public IP* resource and a new subnet in the VNet named `AzureBastionSubnet`. This IP will be assigned to the Bastion host—not the Azure VM:

```
ipName="BastionPublicIP01"

az network public-ip create \
    --resource-group $rgName \
    --name $ipName \
    --sku Standard
```

6. Now create the new subnet, `AzureBastionSubnet`, using the following command. Azure Bastion will be deployed to this subnet:

```
az network vnet subnet create \
    --resource-group $rgName \
    --vnet-name $vnetName \
    --name 'AzureBastionSubnet' \
    --address-prefixes 10.0.1.0/24
```

The subnet name must be exactly `AzureBastionSubnet`; otherwise, the `bastion create` CLI command returns a validation error.

7. Now, you can create an Azure Bastion resource using the following command. Make sure the `$region` variable is populated. See "General Workstation Setup Instructions" on page xii for more details. If you're prompted to install the Bastion extension, answer Y:

```
az network bastion create \
    --location $region \
    --name MyBastionHost01 \
    --public-ip-address $ipName \
    --resource-group $rgName \
    --vnet-name $vnetName
```

Provisioning of Azure Bastion may take up to 10 minutes.

8. Wait for the preceding command to succeed. Now, you can connect to the VM using the Bastion host. Log in to the Azure portal and find your new Virtual Machine (*https://oreil.ly/odtzK*). Click on it, and from the top left menu, select Connect > Bastion, as shown in Figure 1-7.

9. Fill in the username. For Authentication type, choose SSH Private Key from Local File and choose your private SSH key file. Then click on the Connect button, as shown in Figure 1-8.

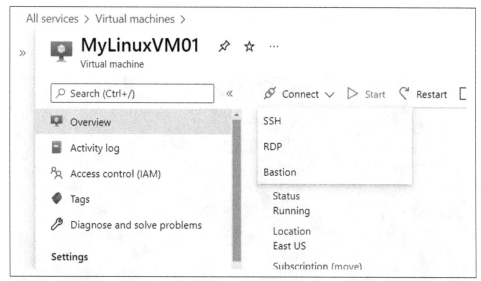

*Figure 1-7. Choosing Bastion as the connection method*

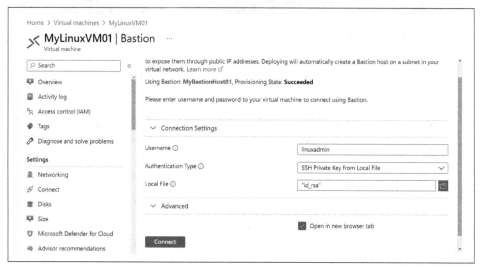

*Figure 1-8. Entering the VM username and uploading the SSH key*

10. You should see the Linux command prompt, as shown in Figure 1-9.

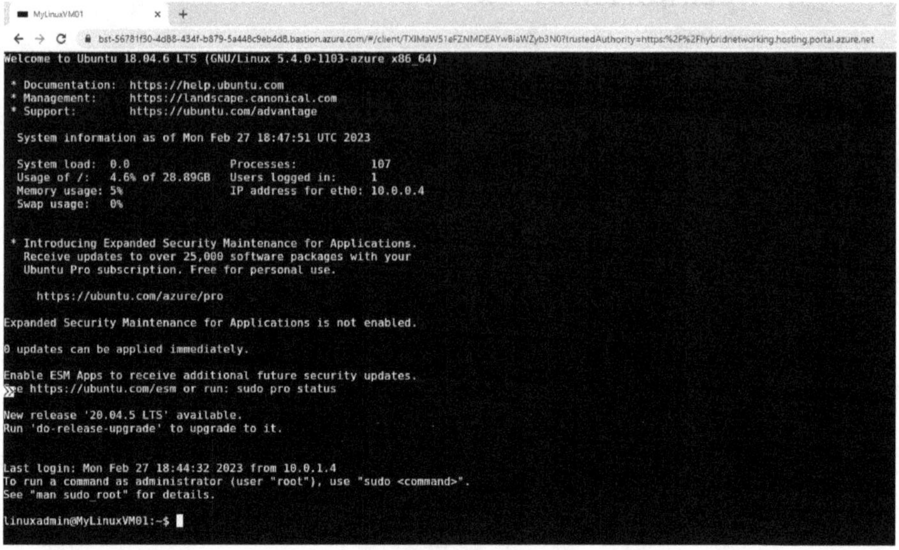

*Figure 1-9. Logging in to the Azure VM using Azure Bastion*

11. Run the following command to delete the resources you created in this recipe:

```
az group delete --name $rgName
```

Azure Bastion is a paid service. Make sure that you run the command in this step to delete the VM, the Bastion host, and their dependencies.

In this recipe, you connected to a private VM using an Azure Bastion host.

## Discussion

Azure Bastion acts as a managed *jump server*, *jump box*, or *jump host*. You use it to manage private Azure VMs. Before the Bastion service was introduced, Azure administrators had to create their own jump box machines, or even expose the Azure VM to the internet via a public IP address. Features such as JIT access or Azure Firewall could be used to improve the security to the connection, but exposing a VM via public IP address is never a good idea.

You can authenticate to Azure Linux VMs with either passwords or SSH keys. Azure Bastion also supports the use of SSH keys with the Linux VMs.

# 1.6 Protecting Azure VM Disks Using Azure Disk Encryption

## Problem

You need to encrypt your Azure VM disks using BitLocker or dm-crypt to protect your data or meet your company's security and compliance standards.

## Solution

Create an encryption key in Azure Key Vault, and use it to configure *BitLocker* (Windows VM) or *dm-crypt* (Linux VM) encryption for your Azure VMs (see Figure 1-10).

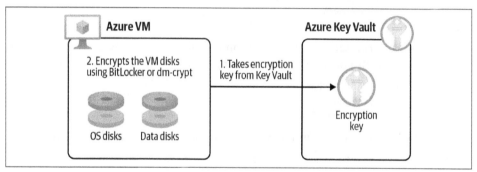

*Figure 1-10. Using Azure Disk Encryption to protect an Azure VM*

### Steps

1. Log in to your Azure subscription in the Owner role and create a new resource group for this recipe. See "General Workstation Setup Instructions" on page xii for details.

2. Create a new Windows VM using the following CLI command. Replace <*vm-password*> with a secure password:

```
vmName="MyWinVM01"

az vm create \
    --resource-group $rgName \
    --name $vmName \
    --image win2016datacenter \
```

```
    --admin-username cookbookuser \
    --admin-password <vm-password>
```

3. You need an *Azure Key Vault* resource to store your disk encryption key in. You can create an Azure Key Vault resource with the following CLI command. The `--enabled-for-disk-encryption` parameter makes this Key Vault accessible to Azure VMs. Replace *<key-vault-name>* with a unique name for your new Azure Key Vault resource:

```
kvName="<key-vault-name>"

az keyvault create \
  --name $kvName \
  --resource-group $rgName \
  --location $region \
  --enabled-for-disk-encryption
```

4. Now the stage is set to enable Azure Disk Encryption for our Windows VM:

```
az vm encryption enable \
  --resource-group $rgName \
  --name $vmName \
  --disk-encryption-keyvault $kvName
```

5. You can confirm Azure Disk Encryption is enabled by logging in to the machine, and check the BitLocker status, or by using the following CLI command:

```
az vm encryption show \
  --name $vmName \
  --resource-group $rgName
```

6. Run the following command to delete the resources you created in this recipe:

```
az group delete --name $rgName
```

We successfully enabled Azure Disk Encryption for our Windows VM using Azure Key Vault and BitLocker. Azure Disk Encryption automatically created a new *secret* in the Key Vault to store the disk encryption key. This encryption is also available for Linux VMs (via dm-crypt). Refer to the Microsoft documentation (*https://oreil.ly/ 2iC_M*) for greater details.

## Discussion

In this scenario, we enabled Azure Disk Encryption for an Azure Windows VM. This encryption happens at the Windows OS level using the familiar BitLocker technology.

Azure VM disks are stored as blob objects in Azure Storage. Microsoft Azure offers another encryption type for Azure VMs as well. This encryption is called *server-side encryption* (*SSE*) and happens at the Azure disk storage level. You can enable both (*https://oreil.ly/hZ-BR*) Azure Disk Encryption and SSE for greater protection.

Encrypting your Azure VM OS and data disks protects your data in the highly unlikely event that the Azure data center machines are compromised. In addition, many organizations require VM disks to be encrypted to meet their compliance and security commitments.

# 1.7 Blocking Anonymous Access to Azure Storage Blobs

## Problem

You need to prevent developers from accidentally granting anonymous public access to Azure Storage blobs and containers.

## Solution

Set the `--allow-blob-public-access` flag to `false` programmatically, or set the "Allow Blob public access" field to Disabled in the Azure portal (see Figure 1-11). This can be set for both new and existing storage accounts.

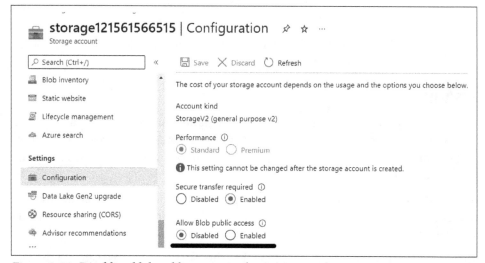

*Figure 1-11. Disabling blob public access in the Azure portal*

### Steps

1. Log in to your Azure subscription in the Owner role and create a new resource group for this recipe. See "General Workstation Setup Instructions" on page xii for details.

2. Create a new Azure storage account. Replace `<storage-account-name>` with the desired name. See the storage account naming documentation for naming rules

and restrictions (*https://oreil.ly/tcXrF*). Set `--allow-blob-public-access` to `false` so that developers can't allow anonymous blob and container access:

```
storageName="<storage-account-name>"
```

```
az storage account create \
   --name $storageName \
   --resource-group $rgName \
   --location $region \
   --sku Standard_LRS \
   --allow-blob-public-access false
```

3. You can use the following CLI command to configure the same safeguard for an existing storage account:

```
az storage account update \
   --name $storageName \
   --resource-group $rgName \
   --allow-blob-public-access false
```

4. Run the following command to delete the resources you created in this recipe:

```
az group delete --name $rgName
```

Refer to "Configure Anonymous Public Read Access for Containers and Blobs" (*https://oreil.ly/tyZap*) for more details.

## Discussion

When a storage account container or blob is configured for public access, any user on the web can access it without any credentials. Disabling `--allow-blob-public-access` prevents developers from accidentally removing protection from storage account blobs and containers.

Setting the `--allow-blob-public-access` flag to `true` does not enable anonymous access for container and blobs. It leaves the door open for developers to accidentally, or intentionally, enable that access.

In some scenarios, you might need to make your blobs publicly available to the web (for example, to host images used by a public website). In these scenarios, it is recommended to create a separate storage account meant only for public access. Never use the same storage account for a mixture of public and private blobs.

You can assign the Azure policy "Storage account public access should be disallowed" (*https://oreil.ly/FP389*) to govern disabling anonymous public access.

---

# 1.8 Configuring an Azure Storage Account to Exclusively Use Azure AD Authorization

## Problem

You want to prevent an Azure storage account from accepting storage keys and SAS tokens for authorization. Doing this leaves users with the more secure Azure AD authentication/authorization method.

## Solution

Set the `--allow-shared-key-access` flag to `false` programmatically, or set the "Allow storage account key access" field to Disabled in the Azure portal (see Figure 1-12). This can be configured for both new and existing storage accounts.

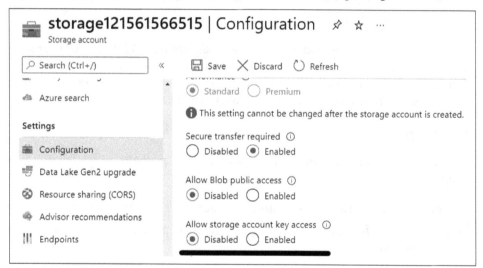

*Figure 1-12. Setting "Allow storage account key access" to Disabled in the Azure portal*

### Steps

1. Log in to your Azure subscription in the Owner role and create a new resource group for this recipe. See "General Workstation Setup Instructions" on page xii for details.

2. If you have an existing storage account, skip to the next step. If not, use this command to create a new storage account. Replace *<storage-account-name>* with the desired name and set the `--allow-shared-key-access` flag to `false`:

```
storageName="<storage-account-name>"

az storage account create \
  --name $storageName \
  --resource-group $rgName \
  --location $region \
  --sku Standard_LRS \
  --allow-shared-key-access false
```

3. You can use the following CLI command to configure this setting for an existing storage account:

```
az storage account update \
  --name $storageName \
  --resource-group $rgName \
  --allow-shared-key-access false
```

4. Run the following command to delete the resources you created in this recipe:

```
az group delete --name $rgName
```

You disabled Allow storage account key access (*https://oreil.ly/eLPmW*) for your storage account. This means that clients such as Azure Functions, App Services, etc. can access this storage account using only Azure AD authentication/authorization. Any request using storage account keys or SAS tokens will be denied.

## Discussion

Azure storage accounts support multiple authorization methods, which fall into two groups:

- Key-based access, such as using storage account keys, or SAS tokens
- Azure Active Directory access using an Azure AD principal, user, or group, and an RBAC role

Some organizations prefer the second method, because no password, account key, or SAS token needs to be stored or maintained, resulting in a more secure solution.

See the Azure documentation for greater details on storage account authentication and authorization (*https://oreil.ly/BRnQj*).

> You can assign the Azure policy "Storage accounts should prevent shared key access" to govern storage accounts to only accept Azure AD-based requests. See the Azure documentation (*https://oreil.ly/UHWWc*) to read more about this policy.

# 1.9 Storing and Retrieving Secrets from Azure Key Vault

## Problem

You need to safely store and retrieve passwords, database connections, and other sensitive data in Azure.

## Solution

Store your secrets, keys, and certificates in the *Azure Key Vault* service. Give access to clients to read the secrets from the Key Vault when needed. The flow is shown in Figure 1-13.

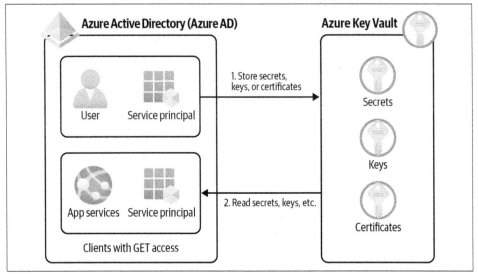

*Figure 1-13. Storing and accessing keys, secrets, and certificates in Azure Key Vault*

### Steps

1. Log in to your Azure subscription in the Owner role and create a new resource group for this recipe. See "General Workstation Setup Instructions" on page xii for details.

2. First create a new Azure Key Vault service using this CLI command. Replace *<key-vault-name>* with a valid, globally unique name:

```
kvName="<key-vault-name>"

az keyvault create --name $kvName \
  --resource-group $rgName \
  --location $region
```

3. Now use this command to create a secret in the Key Vault:

```
az keyvault secret set \
  --name MyDatabasePassword \
  --vault-name $kvName \
  --value P@$$w0rd
```

4. Your secret is now stored in the Azure Key Vault. Only clients with "Get" secret access policy can read this secret from the vault. This permission can be given to managed identities, Azure AD service principals, or even user and groups. You already logged in to the CLI as the Owner account, so you should be able to read the secret value back. Look for the value property in the command output:

```
az keyvault secret show \
  --name MyDatabasePassword \
  --vault-name $kvName
```

5. Run the following command to delete the resources you created in this recipe:

```
az group delete --name $rgName
```

## Discussion

Azure Key Vault is Azure's safe to store sensitive data. Three types of entities can be stored in a vault:

*Secrets*
Any custom value you need to safeguard, such as database connection strings or account passwords

*Keys*
Encryption keys used by other Azure services to encrypt disks, databases, or storage accounts

*Certificates*
X.509 certificates used to secure communications between other services

Entities stored in the Key Vault can be accessed by other client Azure services, provided that the client has the right access to the vault. This access can be defined by either the Azure Key Vault Access Policy (*https://oreil.ly/L62D-*) or the Azure Key Vault RBAC (*https://oreil.ly/c-8QL*).

Here are a few of these client services and what they are used for:

- Azure Function Apps and App Services, so secrets such as database connection strings can be fetched from the Key Vault at runtime
- Azure Cosmos DB or Azure Storage, so customer managed keys for encryption can be used for Cosmos DB encryption at rest

- Azure VMs, so encryption keys from the vault can be used to encrypt VM managed disks
- Azure Application Gateway, so SSL certificates in the key vault can be used to secure HTTPS communications

There are several other use cases for Azure Key Vault, which we will discuss throughout this book.

# 1.10 Enabling Web Application Firewall (WAF) with Azure Application Gateway

## Problem

You need to protect your Azure web applications from common web attacks such as SQL injection.

## Solution

Deploy an *Azure Application Gateway* resource in front of your web application, and enable WAF on it, as shown in Figure 1-14.

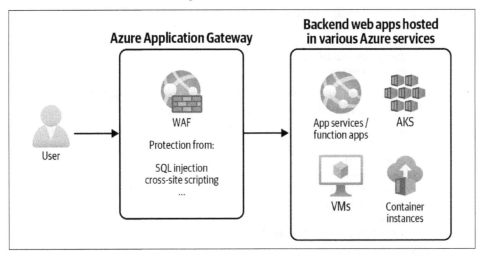

*Figure 1-14. Protecting your web applications with Azure Application Gateway WAF*

WAF is one of the *Azure Application Gateway* features. Azure Application Gateway is a web load balancer with a rich set of capabilities. Setting up an Azure Application Gateway involves creating HTTP listeners, routing rules, etc. See Application Gateway CLI documentation (*https://oreil.ly/BtvDk*) for details.

## Steps

1. Log in to your Azure subscription in the Owner role and create a new resource group for this recipe. See "General Workstation Setup Instructions" on page xii for details.

2. First create a simple App Service plan and an Azure web app in it. Your goal is to protect this web application from common web attacks. Replace *<web-app-name>* with the desired name:

```
appName="<web-app-name>"
planName=$appName"-plan"

az appservice plan create \
  --resource-group $rgName \
  --name $planName

az webapp create \
  --resource-group $rgName \
  --plan $planName \
  --name $appName
```

3. With the web application created, use this command to save its URL in a variable. We will use this variable when configuring Application Gateway:

```
appURL=$(az webapp show \
  --name $appName \
  --resource-group $rgName \
  --query "defaultHostName" \
  --output tsv)
```

4. Azure Application Gateway is deployed to an Azure VNet. So, first use this command to create a new Azure VNet, with a default subnet:

```
vnetName="AppGWVnet"

az network vnet create \
  --resource-group $rgName \
  --name $vnetName \
  --address-prefix 10.0.0.0/16 \
  --subnet-name Default \
  --subnet-prefix 10.0.0.0/24
```

5. Your Azure App Service web application will be accessible through the new Azure Application Gateway, so you need to create a new public IP address to be assigned to the Application Gateway. Use the following command to provision the public IP address:

```
gwIPName="appgatewayPublicIP"

az network public-ip create \
  --resource-group $rgName \
```

```
    --name $gwIPName \
    --sku Standard
```

6. Web Application Firewall Policies (*https://oreil.ly/tPMFw*) contain all the Application Gateway WAF settings and configurations, including managed security rules, exclusions, and custom rules. Let's use the following command to create a new WAF policy resource with the default settings:

```
wafPolicyName="appgatewayWAFPolicy"

az network application-gateway waf-policy create \
    --name $wafPolicyName \
    --resource-group $rgName
```

7. You have all the resources needed to create a new Azure Application Gateway. Make sure to deploy the WAF_Medium, WAF_Large, or WAF_v2 SKUs. The WAF_v2 SKU is the latest WAF release—see the WAF SKUs documentation (*https://oreil.ly/p8UtB*) for details. Replace *<app-gateway-name>* with the desired name:

```
appGWName="<app-gateway-name>"

az network application-gateway create \
    --resource-group $rgName \
    --name $appGWName \
    --capacity 1 \
    --sku WAF_v2 \
    --vnet-name $vnetName \
    --subnet Default \
    --servers $appURL \
    --public-ip-address $ipName \
    --priority 1001 \
    --waf-policy $policyName
```

 An Azure Application Gateway deployment can take up to 15 minutes.

8. You successfully provisioned a new WAF-enabled Azure Application Gateway. Now configure your web application to accept traffic only from the Application Gateway subnet so that end users can't directly access the App Service web app anymore. See Recipe 8.5 for a step-by-step guide. Accessing your web application through Azure Application Gateway (with WAF) protects it from common web attacks (*https://oreil.ly/BjN9z*) such as SQL injection. Run the following command to get the public IP address for your Application Gateway. This IP address

(as well as custom domain names) can be used to access your web application through Azure Application Gateway:

```
IPAddress=$(az network public-ip show \
  --resource-group $rgName \
  --name $gwIPName \
  --query ipAddress \
  --output tsv)

echo $IPAddress
```

 Before your App Service can be accessed through Azure Application Gateway, HTTP listeners, health probes, routing rules, and backends should be properly configured. Check the Azure Application Gateway documentation (*https://oreil.ly/JWi7z*) and Application Gateway HTTP settings configuration (*https://oreil.ly/N6LGG*) for details.

9. Run the following command to delete the resources you created in this recipe:

```
az group delete --name $rgName
```

## Discussion

At the time of authoring this book, two Azure services support the WAF feature:

- Azure Application Gateway for backends in the same Azure region
- Azure Front Door for backends in different regions

WAF protects your web applications against common web attacks such as:

- SQL injection
- Cross-site scripting
- Command injection
- HTTP request smuggling
- HTTP response splitting
- Remote file inclusion
- HTTP protocol violations

Check the WAF features documentation (*https://oreil.ly/dJDro*) for a complete list of supported features.

## CHAPTER 2

# Networking

Every Azure service needs the right network connectivity to securely communicate with other dependencies and service clients. The processed data should be fed to downstream services over a secure connection. To reduce the attack surface, services such as Azure Cosmos DB need to limit the incoming requests to desired networks only. Microservices deployed to Azure Functions, Azure Kubernetes Service, or Azure Container Instances need to connect to one another in an efficient and secure manner. These are just a few examples of the hundreds of services that are available. Under the hood, these communications are achieved using Azure networking infrastructure. At the core of this infrastructure sits *Azure Virtual Network*.

If you are a developer, DevOps, or infrastructure professional, understanding Azure networking helps you to correctly (and securely) configure your Azure solutions and to see the bigger picture when doing so. Long story short, networking is the foundation of almost every Azure service we discuss in this book.

The recipes in this chapter are carefully selected to convey key Azure networking concepts. They are also easy to implement using a personal Azure subscription. You can find details on more advanced services such as ExpressRoute, VPNs, and Azure Virtual WAN in this chapter's GitHub repository (*https://oreil.ly/wq3WD*).

 Similar to other Azure services, Azure networking is continuously changing for the better. Consult the Microsoft documentation (*https://oreil.ly/O_MH6*) for new updates and apply the relevant changes to your cloud networking solutions.

## Workstation Configuration

You will need to prepare your workstation before starting on the recipes in this chapter. Follow "What You Will Need" on page xi to set up your machine to run Azure CLI commands. Clone the book's GitHub repository using the following command:

```
git clone https://github.com/zaalion/AzureCookbook.git
```

# 2.1 Creating an Isolated Private Network by Provisioning an Azure Virtual Network

## Problem

You need to create an isolated private network in Azure to protect your resources from requests originated from unwanted networks and IP addresses.

## Solution

Provision an Azure Virtual Network (VNet), create one or more subnets in it, and place your resources, such as Azure VMs, in the desired subnets as shown in Figure 2-1.

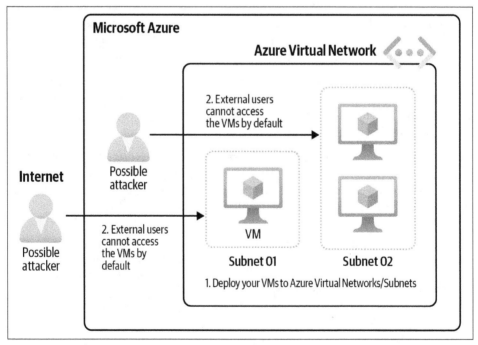

*Figure 2-1. Isolate your Azure resources by deploying them to Azure VNet subnets*

**Steps**

1. Log in to your Azure subscription in the Owner role and create a new resource group for this recipe. See "General Workstation Setup Instructions" on page xii for details.

2. Create a new Azure VNet, and a default subnet using the following CLI command. Replace *<vnet-name>* with the desired network name:

```
vnetName="<vnet-name>"

az network vnet create \
    --resource-group $rgName \
    --name $vnetName \
    --address-prefix 10.0.0.0/16 \
    --subnet-name Subnet01 \
    --subnet-prefix 10.0.0.0/26
```

> Pass the desired CIDR range (*https://oreil.ly/QUWJM*) to the `--address-prefix` and `--subnet-prefix` parameters to set the size of your VNet and its subnets. 10.0.0.0/16 will give you 65,536 IP addresses.

3. By doing this, you created a new Azure VNet, with 65,536 IP addresses, and a child subnet with 64 IP addresses (10.0.0.0/26). In Recipe 2.2, you'll add more subnets to your VNet. Use the following CLI command to get details on your new Azure VNet:

```
az network vnet show \
    --resource-group $rgName \
    --name $vnetName
```

In this recipe, you successfully provisioned a new Azure Virtual Network. You will use this network in the other recipes in this chapter.

## Discussion

Azure VNet is the building block of your private network in the Azure cloud. Azure resources (VMs, App Services, Function Apps, etc.) use Azure VNets to securely communicate with each other, the internet, and even on-premises (local) networks.

Many Azure resources (*https://oreil.ly/lNjSQ*) support virtual network integration. Use the virtual network integration feature to isolate those resources from public networks and the internet. For instance, you can configure a Cosmos DB database to accept requests only from a specific Virtual network. This protects your database from unwanted clients and attackers, and improves your Azure subscription security posture (*https://oreil.ly/_l-gL*).

## 2.2 Creating a Network Layout in Azure Virtual Networks Using Subnets

### Problem

You want to divide your Azure VNet into several subnetworks (subnets) for organization, and security. Later you will deploy Azure resources into these subnets.

### Solution

Create one or more subnets in your Azure VNet. Then, multiple resources can be placed into these subnets (see Figure 2-2).

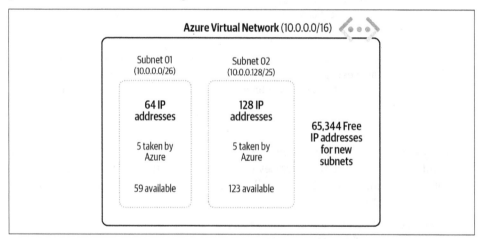

*Figure 2-2. Dividing your Azure VNet into several subnets and deploying resources into them*

### Steps

1. Log in to your Azure subscription in the Owner role and create a new resource group for this recipe. See "General Workstation Setup Instructions" on page xii for details.

2. Create an Azure VNet. Refer to Recipe 2.1 if you're unsure of the steps.

3. Our VNet, which we created in Recipe 2.1, already has one subnet, Subnet01. You can use the following command to list all the subnets within an Azure VNet. Replace *<vnet-name>* with the desired VNet name:

```
vnetName="<vnet-name>"

az network vnet subnet list \
    --resource-group $rgName \
    --vnet-name $vnetName \
    --query "[].name"
```

4. Your VNet already has a subnet with the 10.0.0.0/26 address prefix (address space). This makes the last used IP 10.0.0.64. Create the second subnet with 128 IP addresses, and let's choose a new address space, such as 10.0.0.128/25, for the new subnet using the following command:

```
az network vnet subnet create \
    --resource-group $rgName \
    --vnet-name $vnetName \
    --name Subnet02 \
    --address-prefixes 10.0.0.128/25
```

5. Run the CLI command in step three to list all the subnets in your VNet. You should see two subnets.

## Discussion

Azure subnets are the main Azure network security pillar. Resources such as VMs should be deployed to an Azure subnet. Other Azure resources, such as Azure App Service Environment, Azure API Management, Azure Functions Premium, and more can be deployed to subnets. Almost all Azure network security services such as Azure Firewall, network security groups (NSGs), and Azure route tables are designed to work with Azure subnets.

Before creating a new subnet in your VNet, make sure you know which IP ranges are already taken by existing subnets, and choose the next available free range. Subnets within the same Azure VNet can't have any overlapping address. You can resize deployed Azure subnets, if there is available growing space in the parent VNet. It is a good practice to understand how big your subnet needs to be and allocate the right address space in the first place.

In this recipe we created a new subnet. Keep this subnet; we will configure its egress traffic to go through Azure Firewall later in this chapter.

> Azure reserves the first four and the last IP addresses within each subnet. For instance, the 10.0.0.0/26 address prefix gives you only 59 free IP addresses. See the Azure documentation (*https://oreil.ly/vOMV9*) for details.

# 2.3 Routing Network Traffic Using User-Defined Routes

## Problem

You need to route outgoing subnet traffic to Azure and/or on-premises networks and/or internet resources.

## Solution

Create an Azure route table, add one or more custom routes to it, and associate the new route table with your subnets as shown in Figure 2-3.

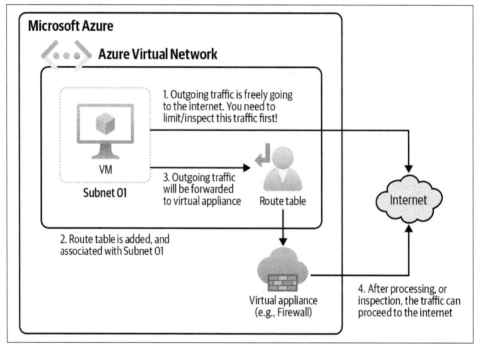

*Figure 2-3. Routing outgoing subnet traffic to Azure, on-premises, or internet resources*

### Steps

1. Log in to your Azure subscription in the Owner role and create a new resource group for this recipe. See "General Workstation Setup Instructions" on page xii for details.

2. Create an Azure VNet. Refer to Recipe 2.1 for details.

3. Our VNet already has two subnets. Use the following command to list the subnets within your VNet. Replace *<vnet-name>* with the desired VNet name:

```
vnetName="<vnet-name>"

az network vnet subnet list \
    --resource-group $rgName \
    --vnet-name $vnetName \
    --query "[].name"
```

4. Create a new *route table* resource using the following command. Replace *<route-table-name>* with your desired name:

```
routeTableName="<route-table-name>"

az network route-table create \
    --resource-group $rgName \
    --name $routeTableName
```

5. Our goal is to forward all egress (outgoing) subnet traffic to the internet. Use the `--next-hop-type` parameter to set the type of Azure hop the packet should be sent to. Accepted values are `Internet`, `None`, `VirtualAppliance` (for example an Azure Firewall service), `VirtualNetworkGateway`, and `VnetLocal`. See the Azure documentation (*https://oreil.ly/A_LVQ*) for details. Now, use the following command to add your first custom route to the new route table. Replace *<custom-route-name>* with the desired name for your custom route table:

```
routeName="<custom-route-name>"

az network route-table route create \
    --resource-group $rgName \
    --route-table-name $routeTableName \
    --name $routeName \
    --next-hop-type Internet \
    --address-prefix 0.0.0.0/0
```

 The 0.0.0.0/0 address prefix will match any destination address (*https://oreil.ly/ZBsVi*) that does not have routes already defined.

6. Now we need to associate this route table with our subnet. As you remember, the name of our default subnet was Subnet01:

```
az network vnet subnet update \
    --resource-group $rgName \
    --name Subnet01 \
    --vnet-name $vnetName \
    --route-table $routeTableName
```

7. From this point, all egress traffic from Subnet01 will be forwarded to the internet. This is useful when you have a resource such as an Azure VM that needs to access the internet from your subnet.

8. Run the following command to delete the resources you created in this recipe:

```
az group delete --name $rgName
```

## Discussion

Microsoft Azure automatically creates a system (default) route table for each subnet and adds system default routes (*https://oreil.ly/iiELF*) to it. You can't update or delete these routes, but you can override them. In this recipe, you learned how to override these system routes by creating and assigning a custom route table.

One of the main use cases for custom routes (route tables) is to forward all the outgoing subnet traffic to a *virtual appliance* such as the Azure Firewall service. This enables you to monitor, secure, and limit the subnet traffic. We will look at this scenario in the next recipe.

# 2.4 Securing Azure Virtual Networks with Azure Firewall

## Problem

You need to improve your Azure network infrastructure security by forwarding all the egress subnet traffic to Azure Firewall.

## Solution

Provision a new Azure Firewall resource and use a route table to forward all the egress subnet traffic to the Azure Firewall as shown in Figure 2-4.

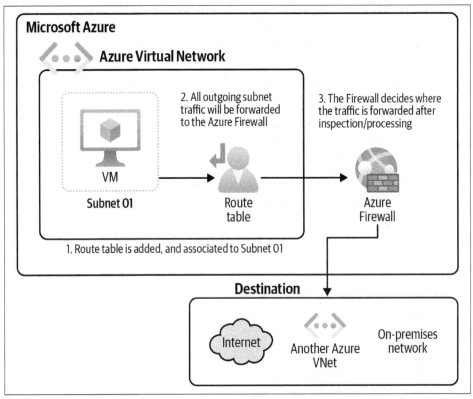

Microsoft Azure

Azure Virtual Network

VM

Subnet 01

2. All outgoing subnet traffic will be forwarded to the Azure Firewall

Route table

3. The Firewall decides where the traffic is forwarded after inspection/processing

Azure Firewall

1. Route table is added, and associated to Subnet 01

Destination

Internet

Another Azure VNet

On-premises network

*Figure 2-4. Routing outgoing subnet traffic to the Azure Firewall*

## Steps

1. Log in to your Azure subscription in the Owner role and create a new resource group for this recipe. See "General Workstation Setup Instructions" on page xii for details.

2. Create an Azure VNet. Refer to Recipe 2.1 for details.

3. We need to create a new subnet for the Azure Firewall. Use the following command to create this subnet. The subnet name for the Azure Firewall resource should be AzureFirewallSubnet:

```
vnetName="<vnet-name>"

az network vnet subnet create \
    --resource-group $rgName \
    --vnet-name $vnetName \
    --name AzureFirewallSubnet \
    --address-prefixes 10.0.1.0/26
```

4. Now that you have the subnet deployed, you can provision a new Azure Firewall resource. The following command will deploy an Azure Firewall instance. If you're prompted to install the Azure Firewall extension, answer Y:

```
vnetName="<vnet-name>"
firewallName="<firewall-name>"

az network firewall create \
    --resource-group $rgName \
    --name $firewallName \
    --tier Standard
```

 Run the command `az config set extension.use_dynamic_install=yes_without_prompt` so any required CLI extension is automatically installed without prompting.

5. Every Azure Firewall instance needs a public IP address. Use the following command to create a public IP resource and assign it to your Azure Firewall:

```
pIPName="<public-ip-name>"

az network public-ip create \
    --resource-group $rgName \
    --name $pIPName \
    --sku Standard


az network firewall ip-config create \
    --resource-group $rgName \
    --name fwIPConfiguration01 \
    --firewall-name $firewallName \
    --public-ip-address $pIPName \
    --vnet-name $vnetName
```

6. By default, all traffic is blocked by the Azure Firewall. You can create three sets of rules for Azure Firewall (*https://oreil.ly/P7rdn*): *DNAT* rules, *network* rules, and *application* rules. In this recipe, we will focus on application rules. Let's create a new application rule that allows outgoing subnet HTTPS traffic to the *www.contoso.com* domain:

```
az network firewall application-rule create \
    --resource-group $rgName \
    --collection-name Application_Rule_Collection \
    --firewall-name $firewallName \
    --name Allow_Contoso \
    --protocols Https=443 \
    --action Allow \
```

```
--target-fqdns www.contoso.com \
--priority 1000
```

7. Now that we've created your Azure Firewall resource and defined its rules, we need to route the subnet traffic to this Azure Firewall instance. As you saw in Recipe 2.3, this can be done with route tables. Create a new route table using the following command. Replace *<fw-route-table-name>* with your desired name:

```
routeTableName="<fw-route-table-name>"

az network route-table create \
    --resource-group $rgName \
    --name $routeTableName
```

8. You need to find the Azure Firewall internal IP address, so it can be passed to the routing rule:

```
firewallPrivateIP=$(az network firewall show \
    --name $firewallName \
    --resource-group $rgName \
    --query "ipConfigurations[0].privateIpAddress" \
    --output tsv)
```

9. Now, use the following command to add your custom route to your route table:

```
routeName="<custom-route-name>"

az network route-table route create \
    --resource-group $rgName \
    --route-table-name $routeTableName \
    --name $routeName \
    --next-hop-type VirtualAppliance \
    --address-prefix 0.0.0.0/0 \
    --next-hop-ip-address $firewallPrivateIP
```

10. Finally, associate your custom route with your desired subnet(s). We created a second subnet in Recipe 2.2, named Subnet02. Let's use that:

```
az network vnet subnet update \
    --resource-group $rgName \
    --name Subnet02 \
    --vnet-name $vnetName \
    --route-table $routeTableName
```

11. Run the following command to delete the resources you created in this recipe:

```
az group delete --name $rgName
```

In this recipe, you successfully forwarded all outgoing traffic from Subnet02 to your Azure Firewall virtual appliance with the address 10.0.1.4. To forward the traffic to the correct destination, you need to also add DNAT rules to your firewall. In addition, you should add network and application rules to allow/deny egress traffic from your VNets. Any traffic with no matching rule will be blocked.

## Discussion

In this recipe, we used Azure Firewall to inspect egress traffic from an Azure VNet subnet. By default, all traffic is blocked unless there is a matching firewall rule for it. See the Azure Firewall rule processing logic documentation (*https://oreil.ly/tQflT*) for details. As you saw, there are three sets of Azure Firewall classic rules:

*DNAT rules*
> For inbound traffic into your subnets. DNAT rules will be processed first.

*Network rules*
> For outgoing traffic from your subnets. You can allow or block traffic based on IP address and port number. Network rules are processed after DNAT rules.

*Application rules*
> Finally, if you need to allow outgoing traffic for HTTP, HTTPS, or MSSQL protocols, use these rules. Application rules are processed last.

> You can optionally use an Azure Firewall Policy (*https://oreil.ly/mx-YV*) instead of directly defining rules in the Azure Firewall resource. This policy can then be assigned to one or more Azure Firewall instances.

Azure Firewall also offers threat intelligence-based filtering (*https://oreil.ly/LtfDs*) to alert and/or deny traffic from Microsoft's list of malicious IP addresses, fully qualified domain names, and URLs.

# 2.5 Securing Azure Virtual Networks with Network Security Groups

## Problem

You need to improve network security by controlling inbound and outbound subnet traffic.

## Solution

Provision a new Azure network security group (NSG) (*https://oreil.ly/nu5J0*) resource and assign it to your subnets, as shown in Figure 2-5.

---

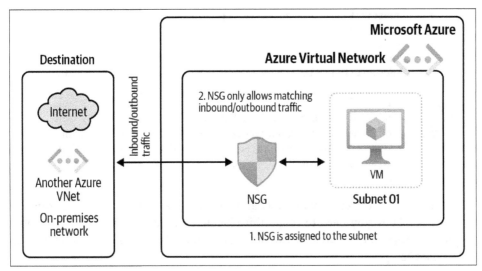

*Figure 2-5. Protecting your subnets by assigning NSGs*

## Steps

1. Log in to your Azure subscription in the Owner role and create a new resource group for this recipe. See "General Workstation Setup Instructions" on page xii for details.

2. Create an Azure VNet. Refer to Recipe 2.1 for the steps.

3. Create a new NSG using the following CLI command:

```
az network nsg create \
    --resource-group $rgName \
    --name nsg01
```

4. By default, all traffic is blocked by Azure NSGs. Using NSG *security rules,* you can allow or deny both inbound (ingress) and outbound (egress) subnet traffic. The priority can be between 100 and 4096. Rules with lower numbers have higher priority and will be processed first. Imagine you deployed a web server Azure VM into your subnet and so need to allow for inbound traffic on ports 80 and 443. Use the following CLI command to create a new security rule allowing incoming internet traffic on these two ports:

```
az network nsg rule create \
    --resource-group $rgName \
    --nsg-name nsg01 \
    --name allow_http_https \
    --priority 100 \
    --source-address-prefixes Internet \
    --source-port-ranges '*' \
    --destination-address-prefixes '*' \
```

```
--destination-port-ranges 80 443 \
--access Allow \
--protocol Tcp \
--direction Inbound \
--description "Allow from internet IP addresses on ports 80 and 443."
```

 At the time of writing this book, every new NSG has three default inbound and three default outbound security rules. You can't edit or delete these rules, but you can override them by adding custom rules with higher priority. See the NSG documentation (*https://oreil.ly/4tdyM*) for details.

5. So far you have created your NSG and allowed inbound HTTP traffic from the internet. Now, you need to assign this NSG to your subnet(s). As you remember from Recipe 2.4, we created two subnets in our VNet. Let's assign this NSG to Subnet02:

```
az network vnet subnet update \
    --resource-group $rgName \
    --name Subnet02 \
    --vnet-name $vnetName \
    --network-security-group nsg01
```

6. Run the following command to delete the resources you created in this recipe:

```
az group delete --name $rgName
```

In this recipe, you configured an Azure NSG so that all inbound internet traffic with destination ports 80 and 443 is allowed in Subnet02. All other traffic is blocked.

## Discussion

In this recipe, we created a new NSG and assigned it to a subnet. NSGs provide basic protection based on source and destination IP address and port numbers. One NSG can be assigned to multiple subnets, but each subnet can have only one NSG assigned.

In Recipe 2.4, we set up Azure Firewall, which is a more sophisticated service. You can use NSGs along with Azure Firewall to provide extra protection for your subnets. If unwanted traffic goes through one, the next will block it, providing *defense in depth* for your Azure network (see Figure 2-6).

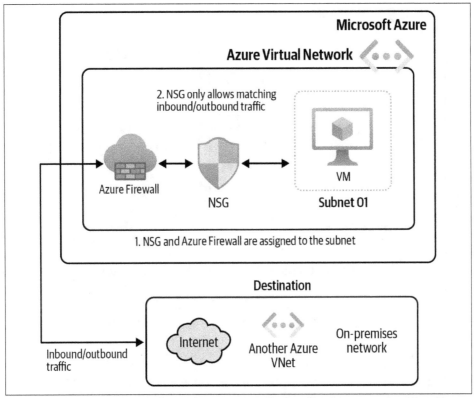

*Figure 2-6. Securing your subnets using NSGs and Azure Firewall*

# 2.6 Connecting Two Azure VNets Using Azure Network Peering

## Problem

You want resources in two separate Azure VNets configured so that they will be able to communicate with each other.

## Solution

Create two new *Azure network peering* resources between your two Azure VNets, so that the resources in the two VNets can see one another (see Figure 2-7).

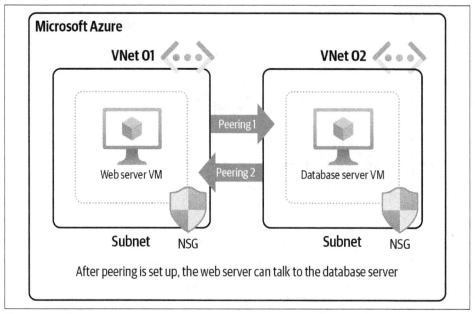

*Figure 2-7. Connecting two Azure VNets using Azure virtual network peering*

**Steps**

1. Log in to your Azure subscription in the Owner role and create a new resource group for this recipe. See "General Workstation Setup Instructions" on page xii for details.

2. Create the first Azure VNet, with a subnet, using the following command:

```
az network vnet create \
    --resource-group $rgName \
    --name VNet01 \
    --address-prefix 10.0.0.0/16 \
    --subnet-name Subnet01 \
    --subnet-prefix 10.0.0.0/26
```

3. Create the second Azure VNet, with a subnet, using the following command. To use network peering between two VNets, they should not have any overlapping IP addresses. So, we choose 10.1.0.0/16 as the address space for the second VNet:

```
az network vnet create \
    --resource-group $rgName \
    --name VNet02 \
    --address-prefix 10.1.0.0/16 \
    --subnet-name Subnet01 \
    --subnet-prefix 10.1.0.0/26
```

4. The two Azure VNets we created are separate networks; therefore, resources deployed to VNet01 can't see VNet02 resources and vice versa. Let's fix this issue by creating an Azure virtual network peering resource:

```
az network vnet peering create \
    --resource-group $rgName \
    --name peering01 \
    --vnet-name VNet01 \
    --remote-vnet VNet02 \
    --allow-vnet-access
```

 To create your network peering (*https://oreil.ly/8Onfe*), your account should have the Network Contributor role assigned over both Azure VNets.

5. At this point, resources in VNet01 can communicate with VNet02 resources, but the opposite is not true. We need to specifically create another peering from VNet02 to VNet01, as follows:

```
az network vnet peering create \
    --resource-group $rgName \
    --name peering02 \
    --vnet-name VNet02 \
    --remote-vnet VNet01 \
    --allow-vnet-access
```

6. Run the following command to delete the resources you created in this recipe:

```
az group delete --name $rgName
```

## Discussion

Imagine you have a web server VM in VNet01 and a database server VM in VNet02. You need a secure method to make sure the web server can talk to the database server. One solution is to create a VNet peering between these two VNets.

In this recipe, we connected two Azure VNets using Azure virtual network peering (*https://oreil.ly/R558V*), which enables you to easily connect two or more virtual networks in Azure.

The two VNets that you are trying to peer should not have any IP address overlaps. In our example, VNet01 uses the 10.0.0.0/16 space and VNet02 uses 10.1.0.0/16 to avoid any overlap.

The traffic between the peered VNets does not go over the public internet; it stays on the Azure backbone network. This makes Azure virtual network peering a secure and low-latency solution.

## 2.7 Verifying Azure VNet Connectivity Using Azure Network Watcher

### Problem

You need to monitor or verify network connectivity between an Azure VM and other destinations, such as the internet or another VM.

### Solution

Create an *Azure Network Watcher connection monitor* and use it to verify connectivity between your IaaS (infrastructure as a service) endpoints (see Figure 2-8).

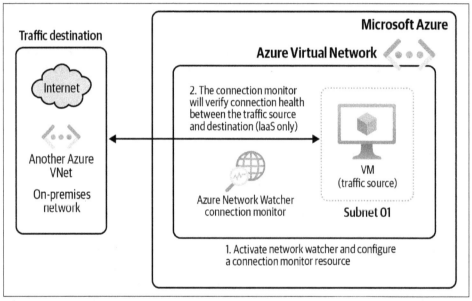

*Figure 2-8. Using Azure Network Watcher to monitor Azure VM connectivity*

### Steps

1. Log in to your Azure subscription in the Owner role and create a new resource group for this recipe. See "General Workstation Setup Instructions" on page xii for details.

2. Create an Azure VNet, with a default subnet, using the following command:

```
az network vnet create \
    --resource-group $rgName \
    --name VNet03 \
    --address-prefix 10.0.0.0/16 \
```

```
    --subnet-name VMSubnet \
    --subnet-prefix 10.0.0.0/26
```

3. Now provision a new Azure VM with the Azure Network Watcher extension installed. This VM will be placed into the VNet you created in the previous step. Replace *<vm-password>* with a secure password:

```
az vm create \
    --resource-group $rgName \
    --name vm001 \
    --image win2016datacenter \
    --vnet-name VNet03 \
    --subnet VMSubnet \
    --public-ip-sku Standard \
    --admin-username cookbookuser \
    --admin-password <vm-password>
```

4. To use Azure Network Watcher to monitor VM network connectivity, you need to install a lightweight agent on it. Run the following command to install the agent:

```
az vm extension set \
    --name NetworkWatcherAgentWindows \
    --version 1.4.2331.0 \
    --resource-group $rgName \
    --vm-name vm001 \
    --publisher Microsoft.Azure.NetworkWatcher
```

> At the time of writing this book, 1.4.2331.0 is the latest version (*https://oreil.ly/GAZFh*) for this extension.

5. Our goal is to check connectivity between our new VM, and 13.107.21.200:80. You can choose a different public IP address or VM based on your scenario. You should see Reachable as the command output, meaning the target IP is reachable from your VM. This comes in handy when troubleshooting connectivity issues between VMs and other endpoints. Now, use the following command to use the connection monitor resource (*https://oreil.ly/KTH7i*) to verify the health of this connection:

```
az network watcher test-connectivity \
    --resource-group $rgName \
    --source-resource vm001 \
    --dest-address 13.107.21.200 \
    --dest-port 80  \
    --query "connectionStatus"
```

6. To avoid getting charged for an idle VM, delete your new VM by running the following command:

```
az vm delete \
    --resource-group $rgName \
    --name vm001 \
    --yes
```

7. Run the following command to delete the resources you created in this recipe:

```
az group delete --name $rgName
```

## Discussion

In this recipe, you verified connectivity for your new Azure VM using Azure Network Watcher connection monitor service (*https://oreil.ly/oyL25*).

 Azure Network Watcher is only intended for IaaS resources such as Azure VMs. This service does not support Azure PaaS (platform as a service) services such as App Services as the source resource.

Here are the steps to use Network Watcher:

1. As soon as an Azure VNet is created, the Azure Network Watcher will be enabled for the VNet region.

2. To use Azure Network Watcher with Azure VMs, a lightweight agent needs to be installed on the VM. Install the Windows (*https://oreil.ly/bltKd*) or Linux (*https://oreil.ly/xarg9*) version, depending on your VM's OS.

3. Create a connection monitor resource for the desired traffic source and destination, and then query for connectivity status.

Azure Network Watcher can also be used to monitor, troubleshoot, and repair network connectivity for IaaS resources. Check the Azure documentation (*https://oreil.ly/ViGra*) for details.

## CHAPTER 3

# Storage

Almost every solution needs to persist data in a data store, and cloud solutions are no exception. Your data store should be protected by multiple security measures to safeguard the data from hackers and unauthorized users. Data redundancy should be in place in case one or more data centers go offline due to expected—or unexpected—events. Scalability is also a key requirement for modern applications. The data store should accommodate any traffic volume and expand to store more data as it is created.

Azure Storage is Azure's main, general-purpose data storage service. It offers native integration with key Azure services such as Azure Active Directory, Azure Key Vault, managed identities, Azure Functions, Azure Logic Apps, virtual machine disks, Azure Cognitive Search, Event Grid, and Azure Synapse Analytics. Infinite scaling capabilities make it a great choice for storing big data, telemetry, logfiles, images, media files, and both unstructured and NoSQL data.

> Microsoft is continuously updating Azure services to offer richer features. Visit the Azure updates page (*https://oreil.ly/dgjrH*) for the latest updates and to take advantage of new offerings as they become generally available.

Azure Storage offers the following services: blobs, files, queues, tables, and disks. VM disks are stored as blob objects. In this chapter, you will use the Azure Storage services to configure a secure, reliable, and affordable data store in your Azure subscription. Use Azure Storage to:

- Automatically invoke an Azure Function when a new file is added to your Azure Storage

- Index your blob files and build content search APIs for them using Azure Cognitive Search

- Store big data to be analyzed by Azure Databricks or Azure Synapse Analytics

- Use Azure Files to implement traditional SMB (Server Message Block protocol) file shares (*https://oreil.ly/Ey2yE*) for your Windows or Linux workstations

 Multiple options exist for migrating your on-premises data to Azure Storage. Use Azure Data Box (*https://oreil.ly/y-Cq8*) to move large amounts of local data to your Azure storage account, or upload files directly using the portal, CLI, PowerShell, or command-line tools such as AzCopy (*https://oreil.ly/GyjVK*).

## Workstation Configuration

You will need to prepare your workstation before starting on the recipes in this chapter. Follow "What You Will Need" on page xi to set up your machine to run Azure CLI commands. You can clone the book's GitHub repository using the following command:

```
git clone https://github.com/zaalion/AzureCookbook.git
```

# 3.1 Using Azure Key Vault Keys to Configure Azure Storage Encryption at Rest

## Problem

You need to use CMK (customer-managed keys) to encrypt your Azure Storage data at rest.

## Solution

Create a new encryption key in Azure Key Vault and configure Azure Storage to use it instead of the default Microsoft-managed keys (see Figure 3-1).

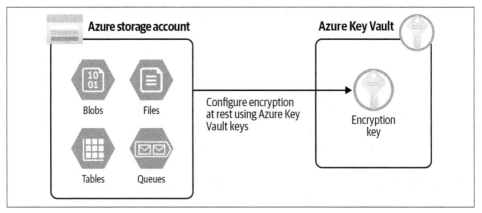

*Figure 3-1. Using Azure Key Vault encryption keys to configure Azure Storage encryption at rest*

## Steps

1. Log in to your Azure subscription in the Owner role and create a new resource group for this recipe. See "General Workstation Setup Instructions" on page xii for details.

2. Create a new Azure Key Vault. You can also use an existing Key Vault. Replace *<kv-Name>* with the desired Key Vault name:

   ```
   kvName="<kv-Name>"
   ```

   ```
   az keyvault create --name $kvName \
     --resource-group $rgName \
     --location $region \
     --enable-purge-protection
   ```

3. You need to use an encryption key to configure Azure Storage encryption. Let's create a new key in your Key Vault resource:

   ```
   az keyvault key create \
       --name storage-cmk-key \
       --vault-name $kvName \
       --kty RSA \
       --size 4096
   ```

    An encryption key has several properties, which you can change based on your scenario. For example, you can create hardware-protected keys if you are in the premium Key Vault tier. The key size, curve, and type can also be configured. See the Key Vault documentation (*https://oreil.ly/S9-wU*) for details.

4. Now create an Azure storage account to test your encryption key using the following command:

```
storageName="<storage-account-name>"

az storage account create \
    --name $storageName \
    --resource-group $rgName \
    --location $region \
    --sku Standard_LRS
```

5. Now let's configure your storage account to use the key you created for encryption at rest (*https://oreil.ly/txZcx*). To access the encryption key from Key Vault, your storage account needs to have the `wrapkey`, `unwrapkey`, and `get` access policies set on the Key Vault. First we'll assign an identity to your storage account; then, the access policy can be set to this identity. Store the identity ID in a variable as follows:

```
az storage account update \
    --name $storageName \
    --resource-group $rgName \
    --assign-identity

storageObjectId=$(az storage account show \
    --name $storageName \
    --query "identity.principalId" \
    --output tsv)
```

6. Now let's configure the access policy (*https://oreil.ly/TtxR2*) for your Key Vault:

```
az keyvault set-policy --name $kvName \
    --object-id $storageObjectId \
    --key-permissions get unwrapKey wrapKey
```

 You must be logged in as the subscription's Owner account to set a Key Vault access policy.

7. Now the stage is set for you to configure your storage account to use your encryption key for data at rest:

```
kvURL=$(az keyvault show \
    --name $kvName \
    --resource-group $rgName \
    --query properties.vaultUri \
    --output tsv)

az storage account update \
```

```
    --name $storageName \
    --resource-group $rgName \
    --encryption-key-source Microsoft.Keyvault \
    --encryption-services blob \
    --encryption-key-vault $kvURL \
    --encryption-key-name storage-cmk-key
```

8. Wait for the command to succeed. You configured your storage account to use your own managed key (*https://oreil.ly/MDVnV*) instead of the default Microsoft managed key. Run the following command to delete the resources you created in this recipe:

```
az group delete --name $rgName
```

## Discussion

Encryption for data at rest is automatically enabled for all Azure storage account instances (*https://oreil.ly/hSKGa*). By default, the encryption key is managed by Microsoft.

However, whether due to security standards, commitments, or for compliance reasons, your organization might want to be in charge of the storage account encryption keys by creating its own keys. You can use this recipe to create your own Key Vault encryption key. This key is stored in the Azure Key Vault, and you are responsible for managing and maintaining its health and availability. If you don't have specific security commitments or compliance needs, it's fine to use the default Microsoft-managed keys. This approach has less administrative overhead for your team.

Keep in mind that when customer-managed keys are enabled for your storage account, Azure Storage queues and tables are not automatically protected by those keys. If needed, you can configure these services to be included in the CMK encryption when you create your storage account. See the Azure documentation (*https:// oreil.ly/tusL6*) for details.

 Losing your CMK key will result in losing your Azure Storage data. Make sure that soft-delete and purge-protection (*https://oreil.ly/ je1Bf*) are enabled on your Key Vault and that the key expiry date and auto-rotation settings (*https://oreil.ly/6xN6f*) are configured as expected.

# 3.2 Controlling Azure Storage Network Access

## Problem

You need to limit Azure storage account network access to one or more Azure VNets.

---

## Solution

Make sure the Public Network Access setting is enabled for your storage account. Then define a network access rule to permit traffic from one or more Azure VNets (see Figure 3-2).

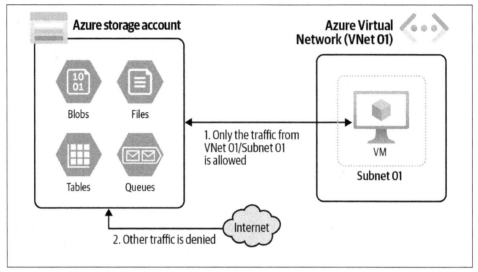

*Figure 3-2. Allowing traffic only from an Azure VNet to reach an Azure storage account*

### Steps

1. Log in to your Azure subscription in the Owner role and create a new resource group for this recipe. See "General Workstation Setup Instructions" on page xii for details.

2. Create a new Azure storage account and make sure the `--public-network-access` setting is set to `Enabled`. This ensures that traffic from public networks (including Azure VNet traffic) is allowed. You also need to set the `--default-action` parameter `Deny`. This denies traffic unless it is allowed in the *virtual network rules*. Use the following CLI command to provision your storage account:

```
storageName="<storage-account-name>"

az storage account create \
    --name $storageName \
    --resource-group $rgName \
    --location $region \
    --sku Standard_LRS \
    --default-action Deny \
    --public-network-access Enabled
```

3. Wait for the command to succeed. Now let's create a new Azure VNet. We'll allow traffic from any resource in this VNet's Subnet01 (for example, from VMs). Use the following command to create your net VNet with a single child subnet:

```
az network vnet create \
    --resource-group $rgName \
    --name VNet01 \
    --address-prefix 10.0.0.0/16 \
    --subnet-name Subnet01 \
    --subnet-prefix 10.0.0.0/26
```

4. You need to allow the egress (outgoing) traffic from your subnet to Azure Storage. You can achieve this by adding a Microsoft.Storage service endpoint (*https://oreil.ly/JPYY5*) to your subnet:

```
az network vnet subnet update \
    --resource-group $rgName \
    --vnet-name VNet01 \
    --name Subnet01 \
    --service-endpoints "Microsoft.Storage"
```

5. Now let's add a storage network rule to allow ingress (incoming) traffic from VNet01/Subnet01 to your storage account:

```
az storage account network-rule add \
    --resource-group $rgName \
    --account-name $storageName \
    --vnet-name VNet01 \
    --subnet Subnet01 \
    --action Allow
```

6. Use the following command to see all storage network rules for your storage account :

```
az storage account network-rule list \
    --account-name $storageName \
    --resource-group $rgName
```

7. Run the following command to delete the resources you created in this recipe:

```
az group delete --name $rgName
```

You have successfully configured your Azure storage account to accept traffic only from one Azure VNet subnet. Any other request from the internet, or any other networks, will fail to reach the storage account.

## Discussion

There are three different network access scenarios for an Azure storage account:

- Allow traffic from all public and private networks (including the internet)

- Allow traffic only from specific Azure VNets
- Allow traffic only from private endpoints with no public network access

The first option is the default behavior when you create a new storage account, unless you explicitly configure other network access settings.

In this recipe, we covered the second option, which allows traffic from one or more VNets. Keep in mind that in this case the traffic still goes through the public internet.

If you need your traffic to only go through Azure's private backbone network, you need to choose the third option to configure private endpoints (*https://oreil.ly/ han2C*). Check the Azure Storage networking documentation (*https://oreil.ly/sLOnW*) for details.

# 3.3 Granting Limited Access to Azure Storage Using SAS Tokens

## Problem

You need a way to grant granular access to Azure Storage services.

## Solution

Instead of Azure Storage Keys, which grant full access, generate shared access signature (SAS) tokens (*https://oreil.ly/ocGNk*) with the desired access and share them with client applications and users (see Figure 3-3).

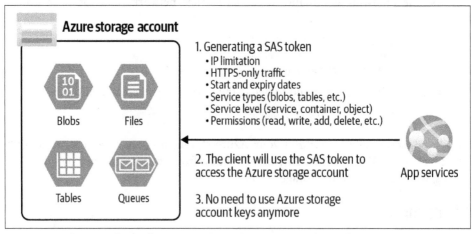

*Figure 3-3. Granting limited access to Azure Storage using SAS tokens*

## Steps

1. Log in to your Azure subscription in the Owner role and create a new resource group for this recipe. See "General Workstation Setup Instructions" on page xii for details.

2. Use the following CLI command to provision a new Azure storage account:

```
storageName="<storage-account-name>"

az storage account create \
    --name $storageName \
    --resource-group $rgName \
    --location $region \
    --sku Standard_LRS
```

3. Wait for the command to succeed. Now, let's imagine a scenario in which an Azure App Service needs access to this storage account. In this situation, you want to grant *read* access to the *blob* and *table* services, and reject any unsecured HTTP (non-HTTPS) traffic. You need this token to expire after 15 minutes. First let's calculate the expiry date for the SAS token using this command:

```
expiryDate=`date -u -d "15 minutes" '+%Y-%m-%dT%H:%MZ'`
```

4. The storage account key is also needed to authenticate the SAS generation command. We only need one storage account key. Use the following command to store key01 in a variable:

```
storageKey=$(az storage account keys list \
    --resource-group $rgName \
    --account-name $storageName \
    --query [0].value \
    --output tsv)
```

5. Now you can use the following command to create the SAS token:

```
sasToken=$(az storage account generate-sas \
    --account-name $storageName \
    --account-key $storageKey \
    --expiry $expiryDate \
    --permissions r \
    --resource-types co \
    --services bq \
    --https-only \
    --output tsv)
```

For `--permissions` you can combine these values: (a)dd, (c)reate, (d)elete, (f)ilter_by_tags, (i)set_immutability _policy, (l)ist, (p)rocess, (r)ead, (t)ag, (u)pdate, (w)rite, (x)delete_previous_version, and (y)permanent_delete. For instance, `rw` means read and write access. For `--services` you can combine these values: (b)lob, (f)ile, (q)ueue, (t)able. See the Azure CLI documentation (*https://oreil.ly/L4c09*) for details.

6. You won't be able to recover this SAS token in the future, so let's store it in a variable (or copy it from the command output). You can grab it using the following command:

```
echo $sasToken
```

7. Run the following command to delete the resources you created in this recipe:

```
az group delete --name $rgName
```

You successfully generated a SAS token with the desired limited access. You can provide this token to clients (users, Function Apps, App Service web apps, etc.) of your storage account so they can use it with the defined access.

## Discussion

The principle of least privilege (*https://oreil.ly/qo8Cs*) requires every service and user to have only the minimum permissions it needs. If your application is meant only to read data, it should not have permissions to write data. SAS tokens are the perfect tool to implement the principle of least privilege for Azure storage accounts.

SAS tokens give you great flexibility in granting access. You can use your client's access requirements to design a SAS token and use the token instead of storage account keys, which have full access to every Azure Storage service.

SAS tokens allow the following granular access to be set:

- Specify start and expiry dates
- Require HTTPS-only traffic
- Choose which storage services to access (blobs, tables, queues, files)
- Choose which resource level to access (service, container, object)
- Specify allowed client IP addresses

Refer to the Azure Storage documentation for more details on generating SAS tokens using CLI (*https://oreil.ly/F4XDf*).

This is a sample of a generated SAS token:

```
se=2022-08-30T19%3A05Z&sp=r&spr=https&
sv=2021-06-08&ss=qb&srt=oc&
sig=E5/XvKCnUd30cRwXNS9cD9Lb4P9g5/W7NVYhGMolEvw%3D
```

 SAS tokens are signed by one of the storage account keys. Rotating/resetting that key will cause all related SAS tokens to be invalidated.

# 3.4 Granting Azure Function Apps Access to Azure Storage Using Managed Identity and RBAC

## Problem

You need to grant storage account read and write access to an Azure Function App without using the storage account key or SAS tokens.

## Solution

Enable managed identities (*https://oreil.ly/AU95f*) (formerly known as Managed Service Identity—MSI) for the Azure Function App and assign the *Storage Blob Data Contributor* built-in RBAC role to them for the storage account scope, as illustrated in Figure 3-4.

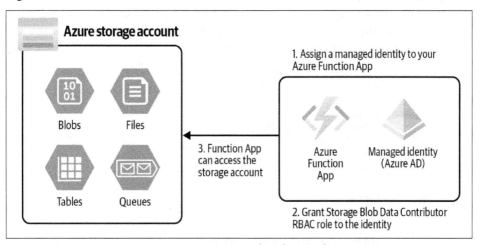

*Figure 3-4. Granting Azure storage account read and write data access to an Azure Function App using RBAC and managed identities*

## Steps

1. Log in to your Azure subscription in the Owner role and create a new resource group for this recipe. See "General Workstation Setup Instructions" on page xii for details.

2. Use the following CLI command to provision a new Azure storage account:

```
storageName="<storage-account-name>"

az storage account create \
    --name $storageName \
    --resource-group $rgName \
    --location $region \
    --sku Standard_LRS
```

3. Wait for the command to succeed. Now, let's create a second storage account to be used for the new Azure Function App's internal operations. Replace *<func-storage-account-name>* with a globally unique name:

```
funcStorageName="<func-storage-account-name>"

az storage account create \
    --name $funcStorageName \
    --resource-group $rgName \
    --location $region \
    --sku Standard_LRS
```

4. Now create your new Azure Function App and assign a managed identity to it. You can choose either system-assigned or user-assigned identities (*https://oreil.ly/ L9MVA*); in the recipe, we use system-assigned for simplicity. Choose the system-assigned identity by passing the `--assign-identity [system]` parameter. Use the following command to create the Function App:

```
planName="<appservice-plan-name>"
funcAppName="<function-app-name>"

az appservice plan create \
    --resource-group $rgName \
    --name $planName \
    --sku S1 \
    --location $region

az functionapp create \
    --resource-group $rgName \
    --name $funcAppName \
    --storage-account $funcStorageName \
    --assign-identity [system] \
    --functions-version 4 \
    --plan $planName \
    --runtime dotnet \
```

```
--runtime-version 6 \
--os-type Windows
```

 As you saw in step 4, you need to create an App Service plan (*https://oreil.ly/CYg4J*) before creating an Azure Function App. We will discuss App Service plans in Chapter 7.

5. So far you have a Function App that needs to access data on the storage account created in step 1. Use the following command to obtain the Function App managed identity ID (GUID), and storage account resource ID. You will need these later to assign an RBAC role to the Function App:

```
storageResourceId=$(az storage account show \
    --name $storageName \
    --resource-group $rgName \
    --query id \
    --output tsv)

funcIdentityObjectId=$(az functionapp show \
    --name $funcAppName \
    --resource-group $rgName \
    --query identity.principalId \
    --output tsv)
```

6. Use this command to store the Storage Blob Data Contributor built-in RBAC role definition ID in a variable:

```
roleDefinitionId=$(az role definition list \
    --name "Storage Blob Data Contributor" \
    --query [].id  --output tsv)
```

7. Now you have all the information you need to assign the Storage Blob Data Contributor RBAC role to your Function App:

```
MSYS_NO_PATHCONV=1 az role assignment create \
    --assignee $funcIdentityObjectId \
    --role $roleDefinitionId \
    --scope $storageResourceId
```

 Git Bash automatically translates resource IDs to Windows paths, which causes this command to fail. Simply add `MSYS_NO_PATH` `CONV=1` in front of the command to temporarily disable this behavior. See the Bash documentation (*https://oreil.ly/2Ni_R*) for details.

8. Run the following command to delete the resources you created in this recipe:

```
az group delete --name $rgName
```

You successfully granted Azure Storage data access to a Function App without using any storage account keys or a SAS token.

## Discussion

Azure Storage offers multiple authentication options (*https://oreil.ly/XjeEX*). You learned about Azure Storage keys and SAS tokens in Recipe 3.3. The issue with these options is their security. There is always a chance that a SAS token or storage key might be accidentally hard-coded and checked into a source control repository. Developers might send these keys over insecure communication lines, such as instant chat or emails. You would need to make sure the keys and SAS tokens were well protected.

There is a better way to authenticate clients to a storage account and any other resource type supporting Azure Active Directory authentication (*https://oreil.ly/cEcu0*). You can create a managed identity for your client resources (in this recipe, we used a Function App as the client), and configure the storage account to allow access to this identity using RBAC roles. Both built-in and custom roles can be used.

Refer to the Azure documentation (*https://oreil.ly/Uonnh*) for a list of Azure services that can use managed identities to access other services.

# 3.5 Creating and Storing Snapshots of Blob Objects

## Problem

You need to create snapshots of a storage account blob file so you have a history of the blob updates.

## Solution

Create blob snapshots (*https://oreil.ly/7q-JL*) for your Azure blob object and store them in an Azure storage account. You can access these snapshots in the future using the datetime they were created, as shown in Figure 3-5.

---

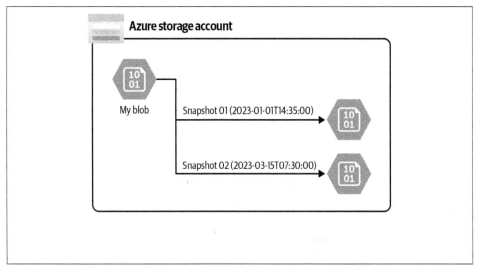

Figure 3-5. Creating Azure blob storage snapshots

**Steps**

1. Log in to your Azure subscription in the Owner role and create a new resource group for this recipe. See "General Workstation Setup Instructions" on page xii for details.

2. Use the following CLI command to provision a new Azure storage account:

```
storageName="<storage-account-name>"

az storage account create \
    --name $storageName \
    --resource-group $rgName \
    --location $region \
    --sku Standard_LRS \
    --default-action Allow
```

3. If your account has required RBAC permissions over the storage account, you can specify login for the --auth-mode parameter. Alternatively, you can store the storage account key in a variable and use it to work with the account in the next steps as this command demonstrates:

```
storageKey1=$(az storage account keys list \
    --resource-group $rgName \
    --account-name $storageName \
    --query [0].value \
    --output tsv)
```

4. Create a container in the storage account using this command:

```
containerName="mycontainer"

az storage container create \
    --name $containerName \
    --account-name $storageName \
    --account-key $storageKey1
```

5. Wait for the command to succeed. Now let's upload a file to the storage account using the following command. Replace *<local-file-path>* with the Linux path to a small text file you created on your machine, for example */path/to/ Myblob01.txt*:

```
blobFileName="Myblob01.txt"

az storage blob upload \
    --account-key $storageKey1 \
    --file <local-file-path> \
    --account-name $storageName \
    --container-name $containerName \
    --name $blobFileName
```

6. So far you have created a blob file in a brand new storage account. Let's create a snapshot of this blob using the following command:

```
az storage blob snapshot \
    --account-key $storageKey1 \
    --account-name $storageName \
    --container-name $containerName \
    --name $blobFileName
```

 You can use the az snapshot create command to create Azure Disks snapshots. See the Azure documentation (*https://oreil.ly/ kZDH5*) and the CLI documentation (*https://oreil.ly/AUgyv*) for details.

7. You successfully created a snapshot of your Azure Storage blob file. This is a read-only copy of your blob at the given time. Run the following command to delete the resources you created in this recipe:

```
az group delete --name $rgName
```

## Discussion

Azure blob snapshots allow you to keep track of blob file changes over time. Think of them as a database backup, allowing you to perform a point-in-time data restore. You can create snapshots of your blob object at specific time intervals and store them as backups. This allows you to easily recover the previous versions on each blob as long as the snapshot for the given time exists.

Keep in mind that blob snapshots take up space and that your Azure subscription will be charged for the extra storage.

Blob versioning (*https://oreil.ly/EllAf*) offers another method to keep track of your blob object changes. Blob versions are automatically created once you enable blob versioning for your storage account. We'll cover blob versioning in Recipe 3.6.

# 3.6 Creating and Accessing New File Versions

## Problem

You need to keep track of all Azure Storage blob changes to recover previous versions if needed.

## Solution

Enable blob versioning (*https://oreil.ly/bkPNu*) for your storage account so that each blob update will create a new blob file version. You can access these versions by their *version ID* when needed, as shown in Figure 3-6.

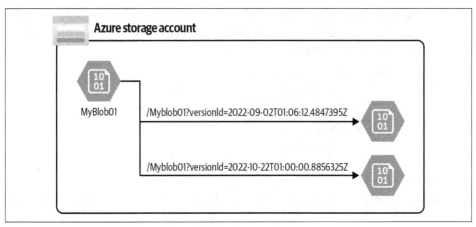

*Figure 3-6. Accessing Azure blob storage versions using a version ID*

### Steps

1. Follow steps 1 through 5 in Recipe 3.5 to create a new Azure storage account and upload a text blob to it. Make sure you run all the commands so that variables such as $storageKey1 are properly initialized.

2. By default, versioning is not enabled on storage accounts. Run the following command to enable it:

```
az storage account blob-service-properties update \
    --account-name $storageName \
    --enable-versioning true
```

 Check the az storage account blob-service-properties update command documentation (*https://oreil.ly/--moK*) for details.

3. Now that you have blob versioning enabled, update your local *Myblob01.txt* and upload it again using this command. The --overwrite true parameter makes sure any file with the same name will be overwritten:

```
az storage blob upload \
    --account-key $storageKey1 \
    --file <local-file-path> \
    --account-name $storageName \
    --container-name $containerName \
    --name $blobFileName \
    --overwrite true
```

4. By uploading *Myblob01.txt* over the existing blob, you automatically created a new blob version. Use this command to get the latest version of your blob file and store versionId in a variable:

```
latestVersion=$(az storage blob show \
    --account-name $storageName \
    --account-key $storageKey1 \
    --container-name $containerName \
    --name Myblob01.txt \
    --query versionId \
    --output tsv)
```

5. You can download any blob version that you wish using this command. Replace <downloaded-file-path> with the local Linux path where you wish to save the file:

```
az storage blob download
    --account-name $storageName \
    --account-key $storageKey1 \
    --container-name $containerName \
    --name Myblob01.txt \
    --file <downloaded-file-path> \
    --version-id $latestVersion
```

6. Run the following command to delete the resources you created in this recipe:

```
az group delete --name $rgName
```

You successfully created multiple versions of a blob file and downloaded the desired version using Azure CLI. You can also download older versions of *Myblob01.txt* by passing the appropriate `versionId`.

## Discussion

Blob versioning is a convenient solution to keep track of your Azure Storage blob changes. This method is better than using blob snapshots because it happens automatically once you activate it, whereas you need to explicitly create snapshots. Keep in mind that as with blob snapshots, blob versions take up space, and your Azure subscription will be charged for that extra storage.

Check the Azure blob documentation (*https://oreil.ly/NopQO*) for more details on blob versioning.

Microsoft recommends that you stop creating blob snapshots after you enable blob versioning. With versioning enabled, taking snapshots does not offer any additional protections for your block blob data. See the blob versioning documentation (*https://oreil.ly/cADoc*) for details.

# 3.7 Using a Lifecycle Management Policy to Save Storage Account Costs

## Problem

You need to move blob objects to less expensive access tiers to save on storage account costs.

## Solution

Configure one or more Azure Storage lifecycle management policies (*https://oreil.ly/5aSco*) to move blob objects from *hot* to *cool* or *cool* to *archive* access tiers based on blob access patterns as illustrated in Figure 3-7.

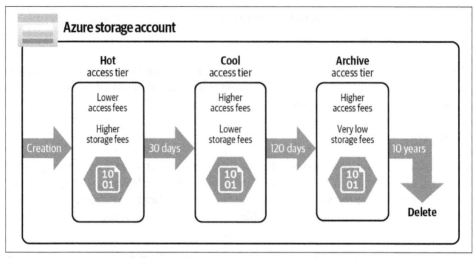

*Figure 3-7. Using lifecycle management policies to optimize storage account costs*

### Steps

1. Log in to your Azure subscription in the Owner role and create a new resource group for this recipe. See "General Workstation Setup Instructions" on page xii for details.

2. Use the `--access-tier` parameter to set the access tier when creating the storage account. The default value is Hot, but we added the parameter for clarity. Accepted values for this parameter are Cool, Hot, and Premium. Use the following CLI command to provision a new Azure storage account in the Hot access tier:

```
storageName="<storage-account-name>"
```

```
az storage account create \
    --name $storageName \
    --access-tier Hot \
    --resource-group $rgName \
    --location $region \
    --sku Standard_LRS \
    --default-action Allow
```

3. In this storage account, by default all new blobs will be saved in the hot tier, which is optimized for frequent access. Let's define a new lifecycle management policy that moves blobs from the hot access tier to the cool if they are unchanged for 60 days, and from the cool access tier to the archive after 120 days of being unchanged. This policy also deletes blobs if they are unchanged for over 8 years (2,920 days). Create a JSON file with the following content and save it as *ACCESS_POLICY.JSON*. You can also find this file in this chapter's GitHub repository (*https://oreil.ly/ChMfH*):

```json
{
  "rules": [
    {
      "enabled": true,
      "name": "sample-rule",
      "type": "Lifecycle",
      "definition": {
        "actions": {
          "baseBlob": {
            "tierToCool": {
              "daysAfterModificationGreaterThan": 60
            },
            "tierToArchive": {
              "daysAfterModificationGreaterThan": 120,
              "daysAfterLastTierChangeGreaterThan": 60
            },
            "delete": {
              "daysAfterModificationGreaterThan": 2920
            }
          }
        },
        "filters": {
          "blobTypes": ["blockBlob"]
        }
      }
    }
  ]
}
```

You can filter which blob types (block, page, etc.) and blob files to include in the access policy, or include blob versions in the policy if required by your scenario. See the storage account documentation (*https://oreil.ly/QYFYU*) for the policy JSON schema details.

4. Use the following command to create the policy for your storage account. Replace *<path-to-folder/ACCESS_POLICY.JSON>* with the Linux-style path to your local policy file created in the previous step:

```
az storage account management-policy create \
    --resource-group $rgName \
    --account-name $storageName \
    --policy <path-to-folder/ACCESS_POLICY.JSON>
```

5. Run the following command to delete the resources you created in this recipe:

```
az group delete --name $rgName
```

You successfully created a lifecycle management policy for your Azure storage account. Data will be moved from the hot to cool access tier after 60 days of being unchanged, and to the archive tier after 120 days of being unchanged. Finally, blobs will be deleted if they are not updated for 8 years (2,920 days).

## Discussion

Azure Storage offers three access tiers (*https://oreil.ly/lRAwQ*) for blob objects:

*Hot tier*
> Optimized for frequent access. You will pay less for accessing a blob object but more for storing it. Use this access tier if you need to access your blob objects frequently.

*Cool tier*
> Use this tier for blob objects that you access less frequently but still need immediate access to on occasion. You will pay less for storing blobs comparing to the hot tier but will pay more to access them. The blob should be at least 45 days old before being moved to this tier.

*Archive tier*
> An offline tier optimized for storing rarely accessed data. Use this tier when you don't need to immediately access the blob objects. When you do need access, it will take several hours to rehydrate the data before it will be available. Data should be at least 180 days old before being moved to the archive tier.

Imagine you use Azure Storage blobs to store system access logs. The auditing application needs to frequently access the logs in the first month. The logs should be still accessible for the next year and must be kept for 10 years due to compliance requirements. You could store all the logs in the hot tier, but you would be overpaying for the expensive storage cost associated with that tier. Instead, you can optimize costs by creating a lifecycle management policy that:

- Moves the logs from the hot tier to cool after 31 days
- Moves data from cool to archive after 365 days (12 months)
- Deletes the logs from the archive tier after 10 years (3,650 days)

> Do not move your blobs to the archive tier if they need to be immediately readable! Blobs in the archive tier cannot be read unless they are first *rehydrated*, a process that may be time-consuming and expensive. For more information, see the archive tier documentation (*https://oreil.ly/9Mk-m*) for details.

Lifecycle management rules can also move blob data to *warmer* tiers if needed. For example, you can create a lifecycle management policy to move a blob from cool to hot as soon as it is accessed.

# 3.8 Using AzCopy to Upload Multiple Files to Azure Storage Blobs

## Problem

You need to upload all the files within a local directory to Azure Storage blobs.

## Solution

Install the AzCopy tool (*https://oreil.ly/RTvgp*) and use it to bulk upload files to an Azure storage account (see Figure 3-8).

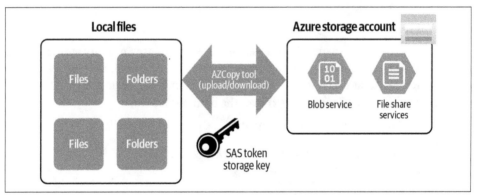

*Figure 3-8. Using AzCopy to bulk upload files to Azure storage blobs or file shares*

### Steps

1. Log in to your Azure subscription in the Owner role and create a new resource group for this recipe. See "General Workstation Setup Instructions" on page xii for details.

2. Use the following CLI command to provision a new Azure storage account and create a new container in it:

   ```
   storageName="<storage-account-name>"

   az storage account create \
        --name $storageName \
        --resource-group $rgName \
        --location $region \
        --sku Standard_LRS \
   ```

```
    --default-action Allow

storageKey1=$(az storage account keys list \
    --resource-group $rgName \
    --account-name $storageName \
    --query [0].value \
    --output tsv)

az storage container create \
    --name "mycontainer" \
    --account-name $storageName \
    --account-key $storageKey1
```

3. Download and install the AzCopy tool for your OS. Check the AzCopy installation documentation (*https://oreil.ly/N3QWr*) for details.

4. Create a local folder on your machine and copy/create several non-sensitive text files in it. Make a note of the local folder path and save it in the `localPath` variable (for example *C:\files*):

    ```
    localPath="<local-folder-path>"
    ```

5. As you probably remember from Recipe 3.3, you can use an Azure storage key or SAS token to grant access to a storage account. Take a look at Recipe 3.3 for a detailed explanation. Run the following commands to create a new SAS token with read and write accesses (rw) over the blob service (b):

    ```
    expiryDate=`date -u -d "60 minutes" '+%Y-%m-%dT%H:%MZ'`

    sasToken=$(az storage account generate-sas \
        --account-name $storageName \
        --account-key $storageKey1 \
        --expiry $expiryDate \
        --permissions rw \
        --resource-types co \
        --services b \
        --https-only \
        --output tsv)
    ```

6. Now use AzCopy to upload all the files within the `localPath` folder to the storage account:

    ```
    containerURL=$(az storage account show \
        --resource-group $rgName \
        --name $storageName \
        --query primaryEndpoints.blob \
        --output tsv)"mycontainer/?"$sasToken

    azcopy copy $localPath"/*" $containerURL
    ```

7. To confirm your files are uploaded, list the blobs within your container using the following command:

```
az storage blob list \
    --account-name $storageName \
    --account-key $storageKey1 \
    --container-name "mycontainer" \
    --query [].name
```

8. Run the following command to delete the resources you created in this recipe:

```
az group delete --name $rgName
```

You successfully uploaded multiple files to the Azure Storage blob service using the AzCopy utility. The same tool can be used to upload files to the storage account file shares as well. We will try this in Recipe 3.9. See the AzCopy documentation (*https://oreil.ly/JOoSP*) for additional details.

## Discussion

AzCopy is a command-line tool that you can use to copy blobs or files to or from a storage account. Both Azure blobs and Azure file shares are supported. Use this tool to migrate your small- to medium-size local datasets to your storage account. For gigabyte-size datasets, you might want to check other services such as Azure Data Box (*https://oreil.ly/m-Prm*).

You can use storage account keys or SAS tokens to authenticate the AzCopy tool into your storage account. A SAS token is recommended because you can grant scoped access that expires after your migration is completed.

# 3.9 Using AzCopy to Upload Multiple Files to Azure Storage File Shares

## Problem

You need to upload all the files within a local directory to Azure Storage file shares.

## Solution

Install the AzCopy tool (*https://oreil.ly/0TdFo*) and use it to bulk upload files to Azure Storage.

## Steps

1. Log in to your Azure subscription in the Owner role and create a new resource group for this recipe. See "General Workstation Setup Instructions" on page xii for details.

2. Use the following CLI command to provision a new Azure storage account and create a new container in it:

```
storageName="<storage-account-name>"

az storage account create \
    --name $storageName \
    --resource-group $rgName \
    --location $region \
    --sku Standard_LRS \
    --default-action Allow

storageKey1=$(az storage account keys list \
    --resource-group $rgName \
    --account-name $storageName \
    --query [0].value \
    --output tsv)

az storage share create \
    --name "myfileshare" \
    --account-name $storageName \
    --account-key $storageKey1
```

3. If you haven't already done so, follow step 3 in Recipe 3.8 to download the AzCopy utility.

4. Create a local folder on your machine and copy/create several nonsensitive text files in it. Make a note of the local folder path and save it in the `localPath` variable (for example *C:\files*):

```
localPath="<local-folder-path>"
```

5. Run the following commands to create a new SAS token with read and write accesses (rw) over the file share service (f):

```
expiryDate=`date -u -d "60 minutes" '+%Y-%m-%dT%H:%MZ'`

sasToken=$(az storage account generate-sas \
    --account-name $storageName \
    --account-key $storageKey1 \
    --expiry $expiryDate \
    --permissions rw \
    --resource-types co \
    --services f \
    --https-only \
    --output tsv)
```

6. Now use AzCopy to upload all the files within the `localPath` folder to your storage account:

```
fileshareURL=$(az storage account show \
    --resource-group $rgName \
    --name $storageName \
    --query primaryEndpoints.file
    --output tsv)"myfileshare/?"$sasToken

azcopy copy $localPath $fileshareURL \
    --recursive=true
```

 The AzCopy tool creates a logfile, which can be consulted in case of problems. You can find the log filepath in the AzCopy command output.

7. To confirm your files are uploaded, list the blobs within your container using the following command:

```
az storage file list \
    --account-name $storageName \
    --account-key $storageKey1 \
    --share-name "myfileshare" \
    --query [].name
```

8. Run the following command to delete the resources you created in this recipe:

```
az group delete --name $rgName
```

You successfully uploaded multiple files to the Azure Storage file share service using the AzCopy utility. If the `--recursive=true` parameter is passed, all the subfolders within the parent directory will be copied to the file share as well.

## Discussion

Many companies are migrating their on-premises network file shares to Azure to take advantage of availability, security, and manageability of Azure storage accounts. You can use the AzCopy utility to conveniently upload your local file shares to Azure storage file shares. For gigabyte-size shares, Azure Data Box (*https://oreil.ly/GaN3m*) remains the most efficient service.

# 3.10 Protecting Azure Storage Blobs from Accidental Deletion

## Problem

You want to protect Azure Storage blob files from accidental deletion.

## Solution

Enable the soft delete option (*https://oreil.ly/wrTfE*) for your Azure Storage blobs and containers. This enables you to recover deleted blobs within a retention period that you set.

### Steps

1. Follow steps 1 through 5 in Recipe 3.5 to create a new storage account and upload a text blob to it. Make sure you run all the commands so that variables such as $storageKey1, $containerName, and $blobFileName are initialized.

2. By default, soft delete is not enabled on storage accounts. Run the following command to enable soft delete for your storage account blobs. The retention period is set to 14 days:

   ```
   az storage account blob-service-properties update \
       --account-name $storageName \
       --enable-delete-retention true \
       --delete-retention-days 14
   ```

    Check the az storage account blob-service-properties update command documentation (*https://oreil.ly/YQKb9*) for details.

3. Now, any deleted blob can be recovered within 14 days of its deletion time. Let's try this by deleting the blob object we uploaded earlier:

   ```
   az storage blob delete \
       --account-name $storageName \
       --account-key $storageKey1 \
       --container-name $containerName \
       --name MyBlob $blobFileName
   ```

4. To confirm your file is deleted, list the blobs within your container using the following command. Make sure you get any empty list, [ ]:

   ```
   az storage blob list \
       --account-name $storageName \
   ```

```
            --account-key $storageKey1 \
            --container-name $containerName \
            --query [].name
```

5. Use the following command to *undelete* your blob object. The `undelete` command will be successful only if it is used within the delete retention period. Also, you can't recover a blob object that is deleted before enabling soft delete. This command succeeds because we are within the 14-day delete retention period:

```
az storage blob undelete \
    --account-name $storageName \
    --account-key $storageKey1 \
    --container-name $containerName \
    --name MyBlob $blobFileName
```

6. To confirm your file is recovered, list the blobs within your container using the following command. Make sure your blob file is back on the list:

```
az storage blob list \
    --account-name $storageName \
    --account-key $storageKey1 \
    --container-name $containerName \
    --query [].name
```

7. Run the following command to delete the resources you created in this recipe:

```
az group delete --name $rgName
```

In this recipe, you added soft delete protection for Azure Storage blobs, so any accidentally deleted blobs can be recovered within the set retention period.

## Discussion

In this recipe, you learned how to enable the soft delete option for your Azure storage accounts containing sensitive or hard-to-replace blob objects. This feature protects your blobs and their snapshots/versions against accidental deletion.

Microsoft recommends the following steps to protect your blob data:

- Enable soft-delete for blobs, snapshots, and/or blob versions. You achieved this in the current recipe.
- Enable soft-delete for containers to protect containers against accidental deletion.
- Enable Azure Storage blob versioning for your storage account.

Check the Azure Storage blobs documentation (*https://oreil.ly/EyMd_*) and soft delete documentation (*https://oreil.ly/JrEyF*) for details.

Enabling soft delete for blobs does not protect parent containers. For complete protection, you should also enable soft delete for containers as recommended in the preceding list.

# 3.11 Protecting an Azure Storage Account from Deletion Using Azure Locks

## Problem

You want to protect your Azure storage account from deletion by users or applications.

## Solution

Create a delete lock (*https://oreil.ly/ZdOxP*) for your storage account, as shown in Figure 3-9.

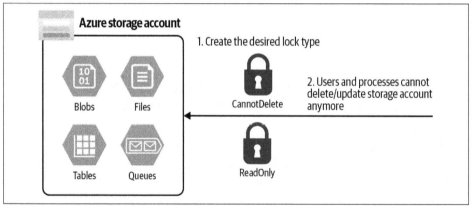

*Figure 3-9. Protecting storage accounts using Azure locks*

### Steps

1. Log in to your Azure subscription in the Owner role and create a new resource group for this recipe. See "General Workstation Setup Instructions" on page xii for details.

2. Use the following CLI command to provision a new storage account and create a new container in it:

```
storageName="<storage-account-name>"

az storage account create \
    --name $storageName \
```

```
    --resource-group $rgName \
    --location $region \
    --sku Standard_LRS
```

3. Create a new Azure `CanNotDelete` lock for your storage account using the following CLI command:

```
az lock create \
    --name MyStorageDeleteLock \
    --lock-type CanNotDelete \
    --resource-group $rgName \
    --resource $storageName \
    --resource-type "Microsoft.Storage/storageAccounts"
```

4. You successfully created a `CanNotDelete` lock for your storage account. The storage account can't be deleted by any user until this lock is deleted. You can use the following command to delete this lock:

```
az lock delete \
    --name MyStorageDeleteLock \
    --resource-group $rgName \
    --resource $storageName \
    --resource-type "Microsoft.Storage/storageAccounts"
```

5. Run the following command to delete the resources you created in this recipe:

```
az group delete --name $rgName
```

> You won't be able to delete the storage account unless the lock is successfully deleted in the previous step.

In this recipe, you successfully created a `CanNotDelete` lock. You can also create a `ReadOnly` lock using the same CLI command.

## Discussion

In this recipe, we learned how to use Azure locks to protect your Azure subscriptions, resource groups, or resources against deletion and updates by other users or processes. Azure offers two lock types:

`CanNotDelete` *lock*
    This prevents the resource from being deleted by users/processes with any permissions level.

**ReadOnly** *lock*

As the name implies, this lock prevents users and processes from updating the resource. They can still read the resource.

See the Azure locks documentation (*https://oreil.ly/M53Kg*) to read more about locks.

 To create or delete locks, you need to have Microsoft.Authorization/* or Microsoft.Authorization/locks/* permissions/actions. Only the Owner and the User Access Administrator built-in roles have such access levels. As you saw in Recipe 1.2, a custom role with such permissions can also be created.

CHAPTER 4

# Persisting Data

Almost every application needs to persist data in some form, and cloud applications are no exception. The data could be in one of the following forms:

- Binary or text files, such as images, videos, music, Apache Avro, CSV, or JSON formats
- Structured or semi-structured data stored in relational or NoSQL databases

In Chapter 3, we talked about Azure Storage, which can store unstructured data such as blob files (text, binary, etc.). In this chapter, we will talk about databases offered by Azure to persist relational and NoSQL data.

The first option is to go with IaaS database offerings (*https://oreil.ly/ncX95*). You can provision an Azure VM and install any database engine that you like, including Microsoft SQL Server, MySQL, or even MongoDB. This option gives you great flexibility because you own the underlying virtual machine; however, it requires a lot of administrative overhead. You are responsible for maintaining, securing, and patching the VM operating system and the database engine.

A second (and better) option, and the one we'll focus on in this chapter, is to go with the Azure managed databases. These are PaaS (platform as a service) offerings (*https://oreil.ly/096Xs*), also called *managed databases*, which allow you to provision a ready-to-use database in minutes. Azure takes care of the underlying VM OS patching and security and many other administrative tasks such as scaling.

Azure SQL, Azure Cosmos DB, and Azure Database for PostgreSQL are a few Azure PaaS databases available to you. Having native integration with other Azure services such as Azure Virtual Networks, Azure Key Vault, and Azure Monitor enables you to easily integrate these databases with your Azure solutions.

This chapter's focus is on the two main managed Azure databases: Azure Cosmos DB and Azure SQL. Topics you will learn about include:

- Enabling customer-managed keys for Cosmos DB encryption at rest
- Working with Azure Cosmos DB and Azure SQL firewalls
- Granting Cosmos DB access to other Azure services using managed identities and RBAC
- Configuring auto-scaling for Azure Cosmos DB

 Azure continuously improves both Azure Cosmos DB and Azure SQL services. Keep an eye on the Azure updates page (*https://oreil.ly/kQstP*) for the latest and greatest features.

## Workstation Configuration

You will need to prepare your workstation before starting on the recipes in this chapter. Follow "What You Will Need" on page xi to set up your machine to run Azure CLI commands. You can clone the book's GitHub repository using the following command:

```
git clone https://github.com/zaalion/AzureCookbook.git
```

# 4.1 Creating a Cosmos DB NoSQL API Account

## Problem

You need to store your NoSQL data as JSON documents in a scalable, globally distributed Azure database.

## Solution

Create a new Azure Cosmos DB NoSQL API account, create a database, and store your JSON data in the containers within the database, as shown in Figure 4-1.

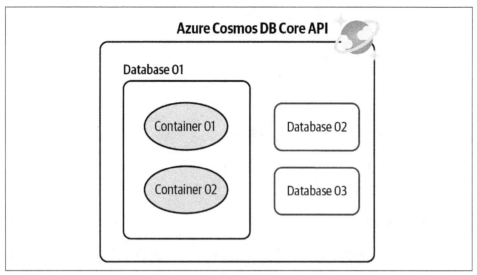

*Figure 4-1. Storing NoSQL data in an Azure Cosmos DB NoSQL API account*

### Steps

1. Log in to your Azure subscription in the Owner role and create a new resource group for this recipe. See "General Workstation Setup Instructions" on page xii for details.

2. Create a new Azure Cosmos DB NoSQL API account. Replace *<cosmos-account-name>* with the desired Cosmos DB account name. This script also configures periodic backups to be created every 240 minutes (4 hours) and to be kept for 12 hours:

```
cosmosAccountName="<cosmos-account-name>"

az cosmosdb create \
    --name $cosmosAccountName \
    --resource-group $rgName \
    --backup-policy-type Periodic \
    --backup-interval 240 \
    --backup-retention 12
```

3. Next, you need to create a database to host your data. You can assign a fixed throughput (RU/s) to your database and/or assign desired throughput at the container (collection) level later. See the Azure documentation (*https://oreil.ly/85GId*) for details. Use this command to create a database named MyCompanyDB in your Cosmos DB account:

```
az cosmosdb sql database create \
   --account-name $cosmosAccountName \
   --name MyCompanyDB \
   --throughput 1000 \
   --resource-group $rgName
```

 Assigning a fixed (provisioned) throughput to a database is not mandatory. You have the option to assign throughput to child containers (*https://oreil.ly/8xi2W*) later. Cosmos DB also offers the *autoscale* and *serverless* deployments, which adjust resources based on the traffic and load. See the Cosmos DB documentation (*https:// oreil.ly/SU-Gk*) for more details.

4. Now the stage is set for you to create your first *container* (collection) in your database. Think of a container as a table in a relational database. Each container should have a partition key, which helps with distributing container documents over logical partitions for better performance (*https://oreil.ly/FAL7k*). Use the following command to create a new collection named People with the fixed throughput of 400 RU/s (request units):

```
MSYS_NO_PATHCONV=1 az cosmosdb sql container create \
   --name People \
   --partition-key-path "/id" \
   --throughput 400 \
   --database-name MyCompanyDB \
   --account-name $cosmosAccountName \
   --resource-group $rgName
```

 Put MSYS_NO_PATHCONV=1 before the Bash command so that /id is not converted in a Linux path.

5. Run the following command to delete the resources you created in this recipe:

```
az group delete --name $rgName
```

In this recipe, you created an Azure Cosmos DB NoSQL API account and a database with a container in it. Now you can persist your NoSQL documents in this database.

# Discussion

Azure Cosmos DB is Microsoft's primary NoSQL database offering in the cloud. Cosmos DB is a globally distributed, secure, multi-model database. At the time of writing this book, Cosmos DB offers the following APIs (models):

*SQL (Core) API*
We recommend this API for all new projects.

*Gremlin (Graph) API*
We recommend this API if you need to persist the graph data structure in your database. For instance, you may want to do this for a social media application.

*API for MongoDB*
Use this API if you are migrating data from MongoDB to Azure Cosmos DB and would like no, or minimal, changes to your application code.

*Cassandra API*
Use this API if you are migrating from Cassandra to Azure Cosmos DB and would like your application to work with Cosmos DB without code changes.

*Table API*
A premium alternative for Azure Table storage users. Migrate your data to Azure Cosmos DB Table API, and your code will work without any required changes.

Check the Azure Cosmos DB SQL (Core) API documentation (*https://oreil.ly/tDoP2*) for details.

In this recipe, we created a SQL (Core) API. This API stores data in JSON document format. You have full control over the interface, service, and the SDK client libraries (*https://oreil.ly/QGaqe*).

Cosmos DB offers the following capabilities as well:

- *Global distribution* and *multi-region writes* so data can be served to clients all over the globe with great performance
- Adjustable consistency level (*https://oreil.ly/dhHgC*) for different consistency and performance requirements
- Zone redundancy (*https://oreil.ly/lqSS1*) for better protection against zonal failures
- Security features such as encryption at rest, encryption in transit, an easy-to-configure firewall, and support for Azure Active Directory authentication

In this chapter, we will go over several Cosmos DB features and capabilities.

# 4.2 Creating a Cosmos DB Apache Gremlin (Graph) API Account

## Problem

You need a scalable, globally distributed graph database in Azure.

## Solution

Create a new Azure Cosmos DB Gremlin API account, create a database, and use it to store your graph objects. See Figure 4-2.

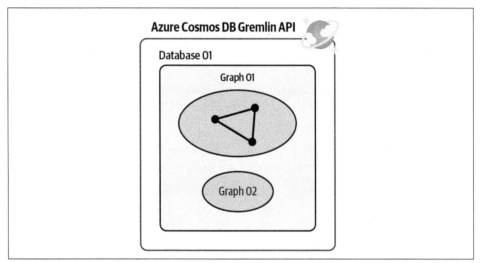

*Figure 4-2. Storing graph data in an Azure Cosmos DB Gremlin API account*

### Steps

1. Log in to your Azure subscription in the Owner role and create a new resource group for this recipe. See "General Workstation Setup Instructions" on page xii for details.

2. Create a new Azure Cosmos DB Gremlin API account. Replace *<cosmos-account-name>* with the desired Cosmos DB account name:

```
cosmosAccountName="<cosmos-account-name>"

az cosmosdb create \
  --name $cosmosAccountName \
  --resource-group $rgName \
  --capabilities EnableGremlin
```

3. Use this command to create a database named `MyGraphDB` in your Cosmos DB account:

```
az cosmosdb gremlin database create \
  --account-name $cosmosAccountName \
  --resource-group $rgName \
  --name MyGraphDB
```

4. Now you can create one or more graphs in `MyGraphDB`. As with containers, each graph should have a partition key (*https://oreil.ly/aVRGb*), which helps with distributing graph data over logical partitions for better performance. Use the following command to create a new graph named `People`:

```
MSYS_NO_PATHCONV=1 az cosmosdb gremlin graph create \
  --resource-group $rgName \
  --account-name $cosmosAccountName \
  --database-name MyGraphDB \
  --name People \
  --partition-key-path "/age"
```

 Put `MSYS_NO_PATHCONV=1` before the Bash command so that `/id` is not converted to a Linux path.

5. Run the following command to delete the resources you created in this recipe:

```
az group delete --name $rgName
```

You successfully created an Azure Cosmos DB Gremlin API account and a database with a graph in it.

## Discussion

Graph databases are NoSQL data stores, which are optimized to persist the graph data structure and query it. Azure Cosmos DB Gremlin API (*https://oreil.ly/Fghq8*) is Microsoft's primary graph database offering in the cloud. It offers high availability, flexible consistency levels, global distribution, and SDKs for many frameworks and languages.

Graph databases are ideal for the following scenarios:

*Internet of Things*
Manage the connection between connected IoT devices

*Social networks*
Model the relationship between people, places, and other entities

---

*Recommendation engines in the retail industry*
Build tailored recommendations per user

*Geospatial*
Find optimized routes in location-enabled applications and products

Check the Azure Cosmos DB Gremlin documentation (*https://oreil.ly/s-FIp*) for more details.

# 4.3 Configuring Azure Cosmos DB Firewall

## Problem

You want to control access to Azure Cosmos DB based on the client IP address or network.

## Solution

Configure the Azure Cosmos DB service firewall to allow access by trusted IP addresses, virtual networks, and private endpoints, while denying all other traffic (see Figure 4-3).

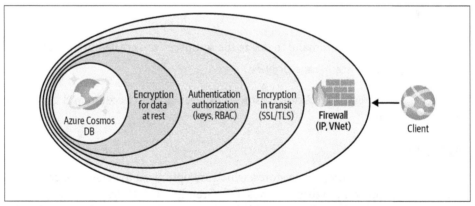

*Figure 4-3. Protecting Azure Cosmos DB using the service firewall*

### Steps

1. Log in to your Azure subscription in the Owner role and create a new resource group for this recipe. See "General Workstation Setup Instructions" on page xii for details.

2. Create a new Azure Cosmos DB account. The service firewall is available for all Cosmos DB APIs. In this recipe, let's go with the SQL (Core) API. Replace `<cosmos-account-name>` with the desired Cosmos DB account name:

```
cosmosAccountName="<cosmos-account-name>"

az cosmosdb create \
  --name $cosmosAccountName \
  --resource-group $rgName
```

3. First, let's add a new *IP filter rule*. After adding this rule, clients will be rejected unless their IP address is present in the rule. Replace *<allowed-ip-range>* with an IP range, comma-separated list of IPs, or a single IP address:

```
allowedIPRange="<allowed-ip-range>"

az cosmosdb update \
  --resource-group $rgName \
  --name $cosmosAccountName \
  --ip-range-filter $allowedIPRange
```

> Updating Azure Cosmos DB can take a few minutes. Please wait until the command completes.

4. You can also create *Cosmos DB network rules* to allow traffic from select Azure VNets. First, use the following command to create a new Azure VNet. Replace *<vnet-name>* with your desired network name:

```
vnetName="<vnet-name>"

az network vnet create \
  --resource-group $rgName \
  --name $vnetName \
  --address-prefix 10.0.0.0/16 \
  --subnet-name Subnet01 \
  --subnet-prefix 10.0.0.0/26
```

5. Your goal is to enable clients in the specified subnet to see and use Azure Cosmos DB. To achieve this, you need to start by adding the Microsoft.AzureCosmosDB service endpoint (*https://oreil.ly/A3yEN*) to the subnet:

```
az network vnet subnet update \
  --resource-group $rgName \
  --name Subnet01 \
  --vnet-name $vnetName \
  --service-endpoints Microsoft.AzureCosmosDB
```

6. Then enable Azure VNet filtering for your Cosmos DB account:

```
az cosmosdb update \
  --resource-group $rgName \
```

```
    --name $cosmosAccountName \
    --enable-virtual-network true
```

7. At this point, your Cosmos DB account only accepts traffic from the IPs specified with $allowedIPRange. Now the stage is set for you to allow traffic originating from Subnet01:

```
az cosmosdb network-rule add \
    --resource-group $rgName \
    --virtual-network $vnetName \
    --subnet Subnet01 \
    --name $cosmosAccountName
```

 This command might take a few minutes to complete. If you get the message "VirtualNetworkRules should be specified only if IsVirtualNetworkFilterEnabled is True," make sure the previous step completed successfully.

8. Use the following command to confirm the Cosmos DB network rule was created:

```
az cosmosdb network-rule list \
    --name $cosmosAccountName \
    --resource-group $rgName
```

9. Run the following command to delete the resources you created in this recipe:

```
az group delete --name $rgName
```

You successfully configured the Azure Cosmos DB firewall to allow client traffic only from your desired IP addresses and Azure VNets.

## Discussion

Many Azure services provide service-level firewalls that provide defense in depth (*https://oreil.ly/X29hp*) to protect your data. Azure SQL, Azure Storage, and Azure Cosmos DB are among these services.

It is a good security practice to always configure service-level firewalls on top of other security safeguards (such as Azure Active Directory authentication). This ensures no unauthorized user from the internet or other networks can access your Azure Cosmos DB data.

Azure Cosmos DB firewall enables you to configure the following restrictions individually or combined:

- Allow traffic based on the client IP address using IP rules (*https://oreil.ly/ExUXV*)
- Allow traffic based on the client virtual network (*https://oreil.ly/YGApP*)

- Allow private traffic via Azure private endpoints (*https://oreil.ly/p7Qoe*)

Use IP rules for clients that have static IP addresses, such as public virtual machines, or when you need to access Cosmos DB from your own local machine. Use virtual network rules to allow services such as Azure virtual machines or App Service Environments, which are deployed to an Azure VNet subnet.

> We strongly recommend configuring service-level firewalls for any data store in production. These services include (but are not limited to) Azure Cosmos DB, Azure SQL, Azure Storage, Azure Databricks, and Azure Synapse Analytics.

# 4.4 Configuring Azure Cosmos DB Private Access

## Problem

You need clients to access Azure Cosmos DB only through Azure private endpoints.

## Solution

Create a private endpoint for your Azure Cosmos DB account and then disable public network access for Azure Cosmos DB, as shown in Figure 4-4.

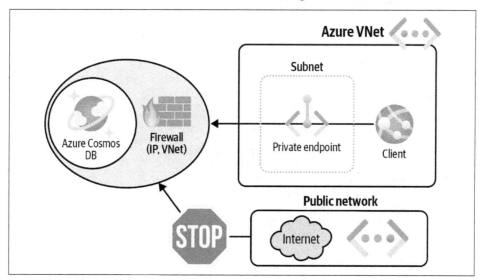

*Figure 4-4. Allowing only private traffic to Azure Cosmos DB using private endpoints*

## Steps

1. Log in to your Azure subscription in the Owner role and create a new resource group for this recipe. See "General Workstation Setup Instructions" on page xii for details.

2. Create a new Azure Cosmos DB account. The service firewall is available for all Cosmos DB APIs. In this recipe, let's go with the SQL (Core) API. Replace *<cosmos-account-name>* with the desired Cosmos DB account name:

```
cosmosAccountName="<cosmos-account-name>"

az cosmosdb create \
  --name $cosmosAccountName \
  --resource-group $rgName
```

3. Use the following command to create a new Azure VNet. Replace *<vnet-name>* with your desired network name:

```
vnetName="<vnet-name>"

az network vnet create \
  --resource-group $rgName \
  --name $vnetName \
  --address-prefix 10.0.0.0/20 \
  --subnet-name PLSubnet \
  --subnet-prefix 10.0.0.0/26
```

4. Now, grab the Cosmos DB account ID and store it in a variable. You will use the variable in the next step:

```
cosmosAccountId=$(az cosmosdb show \
  --name $cosmosAccountName \
  --resource-group $rgName \
  --query id --output tsv)
```

5. Now you are ready to create a private endpoint for your Cosmos DB account:

```
MSYS_NO_PATHCONV=1 az network private-endpoint create \
    --name MyCosmosPrivateEndpoint \
    --resource-group $rgName \
    --vnet-name $vnetName \
    --subnet PLSubnet \
    --connection-name MyEndpointConnection \
    --private-connection-resource-id $cosmosAccountId \
    --group-id Sql
```

6. Your clients can use the new private endpoint in the PLSubnet subnet to communicate with your Cosmos DB account, but this does not prevent public network access. Use the following command to explicitly disable public network access for your Cosmos DB account:

```
az cosmosdb update \
  --resource-group $rgName \
  --name $cosmosAccountName \
  --enable-public-network false
```

7. Run the following command to delete the resources you created in this recipe:

```
az group delete --name $rgName
```

In this recipe, you configured the Azure Cosmos DB firewall to allow client traffic only from a private endpoint.

## Discussion

In Recipe 4.3 we discussed Azure Cosmos DB network access options. We talked about restricting traffic by IP address or the client Azure VNet. Both of these options still allow traffic to go over the public network, which might not be desirable for many organizations.

In this recipe, you configured Azure Cosmos DB to disable public network access and only accept network traffic from a private endpoint. This is by far the most secure option from a networking point of view. Take a look at the Azure Cosmos DB documentation (*https://oreil.ly/sxL3O*) for more details.

Microsoft defines a private endpoint as "a network interface that uses a private IP address from your virtual network." This network interface connects you privately to a service that is powered by Azure Private Link (*https://oreil.ly/fm4RV*). The private endpoint network traffic does not go over the public internet; rather, it uses only Azure's private network infrastructure. You can use private endpoints to connect to many services including:

- Azure Storage
- Azure Cosmos DB
- Azure SQL Database
- Azure App Services
- Azure Function Apps

# 4.5 Granting Function Apps Access to Cosmos DB Using RBAC

## Problem

You need to grant Cosmos DB read and write access to an Azure Function App without using the Azure Cosmos DB Keys.

## Solution

Create a custom Cosmos DB role definition with the desired permissions (actions) and assign it to the Function App identity for the Cosmos DB account scope as illustrated in Figure 4-5.

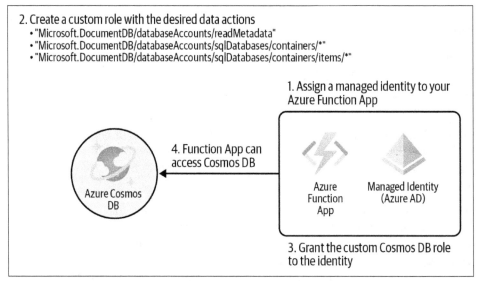

*Figure 4-5. Granting Cosmos DB data access to Azure Function App*

### Steps

1. Log in to your Azure subscription in the Owner role and create a new resource group for this recipe. See "General Workstation Setup Instructions" on page xii for details.

2. Use the following CLI command to create a new Azure Cosmos DB account:

```
cosmosAccountName="<cosmos-account-name>"

az cosmosdb create \
  --name $cosmosAccountName \
  --resource-group $rgName
```

3. Use the following command to create a new Azure Function App and assign a system-assigned managed identity to it:

```
funcStorageAccount="<func-storage-account-name>"
planName="<appservice-plan-name>"
funcAppName="<function-app-name>"

az storage account create \
    --name $funcStorageAccount \
    --resource-group $rgName \
    --location $region \
    --sku Standard_LRS

az appservice plan create \
    --resource-group $rgName \
    --name $planName \
    --sku S1 \
    --location $region

az functionapp create \
    --resource-group $rgName \
    --name $funcAppName \
    --storage-account $funcStorageAccount \
    --assign-identity [system] \
    --functions-version 3 \
    --plan $planName
```

4. Use the following command to obtain the Function App managed identity ID (GUID) and the Cosmos DB account resource ID. You will need these later:

```
cosmosAccountId=$(az cosmosdb show \
  --name $cosmosAccountName \
  --resource-group $rgName \
  --query id \
  --output tsv)

funcObjectId=$(az functionapp show \
    --name $funcAppName \
    --resource-group $rgName \
    --query identity.principalId \
    --output tsv)
```

5. You need to create a custom RBAC role with the desired Cosmos DB permissions. First, create a JSON file with the following content and name it *MyCosmosDBReadWriteRole.json*:

```
{
    "RoleName": "MyCosmosDBReadWriteRole",
    "Type": "CustomRole",
    "AssignableScopes": ["/"],
    "Permissions":
```

```
[
  {
    "DataActions": [
      "Microsoft.DocumentDB/databaseAccounts/readMetadata",
      "Microsoft.DocumentDB/databaseAccounts/sqlDatabases
          /containers/*",
      "Microsoft.DocumentDB/databaseAccounts/sqlDatabases
          /containers/items/*"
    ]
  }
]
}
```

6. Next, you will create the Cosmos DB role definition. Replace *<path-to-MyCosmosDBReadWriteRole.json>* with the Linux-style path to your JSON file, for example *C:/Data/MyCosmosDBReadWriteRole.json*:

```
az cosmosdb sql role definition create \
   --account-name $cosmosAccountName \
   --resource-group $rgName \
   --body <path-to-MyCosmosDBReadWriteRole.json>
```

7. Now you can assign the new MyCosmosDBReadWriteRole custom role to your Function App:

```
MSYS_NO_PATHCONV=1 az cosmosdb sql role assignment create \
   --account-name $cosmosAccountName \
   --resource-group $rgName \
   --role-definition-name MyCosmosDBReadWriteRole \
   --principal-id $funcObjectId \
   --scope "/dbs"
```

 You can narrow down the scope to a single database or even a container in the Cosmos DB account, such as /dbs/mydb/colls/mycontainer. In our case, /dbs, you are assigning the role to all the databases within your Cosmos DB account.

8. Use the following commands to get the role definition ID and pass it to az cosmosdb sql role definition show` to confirm that your role is successfully assigned:

```
# Assuming there is only one role assignment in this Cosmos DB account
roleDefinitionId=$(az cosmosdb sql role assignment list \
   --account-name $cosmosAccountName \
   --resource-group $rgName \
   --query [0].roleDefinitionId --output tsv)

# The last 36 characters will be the role definition ID (GUID)
roleDefinitionGUID=${roleDefinitionId: -36}
```

```
az cosmosdb sql role definition show \
  --account-name $cosmosAccountName \
  --resource-group $rgName  \
  --id $roleDefinitionGUID
```

 At the time of writing this book, you are not able to see Cosmos DB custom role assignments in the Azure portal!

9. Run the following command to delete the resources you created in this recipe:

```
az group delete --name $rgName
```

You successfully granted Azure Cosmos DB access to a Function App without sharing any Cosmos DB keys. Any code deployed to your Function App can have read/write access to Cosmos DB without providing Cosmos DB account keys.

## Discussion

Similar to Azure Storage, Azure Cosmos DB supports Azure Active Directory (Azure AD) authentication through RBAC. This enables you to grant Cosmos DB access to security principals, such as Function app managed identities (*https://oreil.ly/YKW5D*) or Application Registrations (*https://oreil.ly/E5jDr*), without exposing Cosmos DB account keys. This is a recommended security practice.

Azure Cosmos DB supports RBAC access to the following planes:

*Management plane*
This is so that the assignee can manage the Azure Cosmos DB account—for example, configuring backup and restore. The assignee does not have access to the data stored in the database. Azure Cosmos DB provides built-in roles (*https://oreil.ly/ck1XX*) to work with the management plane. If necessary, you have the option to create your own custom roles.

*Data plane*
This is so that the assignee can access the data in the database. In this recipe, you created a custom data plane RBAC role and assigned it to a security principal (Azure Function identity). At the time of writing this book, there are two built-in RBAC roles (*https://oreil.ly/WtTZR*) available for data access, Cosmos DB Built-in Data Reader and Cosmos DB Built-in Data Contributor, in addition to the option of creating custom roles.

We recommend exploring the built-in Cosmos DB RBAC roles for management and data planes before creating your own custom role. You can create custom roles if:

---

- There is no built-in role for the access you need to grant
- The built-in roles give too much access

Although the Cosmos DB Built-in Data Contributor (*https://oreil.ly/lwKvV*) role grants the necessary permissions for our Function App, we decided to create a custom RBAC role for the purpose of learning in this recipe.

# 4.6 Storing Tabular Data in Azure Storage Tables

## Problem

You want to store tabular data in an affordable and scalable NoSQL data storage.

## Solution

Create a *general-purpose v2 storage account* and store your tabular NoSQL data in Azure storage tables as shown in Figure 4-6.

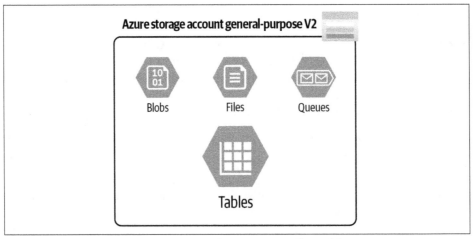

*Figure 4-6. Azure storage account general-purpose v2 offers table service*

### Steps

1. Log in to your Azure subscription in the Owner role and create a new resource group for this recipe. See "General Workstation Setup Instructions" on page xii for details.

2. Create a new Azure storage account using this command. This will be the source of our migration. Replace `<storage-account-name>` with the desired globally unique name:

```
storageName="<storage-account-name>"

az storage account create \
    --name $storageName \
    --resource-group $rgName \
    --location $region \
    --sku Standard_LRS
```

3. Save one of the storage account keys in a variable:

```
storageKey1=$(az storage account keys list \
    --resource-group $rgName \
    --account-name $storageName \
    --query [0].value \
    --output tsv)
```

4. Now, create a table in your storage account, name it `People`, and seed it with two data rows:

```
# creating a table
az storage table create \
  --account-name $storageName \
  --account-key $storageKey1 \
  --name People

# inserting a new row
az storage entity insert \
  --account-name $storageName \
  --account-key $storageKey1 \
  --table-name People \
  --entity PartitionKey=Canada RowKey=reza@contoso.com Name=Reza

# inserting another new row
az storage entity insert \
  --account-name $storageName \
  --account-key $storageKey1 \
  --table-name People \
  --entity PartitionKey=U.S.A. RowKey=john@contoso.com
    Name=John Last=Smith
```

 Each data row in an Azure storage table should have both `Parti`
`tionKey` and `RowKey` properties. Rows with the same `PartitionKey`
will be placed into the same partition for better load balancing. The
`RowKey` should be unique within each partition. Check the Azure
Table service data model documentation (*https://oreil.ly/h7jgl*) for
more details. Make sure you choose the right entities to avoid hot
or cold partitions. In this recipe, we chose the country name as the
`PartitionKey` and email address as the `RowKey`.

5. Use the following command to confirm the two rows were inserted as expected:

```
az storage entity query \
  --table-name People \
  --account-name $storageName \
  --account-key $storageKey1
```

6. Run the following command to delete the resources you created in this recipe:

```
az group delete --name $rgName
```

In this recipe you stored tabular data in Azure storage tables. You can use Azure Storage SDKs, REST APIs, and Azure Storage Explorer (*https://oreil.ly/0GeJA*) to manage your tables and manipulate the data.

## Discussion

At the time of writing this book, Microsoft Azure offers two main managed services to store tabular NoSQL data: *Azure Cosmos DB for Table API* and *Azure Table storage*. While Cosmos DB offers premium performance, latency, and SLA (service level agreements) (*https://oreil.ly/eY5J4*), Azure Table is a more affordable option for many projects.

Check the Azure documentation (*https://oreil.ly/D84va*) for a detailed list of differences between these two table offerings. You can also find Microsoft Azure's introduction on table storage offerings in the Azure documentation (*https://oreil.ly/8qaf7*).

You have a few options to migrate your data from Azure Table storage to Azure Cosmos DB to benefit from global distribution, SLA, and the performance Cosmos DB offers. Depending on the size and nature of your data migration, you can use the Cosmos DB Data Migration Tool, Azure Data Factory, or even custom migrations. See the Azure Cosmos DB documentation (*https://oreil.ly/iZFlv*) for details.

# 4.7 Configuring Autoscale for an Azure Cosmos DB NoSQL API Container

## Problem

You need to make sure an Azure Cosmos DB collection can autoscale to fulfill spikes in the number of requests.

## Solution

Configure autoscale on the Cosmos DB collection (container) and specify the maximum allowed RU/s (*https://oreil.ly/_pLts*).

## Steps

1. Log in to your Azure subscription in the Owner role and create a new resource group for this recipe. See "General Workstation Setup Instructions" on page xii for details.

2. Use the following command to create a new Azure Cosmos DB NoSQL API account:

```
cosmosAccountName="<cosmos-account-name>"

az cosmosdb create \
   --name $cosmosAccountName \
   --resource-group $rgName
```

3. Now, create a new database in your Cosmos DB account. We are not adding any throughput (*https://oreil.ly/RBTiR*) at the database level:

```
az cosmosdb sql database create \
   --account-name $cosmosAccountName \
   --resource-group $rgName \
   --name db01
```

4. Next, use this command to create a new collection (container) in this database and name it People. We are creating this container with a fixed provisioned throughput. This means the container will always have 1000 RU/s (*https://oreil.ly/pSfI6*) to use:

```
MSYS_NO_PATHCONV=1 az cosmosdb sql container create \
   --resource-group $rgName \
   --account-name $cosmosAccountName \
   --database-name db01 \
   --name People \
   --partition-key-path "/id" \
   --throughput "1000"
```

5. Use this command to see the throughput details for the new container. The output should show that the value for the throughput property is 1000 RU/s:

```
az cosmosdb sql container throughput show \
   --resource-group $rgName \
   --account-name $cosmosAccountName \
   --database-name db01 \
   --name People
```

6. In step 4, we could have passed the --max-throughput parameter instead of --throughput to enable autoscaling for the container. Since we didn't, in this step we will *migrate* the container from provisioned (fixed) throughput to autoscale using the following command:

---

```
az cosmosdb sql container throughput migrate \
  --resource-group $rgName \
  --account-name $cosmosAccountName \
  --database-name db01 \
  --name People \
  --throughput "autoscale"
```

7. Run the `az cosmosdb sql container throughput show` command again to see the updated throughput settings. Confirm that the `maxThroughput` property reads 1,000 RU/s:

```
az cosmosdb sql container throughput show \
  --resource-group $rgName \
  --account-name $cosmosAccountName \
  --database-name db01 \
  --name People
```

8. Finally, let's update the container maximum allowed throughput to 2,000 RU/s:

```
az cosmosdb sql container throughput update \
  --resource-group $rgName \
  --account-name $cosmosAccountName \
  --database-name db01 \
  --name People \
  --max-throughput 2000
```

9. Run the following command to delete the resources you created in this recipe:

```
az group delete --name $rgName
```

In this recipe, you created a Cosmos DB SQL API container with a fixed throughput, enabled autoscaling for it, and finally set its maximum allowed throughput.

## Discussion

All Azure Cosmos DB APIs, including the SQL API, allow you to set a fixed provisioned throughput at both the database and the container level. This is an SLA-backed throughput (*https://oreil.ly/kRaaQ*) that will be always assigned to your databases and containers.

Setting up a fixed throughput on containers (and/or databases) gives you a predictable bill at the end of the month; however, spikes in incoming requests might result in poor performance, request throttling, or drops. To make sure that your Cosmos DB databases and containers can scale to accommodate more requests, you can set up autoscaling on databases, containers, or both.

In this recipe, we created a container with a fixed throughput and later migrated it to the autoscale model. You can change the minimum and maximum RU/s to meet your project needs.

Azure Cosmos DB also has a *serverless* (consumption-based) offering. When selecting this option, you don't have to worry about setting minimum and maximum RU/s anymore. Azure Cosmos DB will scale up and down based on your database/container traffic. See the Azure Cosmos DB documentation (*https://oreil.ly/TbSsn*) for details.

# 4.8 Saving Costs on Multiple Azure SQL Single Databases with Varying and Unpredictable Usage Demands

## Problem

You want to save costs and improve manageability of multiple Azure SQL single database instances.

## Solution

Place your single databases into an Azure SQL Database elastic pool (*https://oreil.ly/O3-V0*). Pooled databases are a cost-effective alternative to multiple single databases with unpredictable resource demands, as illustrated in Figure 4-7.

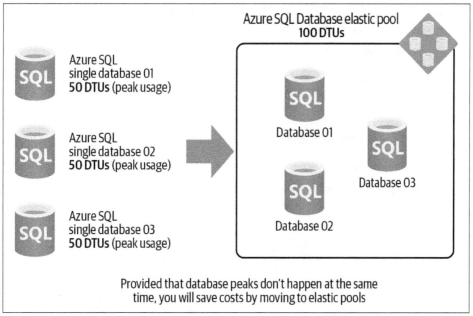

*Figure 4-7. Using Azure SQL Database elastic pools to save costs*

**Steps**

1. Log in to your Azure subscription in the Owner role and create a new resource group for this recipe. See "General Workstation Setup Instructions" on page xii for details.

2. First, you need to provision a *logical Azure SQL server* using the following command. Replace *<logical-sql-server-name>* with the desired server name, *<admin-user>* with the admin username, and *<admin-pass>* with the admin password:

   ```
   logicalServerName="<logical-sql-server-name>"
   sqlAdminUser="<admin-user>"

   # Use a complex password with numbers, upper case characters and symbols.
   sqlAdminPass="<admin-pass>"

   az sql server create \
      --resource-group $rgName \
      --name $logicalServerName \
      --admin-user $sqlAdminUser \
      --admin-password $sqlAdminPass
   ```

3. Now, let's create a new elastic pool. The resources, such as memory and CPU, are allocated to the pool. Use the following command to allocate two vCores (CPU virtual cores) to your new pool:

   ```
   sqlPoolName="MyPool01"

   az sql elastic-pool create \
      --resource-group $rgName \
      --server $logicalServerName \
      --name $sqlPoolName \
      --edition GeneralPurpose \
      --family Gen5 \
      --capacity 2
   ```

4. Let's add two single databases into your new pool. These databases will share the resources assigned to the parent pool:

   ```
   az sql db create \
      --resource-group $rgName \
      --server $logicalServerName \
      --name db01 \
      --elastic-pool $sqlPoolName

   az sql db create \
      --resource-group $rgName \
      --server $logicalServerName \
      --name db02 \
      --elastic-pool $sqlPoolName
   ```

5. You can see all the databases within a given pool by running the following command:

```
az sql elastic-pool list-dbs \
  --resource-group $rgName \
  --name $sqlPoolName \
  --server $logicalServerName \
  --query [].name
```

6. Run the following command to delete the resources you created in this recipe:

```
az group delete --name $rgName
```

In this recipe, you provisioned an Azure SQL Database elastic pool and added two databases to it.

 Azure SQL resources can get expensive. Make sure you clean up the provisioned resources including the elastic pool after concluding this recipe. Check the clean-up section in the chapter repository for details.

## Discussion

Azure SQL offers the following types:

- Azure SQL single database (*https://oreil.ly/mC64x*)
- Azure SQL Database elastic pools (*https://oreil.ly/vZg7r*)
- Azure SQL Managed Instance (*https://oreil.ly/9bEwU*)

*Azure SQL Managed Instance* is the most compatible Azure SQL offering with *Microsoft SQL Server* and is beyond the scope of this recipe.

As the name implies, Azure SQL single database is an independent database with the resources, such as CPU and memory, directly allocated to it. This works perfectly for many scenarios, such as a database with a predictable usage pattern. You simply choose the correct tier (database transaction unit (DTU) (*https://oreil.ly/Zuxk4*) or vCore) and the database will perform as expected.

Now imagine you have three single databases for customers in Japan, the EU, and the Eastern US. Each database needs 50 DTUs at its usage peak. Due to the time difference, none of the databases reaches its peak usage at the same time, but you are paying for 150 DTUs 24x7 that you will not fully use. Azure SQL Database elastic pool is one way to address this issue. (The other way is to go with the serverless tier (*https://oreil.ly/x1Vjw*), which we'll discuss in Recipe 4.9.)

---

Choosing elastic pools, you simply create a new elastic pool, assign 100 DTUs to it, and then add the three databases to the pool. This setup will perform well assuming the three databases never reach their usage peak at the same time.

 You'll need to monitor the pooled databases and adjust the elastic pool resources if needed by assigning more or fewer DTUs. We chose 100 DTUs because there is no load on these databases.

# 4.9 Configuring Serverless Compute Tier for Azure SQL Single Databases

## Problem

You want to ensure your Azure SQL single database has enough allocated resources to accommodate request spikes and that you aren't charged when no request is being processed.

## Solution

Provision your Azure SQL single databases in the serverless compute tier (*https:// oreil.ly/dkCid*). Azure will take care of allocating required resources to your database based on the load, as illustrated in Figure 4-8.

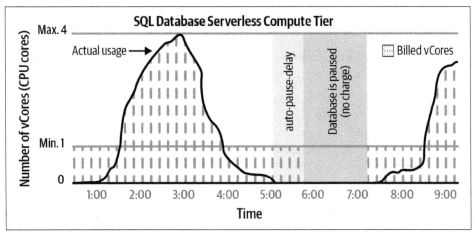

*Figure 4-8. Azure SQL single database serverless compute tier*

## Steps

1. Log in to your Azure subscription in the Owner role and create a new resource group for this recipe. See "General Workstation Setup Instructions" on page xii for details.

2. First provision a logical Azure SQL server. Replace *<logical-sql-server-name>*, *<admin-user>*, and *<admin-pass>* with the desired values:

   ```
   logicalServerName="<logical-sql-server-name>"
   sqlAdminUser="<admin-user>"
   sqlAdminPass="<admin-pass>"

   az sql server create \
     --resource-group $rgName \
     --name $logicalServerName \
     --admin-user $sqlAdminUser \
     --admin-password $sqlAdminPass
   ```

3. Now, let's create a new single database. The following command sets both minimum and maximum limits on the number of vCores (CPU cores) allocated to your database and will configure the database to pause after two hours (120 minutes) of inactivity. The database will automatically scale down and up when needed:

   ```
   # The minimum vCore limit is 1 and the maximum is 4.

   az sql db create \
     --resource-group $rgName \
     --server $logicalServerName \
     --name db01 \
     --compute-model Serverless \
     --edition GeneralPurpose \
     --family Gen5 \
     --auto-pause-delay 120 \
     --min-capacity 1 \
     --capacity 4
   ```

    At the time of writing this book, the serverless compute tier is available only for the Gen5 hardware family. Check Azure SQL single database documentation for details on minimum and maximum supported vCores (*https://oreil.ly/wdeM3*).

4. Finally, use the following command to get the details of your new database:

   ```
   az sql db show \
     --resource-group $rgName \
     --server $logicalServerName \
     --name db01 \
   ```

```
        --query \
        "{Name: name, Sku: currentSku, Edition: edition, MinCapacity:
         minCapacity}"
```

  5. Run the following command to delete the resources you created in this recipe:

```
az group delete --name $rgName
```

In this recipe, you provisioned an Azure SQL single database using the serverless compute tier. You can also move existing Azure SQL single databases from the *provisioned tier* to the serverless tier if needed. Check the Azure SQL documentation (*https://oreil.ly/vVhFP*) for the command details.

## Discussion

When you choose the vCore purchasing model for your Azure SQL single database (*https://oreil.ly/EndIl*) (as opposed to DTU-based), you will have two options for the compute tier: provisioned and serverless.

The provisioned tier requires that you allocate a fixed amount of resources (vCores, memory, etc.) to your database. You will be charged for these resources on a 24x7 basis. The cost does not change if your database is under- or overused. This might result in performance issues when your database receives more requests than expected. You will also keep paying the full bill when your database is not at its usage peak or even when it's completely idle. However, the provisioned compute tier is a great option if you know the exact usage pattern of your database, or when you expect the database will be at the full load most of the time.

Choose the serverless compute tier when you want Azure to take responsibility for resource allocation. You will set the minimum and maximum vCores to be assigned to your single database and leave the rest to Azure. You can also configure *auto-pause delay*, so your database will be paused if it's idle for a specified period. By choosing the serverless tier, you will only get billed when the database is used. Check out the Azure documentation for details on the serverless compute tier (*https://oreil.ly/SWI7R*).

# 4.10 Configuring Azure SQL Firewall IP Rules

## Problem

You want to limit access to your Azure SQL Databases based on the client IP address or an address range.

## Solution

Configure Azure SQL service firewall (*https://oreil.ly/5ZIqt*) to allow only clients with trusted IP addresses, as shown in Figure 4-9.

---

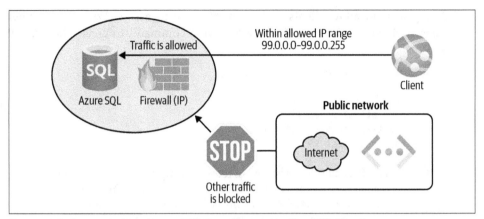

*Figure 4-9. Protecting an Azure SQL Database using firewall IP rules*

## Steps

1. Log in to your Azure subscription in the Owner role and create a new resource group for this recipe. See "General Workstation Setup Instructions" on page xii for details.

2. First, let's provision a logical Azure SQL server and an Azure SQL single database. Replace *<logical-sql-server-name>*, *<admin-user>*, and *<admin-pass>* with the desired values:

```
logicalServerName="<logical-sql-server-name>"
sqlAdminUser="<admin-user>"
sqlAdminPass="<admin-pass>"

az sql server create \
  --resource-group $rgName \
  --name $logicalServerName \
  --admin-user $sqlAdminUser \
  --admin-password $sqlAdminPass

az sql db create \
  --resource-group $rgName \
  --server $logicalServerName \
  --name db01 \
  --compute-model Serverless \
  --edition GeneralPurpose \
  --family Gen5 \
  --auto-pause-delay 60 \
  --min-capacity 1 \
  --capacity 2
```

3. Your goal is to allow clients within an IP range to access Azure SQL. Other requests should be rejected. Use the following command to create the firewall server rule:

```
az sql server firewall-rule create \
  --resource-group $rgName \
  --server $logicalServerName \
  --name allowTrustedClients \
  --start-ip-address 99.0.0.0 \
  --end-ip-address 99.0.0.255
```

 This firewall rule is assigned to the logical Azure SQL server, and it is applied to all the child databases under this server. You can also create database-level-only IP firewall rules by using *Transact-SQL* statements after the server-level firewall is configured. See the Azure documentation (*https://oreil.ly/_UQeI*) for details.

4. So far you allowed a trusted IP range. What if you need to allow all Azure services to access your Azure SQL databases? You can achieve this with the special IP address, 0.0.0.0. Let's add this rule using Azure CLI:

```
az sql server firewall-rule create \
  --resource-group $rgName \
  --server $logicalServerName \
  --name allowAzureServices  \
  --start-ip-address 0.0.0.0 \
  --end-ip-address 0.0.0.0
```

5. You can see the firewall rules assigned to your logical Azure SQL server using the following command:

```
az sql server firewall-rule list \
  --resource-group $rgName \
  --server $logicalServerName
```

6. Run the following command to delete the resources you created in this recipe:

```
az group delete --name $rgName
```

In this recipe, you configured Azure SQL firewall to allow clients from a trusted IP range as well as connections from IP addresses allocated to any Azure service or assets.

## Discussion

Several Azure data services, including Azure Storage, Azure Cosmos DB, Azure Synapse Analytics, and Azure SQL, offer a service-level firewall. Use this firewall to improve the security posture of your Azure data services. Azure SQL firewall is a powerful tool to prevent unwanted clients from accessing your data.

---

When you assign a firewall rule to the logical Azure SQL server, all the child databases will also be protected. Keep in mind that you can also create database-level firewall rules, such that only the database for which the rule is created will be protected. Check the Azure SQL documentation (*https://oreil.ly/McG0U*) for details.

> You can also allow traffic from Azure virtual networks using VNet rules. We will discuss this option in Recipe 4.11.

# 4.11 Configuring Azure SQL Firewall VNet Rules

## Problem

You want to limit access to your Azure SQL Databases based on the client Azure Virtual Network subnet.

## Solution

Configure Azure SQL service firewall (*https://oreil.ly/ccf7p*) to allow clients within a trusted Azure VNet subnet as illustrated in Figure 4-10.

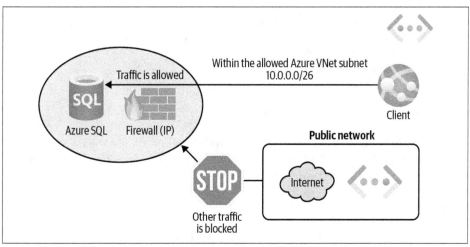

*Figure 4-10. Protecting an Azure SQL Database using the firewall VNet rules*

### Steps

1. Log in to your Azure subscription in the Owner role and create a new resource group for this recipe. See "General Workstation Setup Instructions" on page xii for details.

2. Follow step 1 in Recipe 4.10 to create a new logical Azure SQL server and a single database.

3. Your goal is to allow clients within a trusted Azure VNet subnet to access Azure SQL. Let's create a new Azure VNet and a child subnet:

```
vnetName="<vnet-name>"

az network vnet create \
  --resource-group $rgName \
  --name $vnetName \
  --address-prefix 10.0.0.0/16 \
  --subnet-name Subnet01 \
  --subnet-prefix 10.0.0.0/26
```

4. To enable clients in this subnet to access the Azure SQL Database, we need to add the Microsoft.Sql service endpoint (*https://oreil.ly/ozolY*) to the subnet:

```
az network vnet subnet update \
  --resource-group $rgName \
  --name Subnet01 \
  --vnet-name $vnetName \
  --service-endpoints Microsoft.Sql
```

5. Finally, use the following command to create a new VNet rule for Subnet01:

```
az sql server vnet-rule create \
  --resource-group $rgName \
  --server $logicalServerName \
  --name allowTrustedSubnet \
  --vnet-name $vnetName \
  --subnet Subnet01
```

6. Run the following command to delete the resources you created in this recipe:

```
az group delete --name $rgName
```

You successfully configured Azure SQL firewall to allow clients within Subnet01 to work with your Azure SQL Database. See the Azure SQL service firewall documentation (*https://oreil.ly/DK-Pj*) for details.

## Discussion

Use Azure SQL firewall VNet rules with IP rules to provide protection from incoming requests based on the client IP address and virtual network.

In Recipes 4.10 and 4.11, we talked about Azure SQL firewall IP and VNet rules. These rules protect your Azure SQL Databases against inbound requests. Azure SQL firewall also offers outbound rules to limit egress traffic from your database. See the Azure Firewall documentation (*https://oreil.ly/qwPjz*) for implementation details.

# 4.12 Backing Up Azure SQL Single Databases into Azure Storage Blobs

## Problem

You want to store multiple Azure SQL database backups in an affordable and secure storage to be used later for database recovery.

## Solution

Store Azure SQL backups into Azure Storage blobs using Azure CLI, as shown in Figure 4-11.

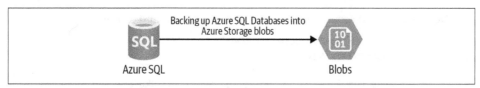

*Figure 4-11. Backing up an Azure SQL Database into Azure Storage blobs*

### Steps

1. Log in to your Azure subscription in the Owner role and create a new resource group for this recipe. See "General Workstation Setup Instructions" on page xii for details.

2. First, let's provision a new Azure SQL single database and seed it with the AdventureWorks sample database. Replace *<logical-sql-server-name>*, *<admin-user>*, and *<admin-pass>* with the desired values:

```
logicalServerName="<logical-sql-server-name>"
sqlAdminUser="<admin-user>"
sqlAdminPass="<admin-pass>"

az sql server create \
  --resource-group $rgName \
  --name $logicalServerName \
  --admin-user $sqlAdminUser \
  --admin-password $sqlAdminPass

az sql db create \
  --resource-group $rgName \
  --server $logicalServerName \
  --name db01 \
  --compute-model Serverless \
  --edition GeneralPurpose \
  --family Gen5 \
```

```
   --auto-pause-delay 60 \
   --min-capacity 0.5 \
   --capacity 2 \
   --sample-name AdventureWorksLT
```

3. You need to allow Azure services to access the new Azure SQL databases for the backup to be created and saved. Use the following command to configure Azure SQL firewall:

```
az sql server firewall-rule create \
   --resource-group $rgName \
   --server $logicalServerName \
   --name allowAzureServices  \
   --start-ip-address 0.0.0.0 \
   --end-ip-address 0.0.0.0
```

4. Now you need to create a new Azure storage account and a child container:

```
storageName="<storage-account-name>"
bakContainerName="sqlbackups"

# we chose the locally redundant storage (LRS) sku but you may need
# to choose a better redundancy for your Azure SQL backups.

az storage account create \
   --name $storageName \
   --resource-group $rgName \
   --sku Standard_LRS

storageKey1=$(az storage account keys list \
   --resource-group $rgName \
   --account-name $storageName \
   --query [0].value \
   --output tsv)

MSYS_NO_PATHCONV=1 az storage container create \
   --name $bakContainerName \
   --account-name $storageName \
   --account-key $storageKey1
```

5. You need write permission to your Azure Storage container. Here we will use the storage account key for authentication. You can also use storage account SAS tokens as an authentication method. See the Azure CLI documentation (*https://oreil.ly/mrZ8O*) for details. Use the following command to create the database backup:

```
storageURL= \
"https://$storageName.blob.core.windows.net/\$bakContainerName
   /sqlbackup01.bacpac"

MSYS_NO_PATHCONV=1 az sql db export \
```

```
    --resource-group $rgName \
    --server $logicalServerName \
    --name db01 \
    --admin-user $sqlAdminUser \
    --admin-password $sqlAdminPass \
    --storage-key $storageKey1 \
    --storage-key-type StorageAccessKey \
    --storage-uri $storageURL
```

6. You can confirm the backup file is created by listing all the files and their sizes in the storage container:

```
MSYS_NO_PATHCONV=1 az storage blob list \
    --container-name $bakContainerName \
    --account-key $storageKey1 \
    --account-name $storageName \
    --query "[].{Name: name, Length: properties.contentLength}"
```

 Because our storage account key contains a forward slash (/), it will be converted to a Linux path in the Bash environment, which causes the CLI command to fail. So we used MSYS_NO_PATHCONV=1 before the CLI scripts to prevent this issue! You can alternatively prefix your commands with two forward slashes (//).

7. Run the following command to delete the resources you created in this recipe:

```
az group delete --name $rgName
```

In this recipe, you successfully backed up an Azure SQL single database into an Azure Storage container (*https://oreil.ly/qdk81*).

## Discussion

Azure Storage offers an affordable, scalable, and secure storage service in the cloud. As you saw in Chapter 3, you can protect your files against accidental deletion by enabling soft delete protection.

The backup files can be stored in the hot, cool, or even archive access tiers (*https://oreil.ly/CE3bV*) to save costs.

In this recipe, we used the cheapest Azure Storage redundancy option, which is locally redundant storage (LRS). If you plan to back up production SQL databases, it is recommended that you choose an option with better redundancy, such as zone-redundant storage (ZRS), geo-redundant storage (GRS), or geo-zone-redundant storage (GZRS). Refer to Chapter 3 or the Azure Storage documentation (*https://oreil.ly/0wWJH*) for details.

## CHAPTER 5

# Messaging and Events

Back in the day, architects used to design applications in one unified codebase, which was then built and deployed to a single host. These applications were referred to as *monolithic applications*. Maintaining such applications was hard and time-consuming. A small change required the whole codebase to be redeployed.

Service-oriented and microservice architecture were introduced to mitigate these issues by simplifying designing, developing, deploying, and maintaining applications. Following this architecture, one big application is broken down into meaningful services in separate codebases, and each service is deployed to an independent host. For instance, imagine an online shop. This shop needs individual services such as ShoppingCardService, PaymentService, AuthenticationService, DeliveryService, and so on. These services need to communicate with each other in a reliable manner. No message should get lost due to networking issues or unavailable destinations. This is when messaging technologies come into the picture.

Messaging technologies enable microservices, applications, and other services to communicate in a safe, secure, and reliable fashion. Queues and topics are notable messaging services to mention.

Microsoft Azure offers several messaging services (*https://oreil.ly/o3Rch*), which provide inter-connectivity between cloud and/or on-premises applications. You can use these services to send and receive messages to/from applications regardless of the destination availability or connectivity status. Each Azure messaging service is tailored to a specific use case. These services include:

- Azure Service Bus queues
- Azure Service Bus topics

- Azure Event Hubs
- Azure IoT Hub

You can also use Azure Event Grid to act on an event generated by an Azure service such as Azure Blob Storage.

In this chapter, our main focus is on Azure messaging and event services. You will learn to:

- Ingest streaming and telemetry data using Azure Event Hubs and Azure IoT Hub
- Configure application communication using Azure Storage queues
- Implement reliable messaging using Azure Service Bus queues
- Implement the publish-subscribe pattern using Azure Service Bus topics and subscriptions
- Work with Azure Event Grid to subscribe to Azure resource events

## Workstation Configuration

You will need to prepare your workstation before starting on the recipes in this chapter. Follow "What You Will Need" on page xi to set up your machine to run Azure CLI commands. You can clone the book's GitHub repository using the following command:

```
git clone https://github.com/zaalion/AzureCookbook.git
```

# 5.1 Ingesting Streaming Data at Scale Using Event Hubs

## Problem

You need to ingest streaming data into Azure, so that downstream services can access and analyze the data.

## Solution

Create a new Azure Event Hubs namespace and a hub and configure your event producer to send events to this service, as shown in Figure 5-1.

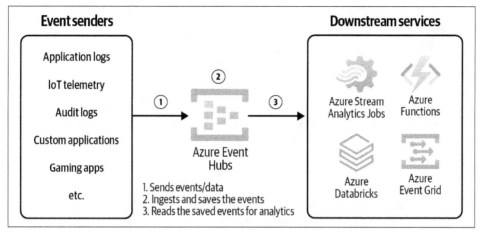

*Figure 5-1. Ingesting streaming data into Azure using Azure Event Hubs*

### Steps

1. Log in to your Azure subscription in the Owner role and create a new resource group for this recipe. See "General Workstation Setup Instructions" on page xii for details.

2. Create a new Azure Event Hubs namespace using the following commands. Replace *<ehub-namespace-name>* with the desired unique namespace name:

   ```
   eventHubNamespaceName="<ehub-namespace-name>"

   az eventhubs namespace create \
     --resource-group $rgName \
     --name $eventHubNamespaceName \
     --sku Standard \
     --enable-auto-inflate \
     --maximum-throughput-units 5
   ```

3. Let's use the following command to create a new *hub* under this namespace and name it hub01:

   ```
   az eventhubs eventhub create \
     --resource-group $rgName \
     --namespace-name $eventHubNamespaceName \
     --name hub01 \
     --message-retention 1 \
     --partition-count 2
   ```

The --message-retention parameter specifies the number of days the messages are saved in the Event Hub. In our case, the messages will be saved for one day and are then deleted.

4. Any client that wishes to send streaming data (events) to Event Hub needs to have the hub's key. Use the following command to get the namespace key and store it in a variable:

```
nsKey1=$(az eventhubs namespace \
  authorization-rule keys list \
  --resource-group $rgName \
  --namespace-name $eventHubNamespaceName \
  --name RootManageSharedAccessKey \
  --query primaryKey)
```

RootManageSharedAccessKey is the default shared access policy (https://oreil.ly/ioTQ4) for the Event Hubs namespace. You can also create your own access policies with a different set of permissions.

5. You successfully created a new Azure Event Hubs namespace and a child hub. Now any client can go ahead and send live data streams to this hub. The data is usually in the form of JSON messages. The data will be ingested into Azure Event Hubs and can be read by downstream Azure services such as Azure Stream Analytics for further processing. Note that the data will be saved for the duration specified by the --message-retention parameter. You can use any client to send messages. These include an application using the Event Hubs SDK or a simple CLI or PowerShell script. In this recipe, you will run the following CLI commands to send a sample data event to hub01:

```
endpoint=\
  "https://$eventHubNamespaceName.servicebus.windows.net/hub01/messages"

event=\
  '{"Name": "John Smith","Email": "john@contoso.com", "Type": "Create"}'

curl -X POST \
  -H "Authorization: \
  SharedAccessSignature \
  sr=$eventHubNamespaceName.servicebus.windows.net\
  &sig=$nsKey1&se=1735693200\
  &skn=RootManageSharedAccessKey" \
  -d "$event" \
```

```
$endpoint \
--verbose
```

 cURL is a command line tool used to make HTTP calls. In the pre-ceding command, we call an Event Hubs HTTP API to send a mes-sage (*https://oreil.ly/NjeYC*). The se parameter is the number of seconds from January 1, 1970, 12:00:00 AM (epoch) to the access policy expiry time, which we set to 2025-01-01 01:00:00 AM. This comes to 1735693200 seconds. See the access policy SAS token documentation (*https://oreil.ly/z2_cp*) for details.

6. Confirm that the command output contains the following line. 68 is the number of bytes in our JSON payload, $event:

    ```
    upload completely sent off: 68 out of 68 bytes
    ```

7. Run the following command to delete the resources you created in this recipe:

    ```
    az group delete --name $rgName
    ```

You successfully sent an event to Azure Event Hubs. This event will be saved in the hub for the configured retention time, which is one day in our case. Downstream services can now read this event from your Azure Event Hub and process it.

## Discussion

Azure Event Hubs is a big data streaming platform that enables you to ingest events at scale. It can receive millions of events per second and these events in turn can be transformed or stored for the duration of the configured retention period. Several downstream Azure services can read events ingested by Azure Event Hubs for later processing. Here follows a few use cases:

- Use Azure Storage blobs to store/archive the ingested events as JSON blobs
- Stream data into Azure Databricks for big data analytics
- Stream data into Azure Stream Analytics for live or near real-time processing, for example, to detect anomaly in the live streaming data

Azure Event Grid (*https://oreil.ly/8vtgm*) supports Azure Event Hubs as an event source. This allows you to handle Azure Event Hubs events using all the supported Event Grid event handlers. For instance, upon an event arrival, you can:

- Trigger an Azure Function or Logic App
- Put a message into an Azure Service Bus queue or topic (*https://oreil.ly/tk7RD*)

- Put a message into an Azure Storage queue
- Run an Azure Automation runbook (*https://oreil.ly/oWeqd*) or an HTTP webhook

# 5.2 Ingesting Telemetry Data from IoT Devices Using Azure IoT Hub

## Problem

You want to ingest telemetry data generated by connected IoT devices, so that Azure services such as Azure Stream Analytics can process this data for insights.

## Solution

Create a new Azure IoT Hub service, register one or more devices with it, and configure your IoT devices to send telemetry data, as shown in Figure 5-2.

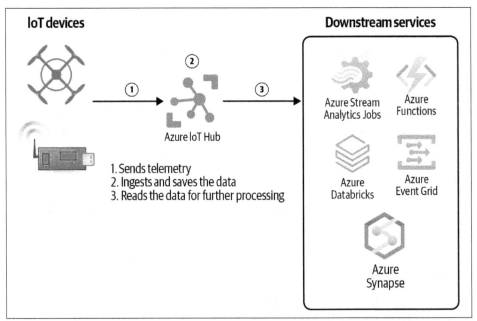

*Figure 5-2. Ingesting IoT device telemetry data into Azure using Azure IoT Hub*

## Steps

1. Log in to your Azure subscription in the Owner role and create a new resource group for this recipe. See "General Workstation Setup Instructions" on page xii for details.

2. First create a new Azure IoT Hub service. Replace *<iot-hub-name>* with the desired unique namespace name:

   ```
   iotHubName="<iot-hub-name>"

   az iot hub create \
      --resource-group $rgName \
      --name $iotHubName \
      --sku S1
   ```

3. To enable devices to send telemetry data, you need to create a *device identity* for your IoT device. Replace *<iot-device-id>* with the desired device ID string:

   ```
   deviceId="<iot-device-id>"

   az iot hub device-identity create \
      --hub-name $iotHubName \
      --device-id $deviceId
   ```

4. Now you are ready to register a physical IoT device with the new IoT Hub. In this recipe, we use a simulated device to send some telemetry data. Use the following command to create a simulated IoT device:

   ```
   az iot device simulate \
      --device $deviceId \
      --hub-name $iotHubName
   ```

5. Leave the `simulate` command window open. Now, open a second CLI session and use the following command to send your first `device-to-cloud` message. This message reports temperatures from an imaginary connected heat sensor:

   ```
   az iot device send-d2c-message \
      --hub-name $iotHubName \
      --device-id $deviceId \
      --data 'temperature=112.8'
   ```

6. Run the following command to delete the resources you created in this recipe:

   ```
   az group delete --name $rgName
   ```

You successfully sent telemetry data from a connected IoT device to Azure. Downstream services such as Azure Stream Analytics can ingest this data for further processing.

You can monitor your device to confirm the messages are successfully sent to the cloud by running the `az iot hub monitor-event` command in a new CLI session. See the command documentation (*https://oreil.ly/SElO3*) for more details. Alternatively, log in to the Azure portal and check the "Device to cloud messages" and Connected Devices charts on your IoT Hub overview page, as shown in Figure 5-3.

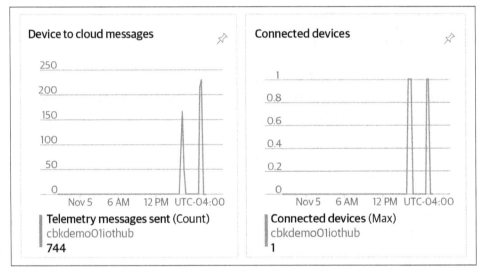

*Figure 5-3. Azure IoT Hub overview page*

## Discussion

Connected IoT devices are increasingly used in our lives. From industrial sensors to smart home devices, most of these small machines have something in common: they send telemetry data to a server for further processing. This data could be temperature, pressure, light, magnetic, or other sensor readings, or pictures taken by a surveillance drone. Azure IoT Hub enables you to ingest telemetry messages from IoT devices and pass them to downstream services that can analyze them for insights.

As you saw in Recipe 5.1, Azure Event Hubs can be used to ingest telemetry data from various senders. This includes IoT devices as well. However, Azure IoT Hub is tailored to IoT scenarios, giving you capabilities that are not available in Azure Event Hubs, including:

- Bidirectional messaging between the device and IoT Hub, including device-to-cloud (d2c) and cloud-to-device (c2d) communication

- d2c messaging, such as file upload (*https://oreil.ly/usQhQ*) and simple messages (*https://oreil.ly/pmYC-*)

- c2d communication, including direct method (*https://oreil.ly/yKUdH*) call and simple messaging (*https://oreil.ly/iBcrN*)

- IoT edge capabilities to enable supporting devices to work offline for an extended amount of time

- Device simulation for testing and development purposes

The collected telemetry data can immediately be used by downstream services for further processing. A couple of scenarios include:

- Use Azure Stream Analytics to process the telemetry data in near real-time. AI models can also be used for scenarios that merit it, such as anomaly detection or predictive analytics.

- Trigger an Azure Function upon the arrival of a new photo from a connected drone. The photo can then be analyzed by Azure Cognitive Services to detect possible intruders.

With the growing number of industrial and commercial IoT devices, the possibilities are endless. See the Azure IoT Hub documentation (*https://oreil.ly/ZNWNN*) for additional details.

# 5.3 Implementing Communication Between Services Using Azure Storage Queues

## Problem

You need to make sure two services can securely and reliably communicate using a queue data structure.

## Solution

Provision a new Azure storage account, create a new queue in it, and configure your applications or services to send and receive messages to/from the queue, as shown in Figure 5-4.

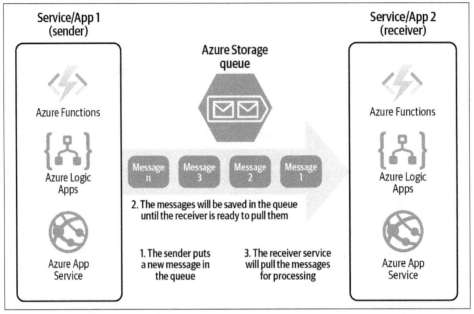

Service/App 1
(sender)

Azure Functions

Azure Logic
Apps

Azure App
Service

Azure Storage
queue

Message n   Message 3   Message 2   Message 1

2. The messages will be saved in the queue
until the receiver is ready to pull them

1. The sender puts
a new message in
the queue

3. The receiver service
will pull the messages
for processing

Service/App 2
(receiver)

Azure Functions

Azure Logic
Apps

Azure App
Service

*Figure 5-4. Enabling two applications or services to communicate using an Azure Storage queue*

### Steps

1. Log in to your Azure subscription in the Owner role and create a new resource group for this recipe. See "General Workstation Setup Instructions" on page xii for details.

2. Create a new general purpose Azure storage account (`StorageV2`) using the following command:

```
storageName="<storage-account-name>"
queueName="ordersqueue"

az storage account create \
    --name $storageName \
    --resource-group $rgName \
    --location $region \
    --sku Standard_LRS \
    --kind StorageV2
```

3. Store the storage account key in a variable. You will need it in the next step:

```
storageKey=$(az storage account keys list \
    --resource-group $rgName \
    --account-name $storageName \
    --query [0].value \
    --output tsv)
```

4. So far you created a *general purpose* storage account, which offers blobs, queues, tables, and file services (all of which you worked with in Chapters 3 and 4). Now use this command to create a new queue in your storage account:

```
az storage queue create \
  --name $queueName \
  --account-name $storageName \
  --account-key $storageKey
```

5. Now your queue is ready to accept messages from senders. Many Azure services have native integration with Azure Storage queues (such as Function Apps). In this recipe, we will simulate both a message sender and receiver using Azure CLI. Use the following command to send (push/put) two new messages into your queue:

```
az storage message put \
  --queue-name $queueName \
  --content '{"order": "1 small pizza"}' \
  --account-name $storageName \
  --account-key $storageKey

az storage message put \
  --queue-name $queueName \
  --content '{"order": "2 large cheese pizzas"}' \
  --account-name $storageName \
  --account-key $storageKey
```

The message content can be up to 64KB in size. For larger messages, use Azure Service Bus queues.

6. Your messages are now safely stored in the queue. Receivers such as Azure Functions can immediately get these messages from the queue and process them. In our case, no receiver is configured, so the messages will stay in the queue until the TTL (time-to-live) period is over. The default TTL is 7 days. Let's simulate a receiver by running the following CLI command to get the first message from the queue:

```
az storage message get \
  --queue-name $queueName \
  --account-name $storageName \
  --account-key $storageKey
```

7. Run the following command to delete the resources you created in this recipe:

```
az group delete --name $rgName
```

You successfully sent and received messages to/from a queue. Different services can now start using this queue by providing the storage account credentials, or using RBAC access as described in Recipe 3.4.

## Discussion

Azure Storage queues provide a reliable communication method between processes, applications, and Azure services. Azure Function Apps, Azure Logic Apps, Azure App Services, and Event Grid have native support for Azure Storage queues. Use queues to implement scenarios such as triggering an Azure Function or Logic App when a new message is put into the queue.

Messages will stay in the queue until the target service or application is ready to pull (dequeue) them, or the configured TTL period is over. You can configure *dead lettering* so that if the target service fails to process the message, it is moved to a special queue called the dead-letter queue (*https://oreil.ly/PqbOa*) for further investigation.

Microsoft Azure offers another queuing service called Azure Service Bus queues. Use Service Bus queues when Storage queues don't meet your needs, for example when your message content could go over 64KB in size. See the Azure documentation for a detailed comparison between these queue offerings (*https://oreil.ly/kaGx7*). We will look into Azure Service Bus queues in the next recipe.

# 5.4 Implementing Communication Between Services Using Azure Service Bus Queues

## Problem

You want to make sure two services can securely and reliably communicate using a queue data structure.

## Solution

Provision a new Azure Service Bus namespace, create a queue in it, and configure your services to send and receive messages to/from this queue as shown in Figure 5-5.

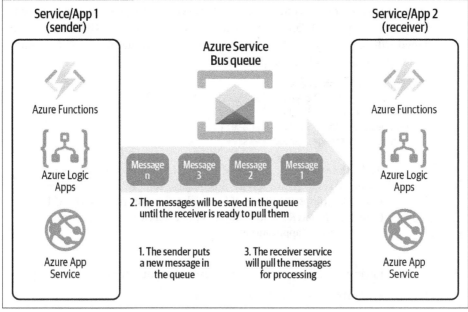

*Figure 5-5. Enabling two applications or services to communicate using an Azure Service Bus queue*

## Steps

1. Log in to your Azure subscription in the Owner role and create a new resource group for this recipe. See "General Workstation Setup Instructions" on page xii for details.

2. Create a new Azure Service Bus namespace using the following CLI command. Replace <*servicebus-namespace-name*> with a unique name:

   ```
   namespaceName="<servicebus-namespace-name>"

   az servicebus namespace create \
     --resource-group $rgName \
     --name $namespaceName \
     --sku Standard
   ```

3. Now use this command to create a new queue in your namespace:

   ```
   az servicebus queue create \
     --resource-group $rgName \
     --namespace-name $namespaceName \
     --name ordersqueue
   ```

4. Any client who wishes to send messages to Service Bus queues needs to have the namespace's (or queue's) connection string or have the correct RBAC permissions assigned (*https://oreil.ly/eamSl*). Use the following command to get the connection string as well as both namespace keys:

```
az servicebus namespace \
  authorization-rule keys list \
  --resource-group $rgName \
  --namespace-name $namespaceName \
  --name RootManageSharedAccessKey
```

 At the time of writing this book, Azure CLI does not support sending messages to Azure Service Bus queues. You can use the Service Bus SDK (*https://oreil.ly/ro4SF*) or the Service Bus REST API (*https://oreil.ly/kzRSZ*) to send or receive Service Bus queue messages from your applications.

5. Run the following command to delete the resources you created in this recipe:

```
az group delete --name $rgName
```

You successfully created an Azure Service Bus queue. Later, in Recipe 7.5, you will use this queue to establish communication between two Azure Functions.

## Discussion

Use Azure Service Bus queues to establish reliable communication between applications and Azure services. Azure Function Apps, Azure Logic Apps, Azure App Services, and Event Grid have native Azure Service Bus support. Use queues to implement scenarios such as triggering an Azure Function, Event Grid Topics, or Logic App when a new message arrives.

As with Azure Storage queues, messages will stay in the Service Bus queue until the target service or application is ready to pull them, or the configured TTL period is over. Dead lettering is automatically enabled so that if the target service fails to process the message, it is moved to the dead-letter queue (*https://oreil.ly/C7fkQ*) for further investigation.

Azure Service Bus queues support messages up to 256KB or 1MB in size, depending on the service tier (*https://oreil.ly/NKnqn*). See the Azure documentation for a comparison (*https://oreil.ly/1cGpq*) between Service Bus queues and storage account queues.

# 5.5 Implementing a Publish-Subscribe Pattern Using Azure Service Bus Topics

## Problem

You want to set up communication between a message publisher and one or more subscribers, so that when a message is published, all subscribers receive a copy of it.

## Solution

Provision a new Azure Service Bus namespace, create a new topic for the publisher service or application, and create one subscription for each subscriber application, as shown in Figure 5-6.

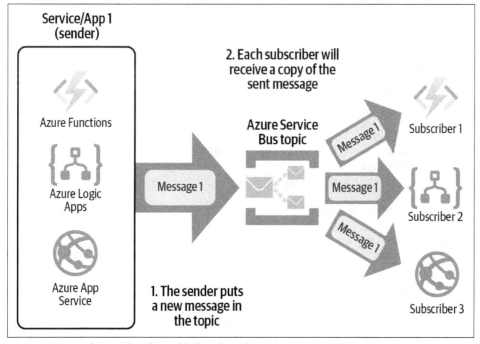

*Figure 5-6. Implementing the publish-subscribe pattern using an Azure Service Bus topic*

### Steps

1. Log in to your Azure subscription in the Owner role and create a new resource group for this recipe. See "General Workstation Setup Instructions" on page xii for details.

2. Create a new Azure Service Bus namespace using the following CLI command. Replace *<servicebus-namespace-name>* with a unique name:

```
namespaceName="<servicebus-namespace-name>"

az servicebus namespace create \
  --resource-group $rgName \
  --name $namespaceName \
  --sku Standard
```

3. Now create a new topic in your namespace:

```
az servicebus topic create \
  --resource-group $rgName \
  --namespace-name $namespaceName \
  --name notificationsTopic
```

4. Your publisher application or service can now send its messages to the newly created topic. Use the following commands to create two subscriptions for your topic:

```
az servicebus topic subscription create \
  --resource-group $rgName \
  --namespace-name $namespaceName \
  --topic-name notificationsTopic \
  --name subscription01

az servicebus topic subscription create \
  --resource-group $rgName \
  --namespace-name $namespaceName \
  --topic-name notificationsTopic \
  --name subscription02
```

 At the time of writing this book, Azure CLI does not support sending messages to Azure Service Bus topics. You can use the Service Bus SDK (*https://oreil.ly/J-fB0*) or the Service Bus REST API (*https://oreil.ly/hi_CK*) to send or receive messages to Service Bus topics.

5. Run the following command to delete the resources you created in this recipe:

```
az group delete --name $rgName
```

## Discussion

Queues allow processing of a message by a single destination service. In contrast, topics and subscriptions provide one-to-many communication by implementing the publish-subscribe pattern. This is useful when you want to scale the number of receivers for a message or need to trigger multiple processes upon message arrival.

---

In some scenarios, messages with different properties should be processed in different manners. Using rules and actions (*https://oreil.ly/Pq7QB*), you can configure a subscription to receive and act on messages based on a specific condition.

See the Azure Service Bus documentation (*https://oreil.ly/bz6Nr*) for more details on topics and subscriptions.

# 5.6 Queuing Newly Uploaded Blobs for Further Processing Using Azure Event Grid

## Problem

You need to queue uploaded Azure Storage blob files, so they can be processed by a consumer service.

## Solution

Create a new Azure Storage queue and use Azure Event Grid to put a new message in the queue upon new blob file upload, as illustrated in Figure 5-7.

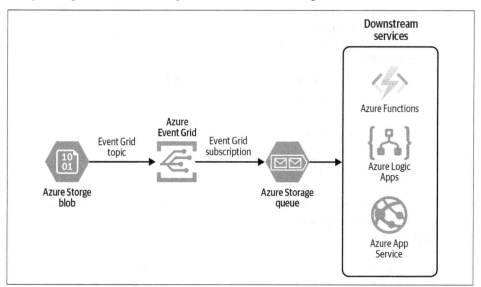

*Figure 5-7. Using Azure Event Grid to queue newly uploaded blob files*

### Steps

1. Log in to your Azure subscription in the Owner role and create a new resource group for this recipe. See "General Workstation Setup Instructions" on page xii for details.

2. Create a new Azure storage account using the following CLI commands. Replace *<storage-account-name>* with the desired unique name:

```
storageName="<storage-account-name>"

az storage account create \
  --name $storageName \
  --resource-group $rgName \
  --sku Standard_LRS \
  --location $region \
  --kind StorageV2
```

3. Store the storage account key in a variable:

```
storageKey=$(az storage account keys list \
  --resource-group $rgName \
  --account-name $storageName \
  --query [0].value --output tsv)
```

4. Create a new Azure Storage blob container and name it `uploadcontainer`. This container will host newly uploaded blob files:

```
containerName="uploadcontainer"

az storage container create \
  --name $containerName \
  --account-name $storageName \
  --account-key $storageKey
```

5. Create a new queue in the same storage account and name it `blobsqueue`:

```
queueName="blobsqueue"

az storage queue create \
  --name $queueName \
  --account-name $storageName \
  --account-key $storageKey
```

 The queue and the blob container do not have to be in the same Azure storage account.

6. Store the storage account and queue IDs in two variables. You will need these IDs in the next step when creating a new Azure Event Grid topic and subscription:

```
storageResId=$(az storage account show \
  --name $storageName \
  --resource-group $rgName \
  --query id --output tsv)
```

```
storageQueueId=\
  "$storageResId/queueservices/default/queues/"$queueName
```

7. Now the stage is set to create a new Azure Event Grid system topic (*https://oreil.ly/pl9s8*). Use system topics when you plan to capture events generated by Azure services. In this recipe, you plan to capture a blob upload event produced by Azure Storage. Replace *<system-topic-name>* with the desired topic name:

```
topicName="<system-topic-name>"

MSYS_NO_PATHCONV=1 az eventgrid system-topic create \
  --resource-group $rgName \
  --name $topicName \
  --topic-type microsoft.storage.storageaccounts \
  --source $storageResId \
  --location $region
```

8. So far you created an Event Grid topic, which is triggered when an Azure Storage event happens. Although you could filter this topic further to narrow down to a blob file upload, we're going to keep it as is for the sake of simplicity. See the Event Grid documentation (*https://oreil.ly/aZMn9*) for details. Now you need to create one or more subscriptions for the topic. You use the subscription to handle the topic event. The following subscription will put a new message in the Storage queue when a new blob file is uploaded. Replace *<eg-subscription-name>* with the desired name for your Event Grid subscription:

```
subscriptionName="<eg-subscription-name>"

MSYS_NO_PATHCONV=1 az eventgrid system-topic \
  event-subscription create \
  --name $subscriptionName \
  --resource-group $rgName \
  --system-topic-name $topicName \
  --endpoint-type storagequeue \
  --endpoint $storageQueueId
```

9. Let's test your new Event Grid topic and subscription. Use the following command to upload a new blob file to the Storage container. Replace *<local-path>* with the Linux path to a file you have on your machine, for example */path/to/Myblob01.txt*. Replace *<blob-file-name>* with the desired blob name, such as *Myblob01.txt*, and *<local-path>* with the Linux path to a file on your machine, for example */path/to/Myblob01.txt*:

```
blobName="<blob-file-name>"
localPath="<local-path>"

az storage blob upload \
  --account-key $storageKey \
  --name $blobName \
  --file $localPath \
```

```
--account-name $storageName \
--container-name $containerName
```

10. If everything is configured correctly, a new message, containing the blob file properties, should show up in your queue. Use the following command to get a message from the end of your queue. Confirm that one message is dequeued:

```
az storage message get \
--queue-name $queueName \
--account-name $storageName \
--account-key $storageKey
```

11. Run the following command to delete the resources you created in this recipe:

```
az group delete --name $rgName
```

You have successfully configured an Azure Event Grid topic and subscription to integrate an Azure Storage blob service with a queue.

## Discussion

Azure Event Grid (*https://oreil.ly/OyX5k*) is a service that integrates applications and services using events. Events are delivered by Azure Event Grid topics to any configured *topic subscription*.

In this recipe you configured an Azure storage account as a topic and a storage account queue as a subscription. Azure Event Grid supports several topics (event sources) and subscriptions (event handlers). Here are a few supported services that can be used as Event Grid topics:

- Azure Blob Storage
- Azure Event Hubs
- Azure IoT Hub
- Azure Policy
- Azure Service Bus
- Azure resource groups
- Azure subscriptions (not to be confused with Event Grid subscriptions or Service Bus topic subscriptions)

You can use many services, including the following, as Event Grid subscriptions (event handlers):

- Azure Function Apps
- Azure Logic Apps
- Azure Storage queues

- Azure Service Bus queues and topics
- Azure Automation

These enable you to implement the following scenarios:

- Trigger an Azure Function or Logic App when a new resource is added to a resource group
- Run an Azure Automation runbook when an Azure subscription property changes
- Call an Azure Function upon the arrival of new Azure IoT Hub telemetry

You can also create your own custom events and use them with Azure Event Grid. Check the Azure documentation (*https://oreil.ly/9fjYo*) for details.

## CHAPTER 6

# Big Data

In Chapter 5, you learned about Azure Event Hubs, which allow ingesting big data streams from various sources into Azure. Network access logs, application logs, and online banking audit data are a few examples of datasets that you can send to Azure using Azure Event Hubs. Azure IoT Hub is another service, which specializes in ingesting telemetry data from connected IoT devices. For instance, you can configure tens, hundreds, or even thousands of connected sensors to send temperature, humidity, magnetic, pressure, or other data points to your applications. So far you have successfully ingested the raw data on a large scale. So what is next?

Raw data on its own does not bring much value. Think of it as the raw materials you need to come up with a great product. You need to process your big dataset to *mine* trends, patterns, and insights from it. Then you will have actionable information that is useful to your business. Microsoft Azure enables you to process large datasets using well-known products and technologies including Hadoop, Spark, and AI/ML models. For example, these technologies can be used to:

- Run analysis on historical weather data to predict natural disasters in the future
- Monitor live temperature telemetry sent by IoT sensors to catch and act on anomalies
- Monitor live access to an online banking application to detect and remediate fraud
- Calculate data aggregations for business reporting and decision making

This chapter introduces key Azure services that enable you to process *streaming data* (live data) as well as *batch data* (historical data) to mine insights and patterns. You will gain familiarity with:

- Processing stream data using Azure Stream Analytics
- Querying batch data using Azure Synapse Analytics
- Processing data using Azure Databricks
- Moving data using Azure Data Factory pipelines

These services can integrate with Azure AI/ML services (e.g., Azure Cognitive Services and Azure Machine Learning) to utilize the power of machine learning in your projects.

## Workstation Configuration

You will need to prepare your workstation before starting on the recipes in this chapter. Follow "What You Will Need" on page xi to set up your machine to run Azure CLI commands. Clone the book's GitHub repository using the following command:

```
git clone https://github.com/zaalion/AzureCookbook.git
```

# 6.1 Processing Live Data Streams Using Azure Stream Analytics

## Problem

You need to process incoming data streams in near real time to find anomalies.

## Solution

Create an Azure Stream Analytics job to ingest data from the event source, process it, and produce output if any anomaly is deleted, as shown in Figure 6-1.

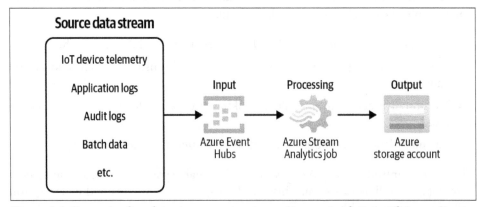

*Figure 6-1. Processing live data streams using Azure Stream Analytics and Azure Event Hubs*

## Steps

1. Log in to your Azure subscription in the Owner role and create a new resource group for this recipe. See "General Workstation Setup Instructions" on page xii for details.

2. First, create a new Azure Event Hubs service. This instance will ingest some live telemetry data (data stream), which will be inputted into your Azure Stream Analytics job. Use the following commands to create the new Event Hubs namespace and hub resources:

```
eventHubNamespaceName="<ehub-namespace-name>"

az eventhubs namespace create \
  --resource-group $rgName \
  --name $eventHubNamespaceName \
  --sku Standard \
  --enable-auto-inflate \
  --maximum-throughput-units 5

az eventhubs eventhub create \
  --resource-group $rgName \
  --namespace-name $eventHubNamespaceName \
  --name inputHub \
  --message-retention 1 \
  --partition-count 2

eventHubprimaryConnectionString=$(az eventhubs namespace \
  authorization-rule keys list \
  --resource-group $rgName \
  --namespace-name $eventHubNamespaceName \
  --name RootManageSharedAccessKey \
  --query primaryConnectionString)
```

3. Your Azure Stream Analytics job will process the live stream and output the result into the configured output. Use the following commands to create a new Azure storage account and a container to be used as the service output:

```
storageAccountName="<storage-account-name>"
containerName="outputcontainer"

az storage account create \
  --name $storageAccountName \
  --resource-group $rgName \
  --sku Standard_LRS

storageKey=$(az storage account keys list \
  --resource-group $rgName \
  --account-name $storageAccountName \
  --query [0].value \
```

```
    --output tsv)

az storage container create \
    --name $containerName \
    --account-name $storageAccountName \
    --account-key $storageKey
```

4. So far, you have created the input and output services. Use the following command to create a new Azure Stream Analytics job:

```
streamJobName="myTemperatureJob"

az stream-analytics job create \
    --resource-group $rgName \
    --name $streamJobName \
    --output-error-policy "Drop" \
    --out-of-order-policy "Drop" \
    --data-locale "en-US"
```

 This command requires the Stream Analytics extension to be installed. If you're prompted to install it, answer Y.

5. It's time to configure the input for your job. Create a new file in your local environment with the following content and name it *inputProperties.json*. This file contains the properties of the input resource, in our case Azure Event Hubs. Replace *<event-hub-name>*, *<event-hub-namespace>*, and *<event-hub-key>* with their values from step 2:

```
{
  "type": "Stream",
  "datasource": {
    "type": "Microsoft.ServiceBus/EventHub",
    "properties": {
      "eventHubName": "<event-hub-name>",
      "serviceBusNamespace": "<event-hub-namespace>",
      "sharedAccessPolicyKey": "<event-hub-key>",
      "sharedAccessPolicyName": "RootManageSharedAccessKey"
    }
  },
  "serialization": { "type": "Json",
  "properties": { "encoding": "UTF8" } }
}
```

6. The stage is set to configure your Azure Stream Analytics job input now:

```
az stream-analytics input create \
  --input-name "temperatureInput" \
  --job-name $streamJobName \
  --resource-group "$rgName" \
  --properties /path/to/inputProperties.json
```

 The `--properties` parameter can be passed inline instead of from an external JSON file. See the command documentation (*https://oreil.ly/73fr0*) for details.

7. Create a new file with the following content and name it *outputProperties.json*. This file contains the properties of your Azure Stream Analytics job output, in our case Azure storage account. Replace *<storage-account-name>* and *<storage-account-key>* with their values from step 3:

```
{
    "type": "Microsoft.Storage/Blob",
    "properties": {
        "storageAccounts": [
            {
                "accountName": "<storage-account-name>",
                "accountKey": "<storage-account-key>"
            }
        ],
        "container": "outputcontainer",
        "pathPattern": "{date}/{time}",
        "dateFormat": "yyyy/MM/dd",
        "timeFormat": "HH"
    }
}
```

8. Create another file with the following content and name it *encoding.json*. This file tells Azure Stream Analytics about the input data format, so it can be deserialized:

```
{
    "type": "Json",
    "properties": {
        "encoding": "UTF8"
    }
}
```

9. Use this command to configure the Stream Analytics job output:

```
az stream-analytics output create \
    --resource-group $rgName \
    --job-name $streamJobName \
    --name temperatureOutput \
    --datasource /path/to/outputProperties.json \
    --serialization /path/to/encoding.json
```

10. Both input and output for your Azure Stream Analytics job are configured. Your job can take the input and create an output based on your business logic. In this recipe, we pretend that connected IoT devices send live temperature data every second. Use the following command to configure your Stream Analytics job to create an output each time the temperature is above 100 degrees:

```
az stream-analytics transformation create \
    --resource-group $rgName \
    --job-name $streamJobName \
    --name AnomalyDetection \
    --streaming-units "1" \
    --saql \
    "SELECT * INTO temperatureOutput FROM temperatureInput
    WHERE Temperature > 100"
```

See Stream Analytics Query Language Reference (*https://oreil.ly/ AiOqP*) for details on the --transformation-query parameter.

11. Your job is now configured. Use the following command to start it:

```
az stream-analytics job start \
    --resource-group $rgName \
    --job-name $streamJobName \
    --output-start-mode JobStartTime
```

12. In a real-world scenario, your Event Hub would accept telemetry data from sources such as live application logs or sensors. Not everyone has access to live environments, so you alternatively can develop a utility application (*https://oreil.ly/ N0rfn*) to send sample data to Azure Event Hubs. You can also install the Visual Studio Code extension Azure Event Hub Explorer (*https://oreil.ly/kZ1c3*) and use it to send test data. Using the utility app, you can send a message batch to your Azure Event Hub as shown in Figure 6-2:

```
{
  "DeviceID": "T - 001",
  "Temperature": <randomized number between 0 and 300>
}
```

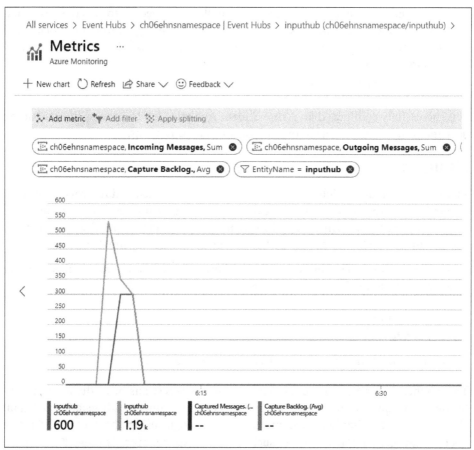

All services > Event Hubs > ch06ehnsnamespace | Event Hubs > inputhub (ch06ehnsnamespace/inputhub) >

**Metrics** ···
Azure Monitoring

+ New chart  ⟳ Refresh  ⤴ Share ∨  ☺ Feedback ∨

⋏ Add metric  ⋎ Add filter  ⋇ Apply splitting

🗔 ch06ehnsnamespace, **Incoming Messages,** Sum ⊗    🗔 ch06ehnsnamespace, **Outgoing Messages,** Sum ⊗

🗔 ch06ehnsnamespace, **Capture Backlog.,** Avg ⊗    ▽ EntityName = **inputhub** ⊗

| inputhub ch06ehnsnamespace | inputhub ch06ehnsnamespace | Captured Messages. (... ch06ehnsnamespace | Capture Backlog. (Avg) ch06ehnsnamespace |
| --- | --- | --- | --- |
| 600 | 1.19 k | -- | -- |

*Figure 6-2. Azure Event Hubs receiving the temperature messages from our utility app*

13. After you send the messages, wait for a few minutes to give the Azure Stream Analytics job time to process the input and generate output blobs. You can see a sample output file on GitHub (*https://oreil.ly/Ks_Jn*). Use the following command to query the output Azure Storage container and confirm you see the new files:

```
az storage blob list \
    --account-name $storageAccountName \
    --account-key $storageKey \
    --container-name $containerName \
    --query [].name
```

14. Finally, use the following command to stop the job:

```
az stream-analytics job stop \
  --job-name $streamJobName \
  --resource-group $rgName
```

15. You should delete the job after you complete this recipe to avoid unexpected costs on your Azure subscription bill. Run the following command to delete the parent resource group you created in this recipe. This will delete all its child resources including your Stream Analytics job:

```
az group delete --name $rgName
```

You successfully configured an Azure Stream Analytics job to process live streaming data and produce output based on your business requirements.

## Discussion

Azure Stream Analytics jobs (*https://oreil.ly/NpXsP*) are designed to process live data streams in near real time and produce outputs that can be used by downstream Azure services. Azure Stream Analytics jobs can also be provisioned in a Docker container and deployed to IoT edge devices (*https://oreil.ly/IhzaS*) for minimal latency.

Azure Stream Analytics jobs support the following services for incoming streaming data input (*https://oreil.ly/Ux-fu*):

- Azure Event Hubs
- Azure IoT Hub
- Azure Blob Storage (and Azure Data Lake Storage Gen2)

The job then uses a SQL-like query language to process (transform) the input data to the desired output. In this recipe, we used a very simple query with a static condition. However, you can implement complex business logic using the Stream Analytics query language. AI/ML functions such as `AnomalyDetection_SpikeAndDip` can be used in the queries to solve complex business problems such as detecting anomalies (*https://oreil.ly/qtVs1*) in the data stream. You can also call external Azure ML models (*https://oreil.ly/oIvEb*) right from your queries.

Once the output is generated, it will be sent to the configured job outputs. At the time of writing this book, the following outputs (*https://oreil.ly/JtSQs*) are supported:

- Azure Functions
- Azure Data Lake Storage Gen1
- Azure Blob Storage and Azure Data Lake Storage Gen2
- Azure Data Explorer
- Azure Database for PostgreSQL
- Azure SQL Database
- Azure Cosmos DB

- Azure Synapse Analytics
- Azure Event Hubs
- Power BI
- Azure Table storage
- Azure Service Bus queues and topics

As you learned, Azure Stream Analytics has native integration with many Azure services, which makes it a powerful option to process live streaming data at scale.

# 6.2 Querying CSV File Content Using Azure Synapse Analytics Serverless Pool

## Problem

You want to query data in multiple CSV files using the familiar SQL language.

## Solution

Upload your CSV files to an Azure Data Lake Gen2 storage and use Azure Synapse Analytics serverless pool to run SQL queries against your file contents, as shown in Figure 6-3.

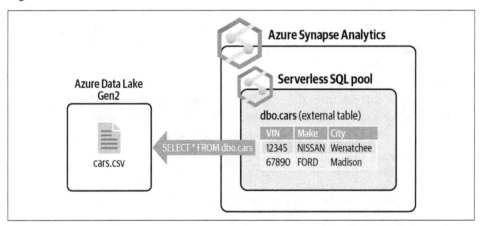

*Figure 6-3. Analyzing CSV file content using Azure Synapse Analytics serverless pool*

### Steps

1. Log in to your Azure subscription in the Owner role and create a new resource group for this recipe. See "General Workstation Setup Instructions" on page xii for details.

2. First, create a new Azure Data Lake Storage Gen2 resource (*https://oreil.ly/nj9HH*). This resource is built on top of Azure Storage blobs and provides data storage for raw data files such as CSV or JSON files. Azure Synapse Analytics will use this storage for big data analysis. By passing `--enable-hierarchical-namespace true`, you are creating an Azure Data Lake Storage Gen2 resource:

```
storageAccountName="<storage-account-name>"

az storage account create \
    --name $storageAccountName \
    --resource-group $rgName \
    --sku Standard_LRS \
    --enable-hierarchical-namespace true
```

3. Now let's create a filesystem (*https://oreil.ly/nruFX*) in your Data Lake Gen2 account. File systems are similar to blob containers in Azure Storage:

```
storageKey=$(az storage account keys list \
    --resource-group $rgName \
    --account-name $storageAccountName \
    --query [0].value \
    --output tsv)

az storage container create \
    --name "rawdata" \
    --account-name $storageAccountName \
    --account-key $storageKey
```

4. Upload your data files to the new file system. In this recipe, we'll query a sample CSV file containing a list of battery electric vehicles (BEVs) and plug-in hybrid electric vehicles (PHEVs) (*https://oreil.ly/7cxGv*) currently registered through the Washington State Department of Licensing (DOL). You can download the first 500 rows of this file from the chapter repository (*https://oreil.ly/7cryh*). Save this file on your local machine and upload it to the file system using the following command. Replace <*local-path*> with the path to the data file:

```
az storage blob upload \
    --account-key $storageKey \
    --file <local-path> \
    --account-name $storageAccountName \
    --container-name "rawdata" \
    --name "cars.csv"
```

5. Now that your data is ready, proceed with creating a new Azure Synapse Analytics workspace. This resource enables you to process files stored in Azure Data Lake Gen2 storage using familiar SQL queries. Replace <*synapse-workspace-name*> with the desired workspace name. You also need to provide a username and password, which will be used to log in to the SQL pools. Replace <*sql-username*> and <*sql-password*> with your values as well:

```
synapseWorkspaceName="<synapse-workspace-name>"
sqlUser="<sql-username>"
sqlPassword="<sql-password>"

az synapse workspace create \
  --name $synapseWorkspaceName \
  --resource-group $rgName \
  --storage-account $storageAccountName \
  --file-system "rawdata" \
  --sql-admin-login-user $sqlUser \
  --sql-admin-login-password $sqlPassword
```

> You can use `--sql-admin-login-user` and `--sql-admin-login-password` to connect to your Synapse pool using any SQL client, such as Microsoft SQL Server Management Studio or Azure Data Studio (*https://oreil.ly/jjqxH*). Alternatively, you can log in to the Synapse Studio portal using your Azure subscription account, as you will see in the next steps.

6. Wait for the preceding command to execute; it might take several minutes. Then, use the following command to get the URL for your *Azure Synapse Studio* portal. You will use this portal to configure the workspace and analyze your data:

```
workspaceURL=$(az synapse workspace show \
  --name $synapseWorkspaceName \
  --resource-group $rgName \
  | jq -r '.connectivityEndpoints | .web')
```

7. Similar to Azure SQL Database, Azure Synapse Analytics blocks all calls to the workspace. Use the following command to configure the Synapse firewall to allow your public IP (v4) address. Replace *<your-public-ip-address>* with your public IP address:

```
clientIP="<your-public-ip-address>"

az synapse workspace firewall-rule create \
  --end-ip-address $clientIP \
  --start-ip-address $clientIP \
  --name "Allowing My IP" \
  --resource-group $rgName \
  --workspace-name $synapseWorkspaceName
```

> You can visit ipaddress.com to find your public IP address. Alternatively, you can derive your public IP from the Synapse Dev workspace as described in step 5 in this document (*https://oreil.ly/29Dbl*).

---

8. You are ready to work with your Synapse workspace. Open the address stored in the $workspaceURL variable in a browser and confirm that you can see the Synapse Studio interface. Use the following command to see the value of this variable:

```
echo $workspaceURL
```

9. If prompted, use the same credentials you used in step 1 to log in to the Synapse portal. Upon successful login, you should land on the dashboard page, as shown in Figure 6-4.

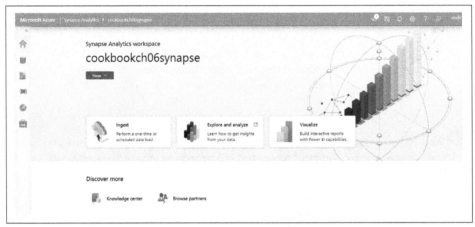

*Figure 6-4. Azure Synapse Studio dashboard*

10. It's time to query your CSV file. Click on the New button and select "SQL script" as shown in Figure 6-5.

11. Azure Synapse uses servers called *pools* to analyze your big data. A *serverless SQL pool* (built-in) is already created for you and selected in the "Connect to" dropdown. Paste the following command into the script editor. This command creates a new database called electricCarsDB in your serverless (built-in) server pool. Select the command and click the Run button as shown in Figure 6-6:

```
CREATE DATABASE electricCarsDB
    COLLATE Latin1_General_100_BIN2_UTF8
```

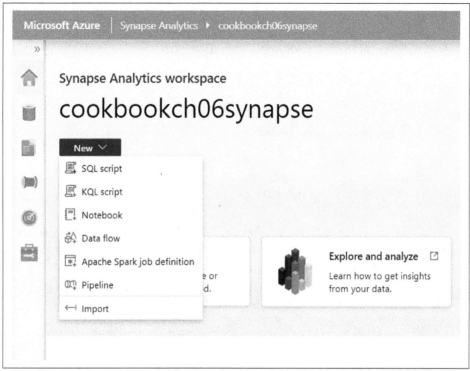

*Figure 6-5. Creating a new SQL script*

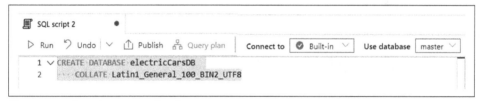

*Figure 6-6. Creating a new database*

12. Confirm that you see a "Query executed successfully" message at the bottom, as shown in Figure 6-7.

*Figure 6-7. Confirming the SQL command executed successfully*

13. Now that you have a new database, let's select it from the "Use database" drop-down list. You might need to click the small refresh button at the right to see the new database in the list, as shown in Figure 6-8.

*Figure 6-8. Selecting the active database*

14. Paste the following SQL script after the CREATE DATABASE command, select it, and click the Run button. This specifies where Synapse should load the data files (CSV files) from, and the column delimiters used in the CSV. Confirm that the scripts are executed successfully:

```
CREATE EXTERNAL DATA SOURCE csvfiles
WITH (
    LOCATION = 'https://synapsecookdl01.blob.core.windows.net/rawdata/'
)


CREATE EXTERNAL FILE FORMAT CsvFileFormat
    WITH (
        FORMAT_TYPE = DELIMITEDTEXT,
        FORMAT_OPTIONS(
            FIELD_TERMINATOR = ',',
            STRING_DELIMITER = '"',
            FIRST_ROW  = 2
        )
    );


CREATE EXTERNAL TABLE dbo.electricHybridCars
(
    VIN VARCHAR(11),
    Country VARCHAR(20),
    City VARCHAR(20),
    [State] VARCHAR(2),
    [Postal Code] VARCHAR(5),
    [Model Year] VARCHAR(4),
    Make VARCHAR(20)
)
WITH
(
```

```
        DATA_SOURCE = csvfiles,
        LOCATION = '*.csv',
        FILE_FORMAT = CsvFileFormat
    );
```

In this recipe, we used a single file (*cars.csv*); however, you can upload multiple files to the *csvfiles* file system and all those files will be included in the data source.

15. So far you have created the `dbo.electricHybridCars` external table, which points to the *cars.csv* content. Now you can use SQL commands to query the CSV file content. Paste and run the following query to get a list of registered car numbers for each car make, as shown in Figure 6-9:

```
-- Find the number of registered cars per make

SELECT Make, COUNT(*) as Sold FROM dbo.electricHybridCars
GROUP BY Make
ORDER BY Sold DESC
```

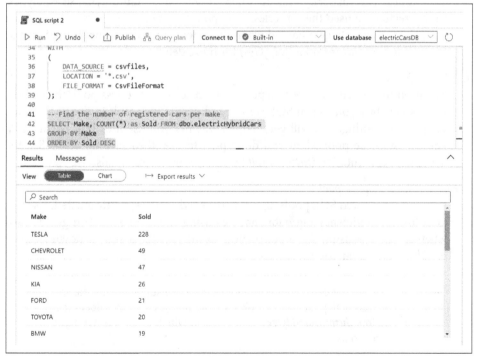

*Figure 6-9. Querying the CSV file using an Azure Synapse external table*

16. Run the following command to delete the resources you created in this recipe:

```
az group delete --name $rgName
```

You successfully queried data stored in a CSV file using Azure Synapse Analytics external tables.

## Discussion

Azure Synapse Analytics (*https://oreil.ly/73WuB*) enables you to use SQL and Spark technologies to analyze big data, offers a Data Explorer for log and time series data analytics, and can persist data in its native data warehouse. You can create data integration pipelines (similar to Azure Data Factory pipelines) for ETL/ELT processes. It has native integration with Azure Storage, Azure Data Lake Gen1 and Gen2, Power BI, Cosmos DB, and Azure ML to enrich your data processing pipelines.

An Azure Synapse *pool* is one or more servers that processes your data. As you saw in Figure 6-9, you ran a SQL script on a built-in SQL pool. You can save the analytics results into the pool, as you would on an Azure SQL database. At the time of writing this book, Azure Synapse offers three pool types:

*Serverless SQL pool (built-in pool)*
This pool is automatically created when provisioning Azure Synapse Analytics. In this recipe, we used the serverless SQL pool to query a CSV file in Azure Data Lake Gen2. You only get charged when this pool is in use. See the Azure Synapse documentation (*https://oreil.ly/KqGys*) for more details.

*Dedicated SQL pool*
You need to explicitly create this pool. Similar to the serverless pool, the dedicated pool enables you to run SQL scripts and persist the result in the pool. When the pool is running, you will get charged whether you use it or not. Fortunately, you can stop the pool when you don't plan to use it, to save on costs. See the Synapse documentation (*https://oreil.ly/CAQ_n*) for more details.

*Serverless Apache Spark pool*
Similar to dedicated SQL pools, Spark pools need to be explicitly created. Use this pool for high-efficiency big data analytics using Apache Spark. You get charged whether you are using this pool or not, so make sure to shut it down (*https://oreil.ly/Y9DzI*) after you finish using it.

Not all the dedicated SQL pool features are supported by the serverless SQL pool. Take a look at the Azure Synapse pools documentation (*https://oreil.ly/zge7B*) to decide which SQL pool type you need to use.

---

Similar to other Azure Data services, Azure Synapse Analytics offers a service-level firewall (*https://oreil.ly/erwHX*), which allows IP-filtering for incoming requests. You should also consider configuring private endpoints (*https://oreil.ly/TT_Sh*) for your Azure Synapse Analytics, if applicable.

# 6.3 Saving Costs on Idle Azure Synapse Dedicated SQL and Spark Pools

## Problem

You need to make sure that idle Azure Synapse pools don't incur charges.

## Solution

If you use dedicated SQL pools, *pause them* (*https://oreil.ly/2eyeF*) when they are not in use. In the case of Spark pools, configure the *automatic pause feature* (*https://oreil.ly/DOUDQ*) so the pool stops when idle for a set period.

 You can use the Microsoft Cost Management and Billing tools (*https://oreil.ly/dl_W2*) to monitor and optimize cost for your resources, including Azure Synapse pools. See Recipe 11.3 for step-by-step instructions.

### Steps

1. Log in to your Azure subscription in the Owner role and create a new resource group for this recipe. See "General Workstation Setup Instructions" on page xii for details.

2. Follow steps 2 to 7 in Recipe 6.2 to create and configure an Azure Synapse Analytics workspace.

3. In this recipe, you will create a dedicated SQL pool as well as a Spark pool. First use the following command to create a dedicated SQL pool in your workspace. Replace *<dedicated-pool-name>* with the desired name for your pool:

```
dedicatedSQLPoolName="<dedicated-pool-name>"

az synapse sql pool create \
    --name $dedicatedSQLPoolName \
    --performance-level "DW1000c" \
    --workspace-name $synapseWorkspaceName \
    --resource-group $rgName \
    --collation "SQL_Latin1_General_CP1_CS_AS"
```

4. Use the following command to check the pool status. You should see a status of "online":

```
az synapse sql pool show \
  --name $dedicatedSQLPoolName \
  --workspace-name $synapseWorkspaceName \
  --resource-group $rgName \
  --query status
```

5. While the pool is running, you get charged whether you use it or not. You can pause the pool when it is not in use to save on costs:

```
az synapse sql pool pause \
  --name $dedicatedSQLPoolName \
  --workspace-name $synapseWorkspaceName \
  --resource-group $rgName
```

6. Run step 4 again to see the pool status. The status should be "paused," which means you are not getting charged for the compute resources. Now you can use the following command to resume the pool:

```
az synapse sql pool resume \
  --name $dedicatedSQLPoolName \
  --workspace-name $synapseWorkspaceName \
  --resource-group $rgName
```

> You won't be charged (*https://oreil.ly/3U8kj*) for compute resources while the dedicated SQL pool is paused. However, you will continue to be charged for the storage space the pool takes.

7. If you are done with this dedicated SQL pool, run the following command to permanently delete it so you don't get charged for an unused pool:

```
az synapse sql pool delete \
  --name $dedicatedSQLPoolName \
  --workspace-name $synapseWorkspaceName \
  --resource-group $rgName
```

8. Let's explore the serverless Spark pools now. Use the following command to create a new serverless Spark pool. Despite the *serverless* name, you get charged whether you are using this pool or not. To avoid charges on an idle (but running) Spark pool, configure the automatic pause feature as follows. Replace *<spark-pool-name>* with the desired name for your Spark pool:

```
sparkPoolName="<spark-pool-name>"

az synapse spark pool create \
  --name $sparkPoolName \
  --workspace-name $synapseWorkspaceName \
```

```
--resource-group $rgName \
--spark-version 2.4 \
--node-count 3 \
--node-size Small \
--enable-auto-pause true \
--delay 10
```

 The automatic pause feature can be configured during the Spark pool creation, as well as for existing pools using the az synapse spark pool update command (*https://oreil.ly/_Tw49*).

9.  Your Spark pool will automatically pause if idle for 10 minutes (set by --delay 10) and will automatically resume when it is needed. Use the following command to get the automatic pause settings of your Spark pool:

```
az synapse spark pool show \
  --name $sparkPoolName \
  --workspace-name $synapseWorkspaceName \
  --resource-group $rgName \
  --query autoPause
```

10. Finally, make sure you delete your Spark cluster to avoid getting charged:

```
az synapse spark pool delete \
  --name $sparkPoolName \
  --workspace-name $synapseWorkspaceName \
  --resource-group $rgName
```

11. Run the following command to delete the resources you created in this recipe:

```
az group delete --name $rgName
```

You successfully optimized costs for both Azure Synapse dedicated SQL and serverless Spark pools.

## Discussion

As you learn in Recipe 6.2, Azure Synapse offers three pool types. These pools are physical servers, which incur costs when running. The cost is different depending on the configured pool size. It is important to make sure no charge incurs when your pools are not in use. Here is how cost management can be implemented for each pool type:

*Serverless SQL pools (built-in)*
    There is no need to explicitly configure automatic pause on these pools. You only get charged when you use the serverless SQL pool.

*Dedicated SQL pools*

You have to manually pause (*https://oreil.ly/2pJih*) and resume dedicated SQL pools in the Azure portal, either programmatically or using Azure CLI and PowerShell.

*Serverless Spark pools*

You can configure automatic pause (*https://oreil.ly/SPyPQ*) on a Spark pool so it stops after a set amount of idle time. The pool starts again when it is needed.

# 6.4 Processing Datafiles Using Azure Databricks

## Problem

You want to load JSON data into in-memory tables to analyze it using Apache Spark.

## Solution

Provision a new Azure Databricks workspace, create a cluster, and load your JSON files into an Apache Spark DataFrame (*https://oreil.ly/gOSh_*). Use Scala, SQL, R, or another supported language (*https://oreil.ly/j1jsY*) to analyze your data as shown in Figure 6-10.

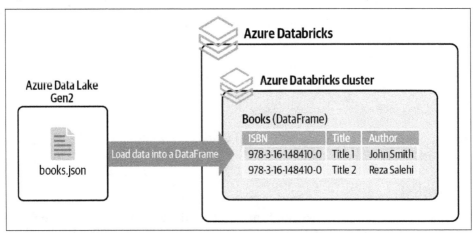

*Figure 6-10. Processing JSON data using Azure Databricks*

## Steps

1. Log in to your Azure subscription in the Owner role and create a new resource group for this recipe. See "General Workstation Setup Instructions" on page xii for details.

---

2. First, create a new Azure Data Lake Storage Gen2 and a child filesystem (container). Azure Databricks can use this storage for big data analysis. By passing `--enable-hierarchical-namespace true`, you are creating an Azure Data Lake Storage Gen2 resource:

```
storageAccountName="<storage-account-name>"

az storage account create \
    --name $storageAccountName \
    --resource-group $rgName \
    --sku Standard_LRS \
    --enable-hierarchical-namespace true

storageKey=$(az storage account keys list \
    --resource-group $rgName \
    --account-name $storageAccountName \
    --query [0].value \
    --output tsv)

az storage container create \
    --name "bigdata" \
    --account-name $storageAccountName \
    --account-key $storageKey
```

3. Create a SAS token for the Azure Data Lake Gen2 resource using the following command. Make a note of the `sasToken` value. You will need it in the following steps:

```
expiryDate=`date -u -d "120 minutes" '+%Y-%m-%dT%H:%MZ'`

sasToken=$(az storage account generate-sas \
    --account-name $storageAccountName \
    --account-key $storageKey \
    --expiry $expiryDate \
    --permissions rwcul \
    --resource-types sco \
    --services b \
    --https-only \
    --output tsv)

echo $sasToken
```

4. In this recipe, you will work with a JSON file containing an array of country names and properties. Download this JSON file (*https://oreil.ly/uXatG*) and save it on your local machine. A single record looks like the following:

```
{
    "name": "United States of America",
    "code": "US",
    "capital": "Washington, D.C.",
    "region": "NA",
```

```
      "currency": {
        "code": "USD",
        "name": "United States dollar",
        "symbol": "$"
      },
      "language": {
        "code": "en",
        "iso639_2": "eng",
        "name": "English",
        "nativeName": "English"
      },
      "flag": "https://restcountries.eu/data/usa.svg"
    }
```

5. Upload *country_list.json* to the `bigdata` filesystem (container) using the follow-ing command. Replace `<local-path>` with the path to *country_list.json* on your local machine:

```
blobName="country_list.json"

az storage blob upload \
    --account-key $storageKey \
    --file <local-path>/country_list.json \
    --account-name $storageAccountName \
    --container-name bigdata \
    --name $blobName
```

6. Use the following command to provision a new Azure Databricks workspace. Replace `<databricks-workspace>` with the desired value. This command might take a few minutes to execute. If you're prompted to install the Databricks exten-sion, answer Y:

```
databricksWorkspaceName="<databricks-workspace>"

az databricks workspace create \
    --resource-group $rgName \
    --name $databricksWorkspaceName \
    --location $region \
    --sku standard
```

7. Open the browser of your choice and navigate to Azure Databricks (*https://oreil.ly/X0MzV*). Click on your new workspace in the list, as shown in Figure 6-11.

*Figure 6-11. Accessing the Azure Databricks page*

8. On the Overview page, click the Launch Workspace button, as illustrated in Figure 6-12. Enter your Azure credentials if prompted.

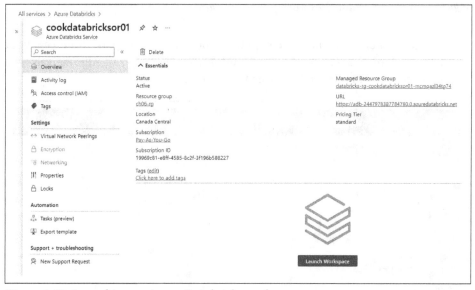

*Figure 6-12. Launching an Azure Databricks workspace*

9. Confirm that you are in the workspace dashboard page as illustrated in Figure 6-13.

*Figure 6-13. Azure Databricks workspace dashboard*

10. You need to create a cluster (compute) to be able to use Spark to process your data. Click on the "Create a cluster" button (see Figure 6-14). Alternatively, you can click on Compute on the left-hand menu (see Figure 6-15).

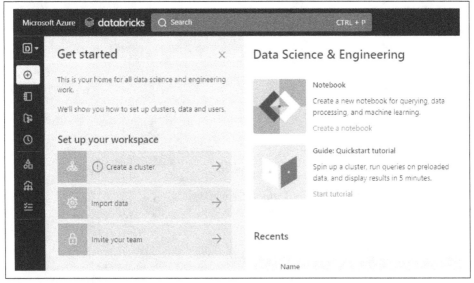

*Figure 6-14. Creating a cluster*

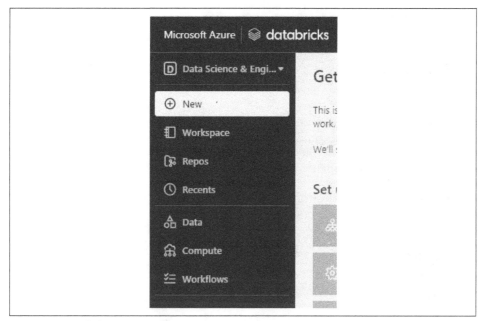

*Figure 6-15. Clicking on Compute*

11. Click on the "Create compute" button as shown in Figure 6-16.

*Figure 6-16. Clicking the "Create compute" button*

12. Fill in the cluster properties. Make sure "Enable autoscaling" is unchecked, number of workers is set to 1, and "Terminate after" is set to 30 minutes. Leave the other default values untouched, as shown in Figure 6-17. Click on the Create Cluster button when done, and then wait for the cluster to be created. It may take several minutes.

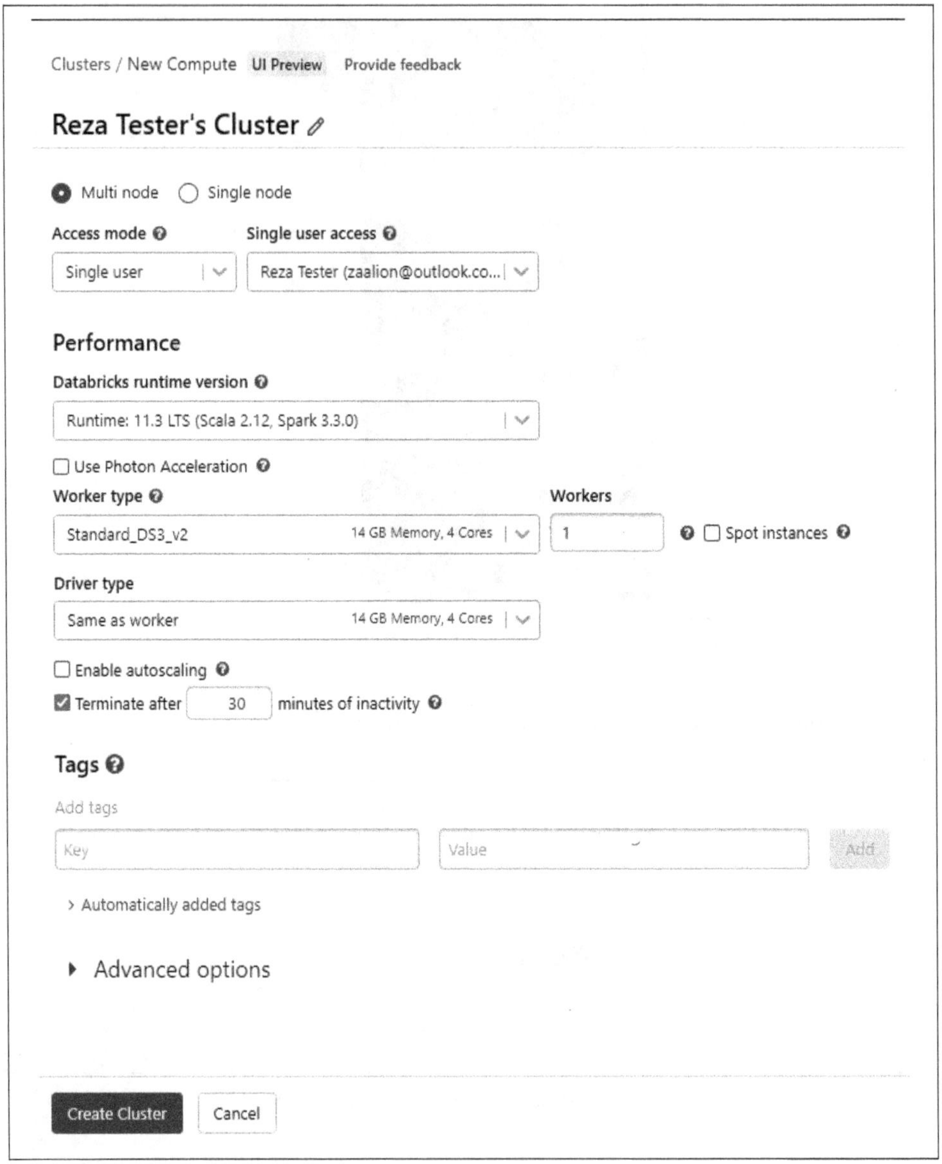

Clusters / New Compute **UI Preview** Provide feedback

# Reza Tester's Cluster ✐

● Multi node   ○ Single node

**Access mode** ❓                **Single user access** ❓

| Single user            | ∨ |     | Reza Tester (zaalion@outlook.co... | ∨ |

## Performance

**Databricks runtime version** ❓

| Runtime: 11.3 LTS (Scala 2.12, Spark 3.3.0)            | ∨ |

☐ Use Photon Acceleration ❓

**Worker type** ❓                                              **Workers**

| Standard_DS3_v2       | 14 GB Memory, 4 Cores  | ∨ |    | 1 |    ❓ ☐ Spot instances ❓

**Driver type**

| Same as worker       | 14 GB Memory, 4 Cores  | ∨ |

☐ Enable autoscaling ❓
☑ Terminate after  | 30 |  minutes of inactivity ❓

## Tags ❓

Add tags

| Key | | Value ˇ | | Add |

> Automatically added tags

▸ Advanced options

**Create Cluster**    Cancel

*Figure 6-17. Specifying the cluster properties*

 Make sure to set the "Terminate after" value for the cluster and, ideally, delete the Azure Databricks workspace resource after you are done with this recipe to avoid unexpected charges on your Azure subscription.

13. Now it's time to create an Azure Databricks notebook (*https://oreil.ly/MTLlU*). You can use notebooks to develop and run code to analyze data and develop data science workflows. From the left menu, click on Workspace > Users > Create > Notebook as shown in Figure 6-18.

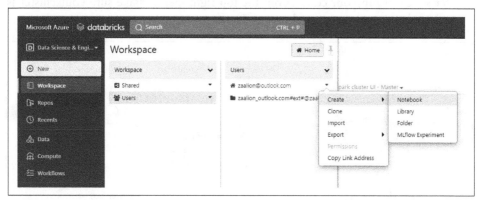

*Figure 6-18. Creating a new notebook*

14. Choose a name for your notebook and select Scala in the Default Language drop-down. Make sure your new cluster is selected to be attached, as illustrated in Figure 6-19.

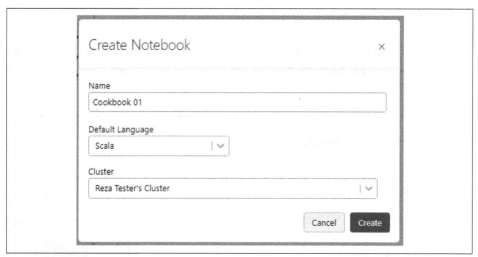

*Figure 6-19. Creating a new Scala notebook*

15. You can add code *cells* to your notebook and run each cell individually to see its result in the notebook. In this recipe, you will develop a notebook that loads data from a JSON file into an in-memory Spark table called `dataframe` and use the Scala language to work with the table. Your notebook must be attached to a cluster so it can run your code. From the top right menu, make sure your cluster is selected and then start it as shown in Figure 6-20.

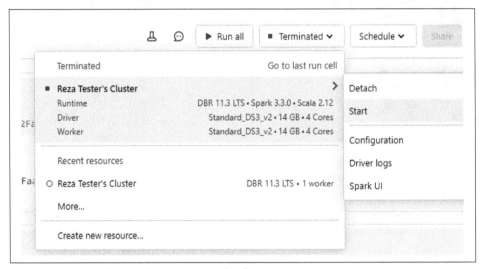

*Figure 6-20. Attaching a cluster to a notebook*

16. As you saw in Figure 6-17, the cluster will automatically stop if idle for more than 30 minutes. If this happens, you will be prompted to start the cluster by clicking the "Start, attach and run" button as shown in Figure 6-21.

*Figure 6-21. Clicking the "Start, attach and run" button on an idle cluster*

17. You are ready to run your first cell. Paste the following code in the first cell of your notebook. Replace *<storage-account-name>*, *<file_system_name>*, and *<SAS-token>* with their values from steps 2 and 3. Then run the cell either by pressing Shift + Enter, or as illustrated in Figure 6-22. As you will see, the code result appears after the cell code:

```
// cell #1
val storageAccountName = "<storage-account-name>"
val fileSystemName = "<file_system_name>"
val SAS = "<SAS-token>"
```

*Figure 6-22. Running a notebook cell*

18. Insert a new cell by pressing Shift + Enter and pasting the following code. This code tells Azure Databricks to use the SAS token to authenticate with the storage account (Azure Data Lake Gen2). Run the cell and confirm the result:

```
// cell #2
spark.conf.set("fs.azure.account.auth.type."
  + storageAccountName + ".dfs.core.windows.net", "SAS")

spark.conf.set("fs.azure.sas.token.provider.type."
  + storageAccountName + ".dfs.core.windows.net",
  "org.apache.hadoop.fs.azurebfs.sas.FixedSASTokenProvider")

spark.conf.set("fs.azure.sas.fixed.token."
  + storageAccountName + ".dfs.core.windows.net", SAS)
```

19. Insert a third cell and run the following code to load *country_list.json* from Data Lake Gen2 (Azure Blob Storage) into a Spark DataFrame. Confirm that the command successfully created the DataFrame as shown in Figure 6-23:

```
// cell #3
val df = spark.read.option("multiLine", true)
  .json("abfss://"
        + fileSystemName + "@" + storageAccountName
        + ".dfs.core.windows.net/country_list.json")
```

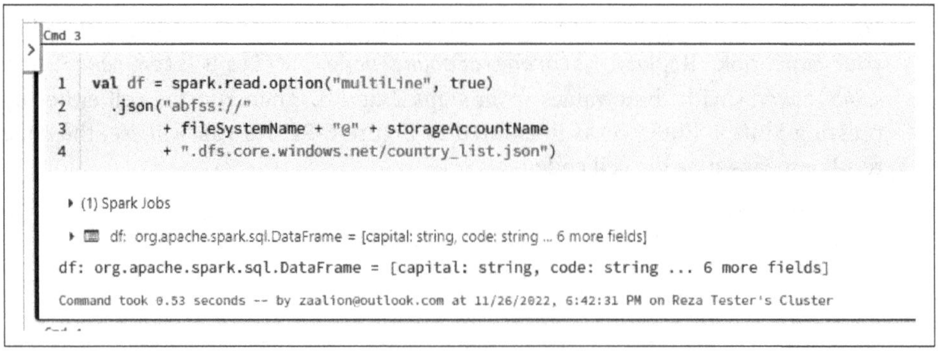

*Figure 6-23. Loading the JSON file into the DataFrame*

20. In a fourth cell, insert the following command to see the DataFrame context as shown in Figure 6-24:

```
// cell #4
df.show()
```

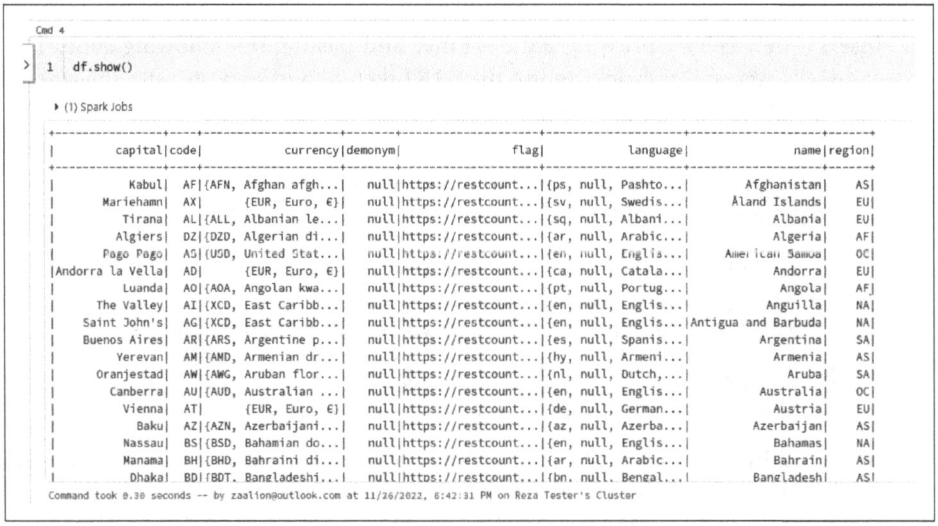

*Figure 6-24. Displaying the DataFrame*

21. Now you can analyze the loaded data by querying the DataFrame. Insert the following command in the fifth cell to select three columns from your data, as shown in Figure 6-25:

```
// cell #5
val selectColDf = df.select("name", "capital", "currency.code")
selectColDf.show()
```

```
Cmd 5

1    val selectColDf = df.select("name", "capital", "currency.code")
2    selectColDf.show()


▶ (1) Spark Jobs

  ▶ 🖼 selectColDf:  org.apache.spark.sql.DataFrame = [name: string, capital: string ... 1 more field]

+-------------------+----------------+----+
|               name|         capital|code|
+-------------------+----------------+----+
|        Afghanistan|           Kabul| AFN|
|      Åland Islands|       Mariehamn| EUR|
|            Albania|          Tirana| ALL|
|            Algeria|         Algiers| DZD|
|     American Samoa|       Pago Pago| USD|
|            Andorra|Andorra la Vella| EUR|
|             Angola|          Luanda| AOA|
|           Anguilla|      The Valley| XCD|
|Antigua and Barbuda|     Saint John's| XCD|
|          Argentina|    Buenos Aires| ARS|
|            Armenia|         Yerevan| AMD|
|              Aruba|      Oranjestad| AWG|
|          Australia|        Canberra| AUD|
|            Austria|          Vienna| EUR|
|         Azerbaijan|            Baku| AZN|
|            Bahamas|          Nassau| BSD|
|            Bahrain|          Manama| BHD|
|         Bangladesh|          Dhaka| BDT|

Command took 0.43 seconds -- by zaalion@outlook.com at 11/26/2022, 6:42:31 PM on Reza Tester's Cluster
```

*Figure 6-25. Selecting specific columns from the DataFrame*

22. In the previous step, we selected the nested `code` property of the `currency` field (`currency.code`). As you saw in Figure 6-25, this column displays as `code` in the result set. Let's rename this column to `currency_code`, and the `name` column to `country_name` for better clarity. Run this command in the sixth cell to do so:

```
// cell #6
val renameColDF = selectColDf.withColumnRenamed("code", "currency_code")
  .withColumnRenamed("name", "country_name")
renameColDF.show()
```

23. You can save the result of your processing back into a JSON file and save it in the */tmp/* folder in the cluster. This JSON file can also be saved into storage account, Data Lake, or even into an Azure Synapse Analytics database:

```
// cell #7
renameColDF.write.json("/tmp/processed_country.json")
dbutils.fs.ls ("/tmp/")
```

24. You can export your notebook as illustrated in Figure 6-26. The exported notebook can be found in the recipe repository (*https://oreil.ly/otEfk*).

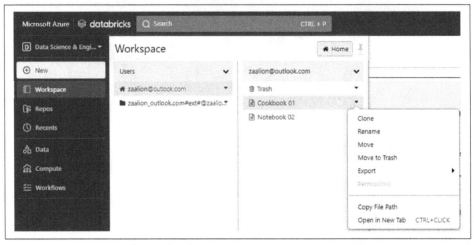

*Figure 6-26. Exporting the notebook*

25. Run the following command to delete the resources you created in this recipe:

```
az group delete --name $rgName
```

You successfully loaded a JSON file into a DataFrame and ran simple analysis on it. You can also import a notebook file into your Azure Databricks workspace as shown in Figure 6-27.

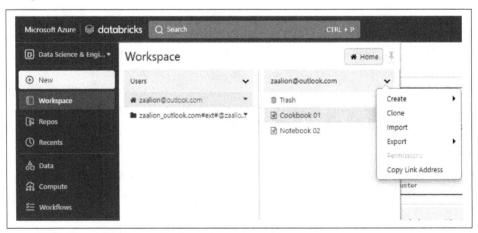

*Figure 6-27. Importing a notebook*

## Discussion

Azure Databricks is Microsoft Azure's implementation of the *Databricks lakehouse* platform (*https://oreil.ly/giRM6*). Azure Databricks (*https://oreil.ly/UbsBV*) provides an integrated set of tools for building, deploying, sharing, and maintaining big data solutions. Integration with Azure Storage, Azure Data Lake Gen1 and Gen2, Azure Key Vault, Azure Virtual Network, Azure Machine Learning, Azure Policy, and Azure RBAC enables you to analyze, process, model, govern, and share your big datasets.

In this recipe, you worked with the Azure Databricks workspace, which provides:

- Interactive notebooks supporting Scala, Python, R, and SQL languages
- Workflow scheduler and manager
- Code editor and dashboards
- Data ingestion and governance
- Data discovery, annotation, and exploration
- Compute (attached cluster) management
- ML experiment tracking
- ML model serving
- Source control integration with Git

Most of the time, you develop your data processing code in a notebook. As you saw in this recipe, a compute resource (running cluster) should be attached to your note-book to execute its commands. This is an Apache Spark cluster, which allows you to efficiently process your big data in RAM.

The source *raw data* can be loaded into a Spark DataFrame from various sources, such as Azure Blob Storage, Azure Data Lake Gen1 and Gen2, or even from a stream-ing data source such as Azure Event Hubs (*https://oreil.ly/loO6a*). You can save the processing result on the cluster, into an Azure Blob Storage (or Azure Data Lake) or in an Azure Synapse Analytics pool (*https://oreil.ly/oL2SA*) for further processing.

Azure Databricks needs proper access to the data source and data destination serv-ices. For example, to enable Azure Databricks to read a JSON file from Azure Data Lake Storage Gen2, you should use the storage account key, SAS token, or configure RBAC permissions for the Azure Databricks managed identity. See the Azure Data-bricks documentation (*https://oreil.ly/gAvR_*) for details.

*Azure HDInsight* is another analytics service, which enables you to process big data using the following cluster types (*https://oreil.ly/lAWYb*): Hadoop, Spark, Kafka, HBase, and Interactive Query. Take a look at the Azure HDInsights documentation (*https://oreil.ly/GrlAH*) for more details.

# 6.5 Performing ETL/ELT Operations on Big Data Using Azure Data Factory (ADF)

## Problem

You want to extract (E) data from a source, transform (T) it, and finally load (L) it into a destination or sink using an Azure data integration service.

## Solution

Provision an Azure Data Factory (ADF) resource and define a data pipeline to perform desired ETL or ELT operations using built-in activities as shown in Figure 6-28.

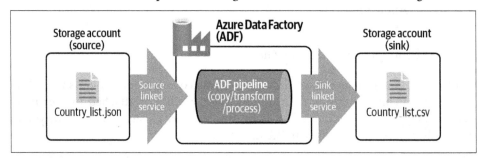

*Figure 6-28. Using ADF to move data files*

## Steps

1. Log in to your Azure subscription in the Owner role and create a new resource group for this recipe. See "General Workstation Setup Instructions" on page xii for details.

2. Create a new Azure storage account with two containers, a *datasource* container and a *datasink* container:

```
storageAccountName="<storage-account-name>"

az storage account create \
    --name $storageAccountName \
    --resource-group $rgName \
    --sku Standard_LRS
```

```
storageKey=$(az storage account keys list \
    --resource-group $rgName \
    --account-name $storageAccountName \
    --query [0].value \
    --output tsv)

az storage container create \
    --name "datasource" \
    --account-name $storageAccountName \
    --account-key $storageKey

az storage container create \
    --name "datasink" \
    --account-name $storageAccountName \
    --account-key $storageKey
```

3. In this recipe you will work with the same JSON file that you used in Recipe 6.4. You will read all the records in this JSON file and transfer the country name, capital city, and flag fields into a destination CSV file. Now upload *country_list.json* to the datasource container. Replace *<local-path>* with the path to *country_list.json* on your local machine:

```
blobName="country_list.json"

az storage blob upload \
    --account-key $storageKey \
    --file <local-path>/country_list.json \
    --account-name $storageAccountName \
    --container-name datasource \
    --name $blobName
```

4. Our goal is to read the JSON file from the source and move select fields into a new CSV file, which is saved into the datasink destination. Use the following command to provision an ADF resource. Replace *<datafactory-name>* with the desired resource name. If you're prompted to install the Data Factory extension, answer Y:

```
adfName="<datafactory-name>"

az datafactory create \
    --resource-group $rgName \
    --factory-name $adfName
```

5. You need to create a *data pipeline* in ADF to process and move your data. This can be done interactively using the ADF Studio GUI or programmatically using Azure CLI. Use the following command to create a *linked service* (*https://oreil.ly/cU8Hy*). A linked service links your data source to the pipeline. You are using a single Azure storage account as both source and destination, so you need only

one linked service. Use the following command to display the storage account connection string. Make a note of it for the next step:

```
storageConnection=$(az storage account show-connection-string \
    --resource-group $rgName \
    --name $storageAccountName \
    --key key1 \
    --output tsv)
```

6. Create a JSON file with your storage account properties and save it on your local machine as *StorageLinkedService.json*. Replace *<connection-string>* with the value from the previous step. All the required files for this recipe can be found in the recipe GitHub repository (*https://oreil.ly/sV880*):

```
{
    "type": "AzureBlobStorage",
    "typeProperties": {
        "connectionString": "<connection-string>"
    }
}
```

7. Use the following command to create your linked service. Replace *<path-to-StorageLinkedService.json>* with the path to the *StorageLinkedService.json* file on your machine:

```
az datafactory linked-service create \
    --resource-group $rgName \
    --factory-name $adfName \
    --linked-service-name SourceSinkStorageLinkedService \
    --properties <path-to-StorageLinkedService.json>
```

8. Your ADF pipeline will read the data from a source dataset. Create another JSON file and name it *InputDataset.json* with the following content. Note that the data-set type is Json and the definition contains the data schema as well:

```
{
    "linkedServiceName": {
        "referenceName": "SourceSinkStorageLinkedService",
        "type": "LinkedServiceReference"
    },
    "annotations": [],
    "type": "Json",
    "typeProperties": {
        "location": {
            "type": "AzureBlobStorageLocation",
            "fileName": "country_list.json",
            "folderPath": "",
            "container": "datasource"
        }
    },
    "schema": {
```

```
        "type": "object",
        "properties": {
          "name": { "type": "string" },
          "code": { "type": "string" },
          "capital": { "type": "string" },
          "region": { "type": "string" },
          "currency": {
            "type": "object",
            "properties": {
              "code": { "type": "string" },
              "name": { "type": "string" },
              "symbol": { "type": "string" }
            }
          },
          "language": {
            "type": "object",
            "properties": {
              "code": { "type": "string" },
              "name": { "type": "string" }
            }
          },
          "flag": { "type": "string" }
        }
      }
    }
```

9. Use the following CLI command to create your source dataset. Replace *<path-to-InputDataset.json>* with the path to the *InputDataset.json* file on your machine:

```
az datafactory dataset create \
   --resource-group $rgName \
   --dataset-name SourceDataset \
   --factory-name $adfName \
   --properties <path-to-InputDataset.json>
```

10. Your pipeline needs an output (sink) dataset as well. Create a JSON file and name it *SinkDataset.json* with the following content. Note that the output file is a CSV file named *country_list.csv* and the output type is `DelimitedText`:

```
{
  "linkedServiceName": {
    "referenceName": "SourceSinkStorageLinkedService",
    "type": "LinkedServiceReference"
  },
  "annotations": [],
  "type": "DelimitedText",
  "typeProperties": {
    "location": {
      "type": "AzureBlobStorageLocation",
      "fileName": "country_list.csv",
```

```
      "folderPath": "",
      "container": "datasink"
    },
    "columnDelimiter": ",",
    "escapeChar": "\\",
    "quoteChar": "\""
  }
}
```

11. Use the following CLI command to create your sink dataset as well. Replace *<path-to-SinkDataset.json>* with the path to the *SinkDataset.json* file on your machine:

```
az datafactory dataset create \
  --resource-group $rgName \
  --dataset-name SinkDataset \
  --factory-name $adfName \
  --properties <path-to-SinkDataset.json>
```

12. With both source and sink datasets defined, you can now create your ADF pipeline. Create a new JSON file named *MoveJsonToCSVPipeline.json* with the following content and save it on your local machine:

```
{
    "name": "JsonToCSVPipeline",
    "properties": {
        "activities": [
            {
                "name": "CopyFromJsonToCSV",
                "type": "Copy",
                "dependsOn": [],
                "policy": {
                    "timeout": "0.12:00:00",
                    "retry": 0,
                    "retryIntervalInSeconds": 30,
                    "secureOutput": false,
                    "secureInput": false
                },
                "userProperties": [],
                "typeProperties": {
                    "source": {
                        "type": "JsonSource",
                        "storeSettings": {
                            "type": "AzureBlobStorageReadSettings",
                            "recursive": true,
                            "wildcardFileName": "country_list.json",
                            "enablePartitionDiscovery": false
                        },
                        "formatSettings": { "type": "JsonReadSettings" }
                    },
                    "sink": {
```

```
                    "type": "DelimitedTextSink",
                    "storeSettings": { "type":
                        "AzureBlobStorageWriteSettings" },
                    "formatSettings": {
                        "type": "DelimitedTextWriteSettings",
                        "quoteAllText": true,
                        "fileExtension": ".csv"
                    }
                },
                "enableStaging": false,
                "translator": {
                    "type": "TabularTranslator",
                    "mappings": [
                        {
                            "source": { "path": "$['name']" },
                            "sink": {
                                "type": "String",
                                "ordinal": 1
                            }
                        },
                        {
                            "source": { "path": "$['capital']" },
                            "sink": {
                                "type": "String",
                                "ordinal": 2
                            }
                        },
                        {
                            "source": { "path": "$['flag']" },
                            "sink": {
                                "type": "String",
                                "ordinal": 3
                            }
                        }
                    ]
                }
            },
            "inputs": [
                {
                    "referenceName": "SourceDataset",
                    "type": "DatasetReference",
                    "parameters": {}
                }
            ],
            "outputs": [
                {
                    "referenceName": "SinkDataset",
                    "type": "DatasetReference",
                    "parameters": {}
                }
```

---

```
            ]
          }
        ],
        "annotations": []
      }
    }
```

13. Use the following command to create your pipeline from the preceding JSON file:

```
az datafactory pipeline create \
  --resource-group $rgName \
  --factory-name $adfName \
  --name CopyFromJsonToCSVPipeline \
  --pipeline <path-to-MoveJsonToCSVPipeline.json>
```

14. Your pipeline is now created. Use the following command to run your pipeline and store the pipeline Run ID in a variable:

```
runID=$(az datafactory pipeline create-run \
  --resource-group $rgName \
  --factory-name $adfName \
  --name CopyFromJsonToCSVPipeline \
  --output tsv)
```

15. Run the following command to check on the pipeline execution status. If the status is "InProgress," wait a few seconds and try again until the command outputs "Succeeded":

```
az datafactory pipeline-run show \
  --resource-group $rgName \
  --factory-name $adfName \
  --run-id $runID \
  --query Status
```

16. At this point, the *country_list.csv* file must be generated in the datasink container. Use the following command to confirm the file is created:

```
az storage blob list \
    --account-name $storageAccountName \
    --account-key $storageKey \
    --container-name "datasink" \
    --query [].name
```

17. Download and open *country_list.csv*. Each row in this file should have three fields as designated in the pipeline. A sample line follows:

```
"United States of America","Washington, D.C.","…/data/usa.svg"
```

18. You can see your pipeline in ADF Studio as well. Visit the Data factories page (*https://oreil.ly/RizfK*) and click on your ADF instance as shown in Figure 6-29.

*Figure 6-29. Visiting the Data factories page in the Azure portal*

19. On the Overview page, click on the "Launch studio" button as shown in Figure 6-30. See the ADF documentation (*https://oreil.ly/CtpOX*) for details.

*Figure 6-30. Launching Azure Data Factory Studio*

20. In ADF Studio, from the left-hand menu, click on your pipeline name, Copy-FromJsonToCSVPipeline, and you will see your pipeline with a single "Copy data" activity as shown in Figure 6-31. You can use ADF Studio to develop your pipelines as well.

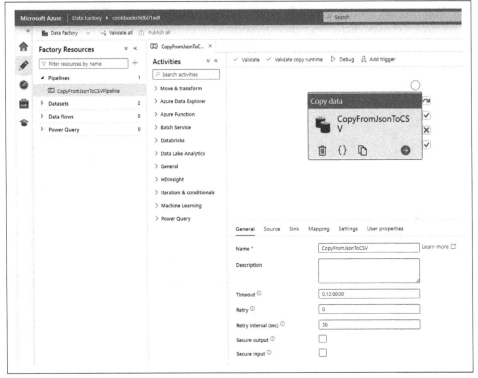

*Figure 6-31. The CopyFromJsonToCSV pipeline*

21. Run the following command to delete the resources you created in this recipe:

```
az group delete --name $rgName
```

You successfully used ADF to process a JSON data resource into a CSV destination.

## Discussion

Azure Data Factory (ADF) (*https://oreil.ly/-PO45*) is a service to create, test, deploy, and run ETL/ELT and data integration pipelines.

Each pipeline consists of one or more activities that read, copy, transform, and write your data. In this recipe, you worked with the Copy activity (*https://oreil.ly/Z7wcL*) to process a JSON file and output the result into a destination CSV file. The following activities are also available:

- Data flow activity (*https://oreil.ly/IkqDd*) to transform data
- Azure Function activity (*https://oreil.ly/SuHNT*) to call Azure Functions
- Databricks activity (*https://oreil.ly/sXUiU*) to run a Databricks notebook

- HDInsight activity (*https://oreil.ly/7deTV*) to work with Azure HDInsight Hive, Pig, Spark, and MapReduce
- Machine Learning activity (*https://oreil.ly/IZGII*) to call Azure Machine Learning models

ADF supports a wide variety of data stores. See the ADF connector documentation (*https://oreil.ly/9ft8l*) for details. A few supported data stores include:

- Azure Storage (blobs, tables, etc.)
- Azure Cosmos DB
- Azure SQL
- Azure Data Lake Storage Gen1 and Gen2
- MongoDB
- Amazon S3
- Google Sheets
- FTP

The combination of supported activities and connectors enables you to address almost any big data processing scenario. A few samples include:

- Read JSON/CSV logfiles from a source Storage blob account, aggregate them, and save the result in an Azure Cosmos DB container.
- For each data row in an Azure SQL table, call an Azure Function, and store the result as JSON files in a sink Azure Blob Storage.
- Run an Azure Databricks notebook on demand or on a schedule.
- Migrate data files stored in an Amazon S3 bucket into Azure Blob Storage.

You can develop, and debug/test your pipeline programmatically, using Azure CLI/ PowerShell or from the ADF Studio GUI. The GUI option is great when you need to quickly create pipelines for testing or proofs of concept. When ready, you can publish the pipeline in production and run it on demand (*https://oreil.ly/BV8Ql*) (as we did in this recipe) or on a schedule (*https://oreil.ly/n2RdW*). At the time of writing this book, ADF offers Git integration with GitHub and Azure DevOps. This enables you to save your work right from ADF Studio. See the ADF documentation (*https:// oreil.ly/ALeH0*) for details.

Azure Synapse Analytics offers a similar pipeline experience to help you perform data extract, transform, and load right from the Synapse Analytics environment. See the Azure Synapse documentation (*https://oreil.ly/Rz1CF*) for details.

## CHAPTER 7

# Azure Functions and Serverless Services

Sometimes the term *serverless computing* gives the impression that a service is not hosted on a server. This is far from the truth. In fact, all Azure services run on servers (either physical or virtual) in Azure data centers. A serverless service (*https://oreil.ly/4ZBK2*) removes the burden of server management from your shoulders. You don't need to worry about managing the underlying platform or server; it's as if it does not exist, hence the term "serverless." Microsoft Azure will take care of the server OS patching, updating, service availability, auto scaling, and more.

Many Azure services are completely serverless or offer a serverless tier (*https://oreil.ly/nVXho*). Here are a few examples:

- Azure SQL Database and Azure Cosmos DB
- Azure Function Apps and Azure Logic Apps
- Azure Kubernetes and Azure Container Apps
- Azure Event Hubs, Azure Services Bus, and Azure Event Grid
- Azure API Management
- Azure Cognitive Services, Azure Machine Learning, and Azure Bot Service

Using "Azure serverless" brings the following values:

*Cost savings*
  You only pay for what is used. For example, a provisioned Azure Function does not cost you anything unless it is called.

*Automatic scaling*
  The service only scales up/out and down/in when needed, to save costs.

*Less management burden*
There is no need to manage any underlying virtual machine, auto-scaling, etc.

This chapter explores Azure Functions as the main serverless compute service in Azure. You will learn to:

- Run an Azure Function on a schedule
- Grant Cosmos DB and storage account access to Azure Functions using managed identity and RBAC
- Implement workflows using Azure Durable Functions
- Deploying Docker containers to Azure Function Apps
- Configure Functions network access restrictions

## Workstation Configuration

You will need to prepare your workstation before starting on the recipes in this chapter. Follow "What You Will Need" on page xi to set up your machine to run Azure CLI commands. You can clone the book's GitHub repository using the following command:

```
git clone https://github.com/zaalion/AzureCookbook.git
```

# 7.1 Implementing a Web API Using Azure Functions

## Problem

You want to use Azure Function Apps to implement an HTTP API.

## Solution

Create an Azure Function App, and then create your API as an *HTTP-triggered* function, as shown in Figure 7-1.

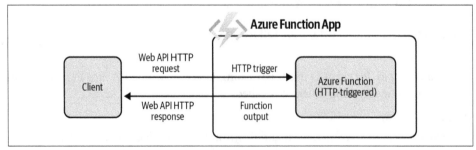

*Figure 7-1. Using Azure Function Apps to implement an HTTP web API*

## Steps

1. Log in to your Azure subscription in the Owner role and create a new resource group for this recipe. See "General Workstation Setup Instructions" on page xii for details.

2. Each Azure Function App needs a dedicated storage account for its internal operations. Let's start by creating a new storage account. Replace *<func-app-storage-account-name>* with the desired value:

```
funcStorageAccountName="<func-app-storage-account-name>"

az storage account create \
    --name $funcStorageAccountName \
    --resource-group $rgName \
    --location $region \
    --sku Standard_LRS
```

3. Now, use the following command to create a new Azure Function App. Replace *<func-app-name>* with the desired name for your app:

```
functionAppName="<func-app-name>"

az functionapp create \
    --resource-group $rgName \
    --name $functionAppName \
    --storage-account $funcStorageAccountName \
    --functions-version 4 \
    --https-only true \
    --consumption-plan-location $region
```

> By passing --functions-version 4, your Azure Function App will use the latest runtime version (at the time of writing this book). See the Azure documentation for a list of the supported frameworks/languages in each Azure runtime (*https://oreil.ly/89YZB*).

4. Navigate to the Function App page (*https://oreil.ly/YAmdg*) using a supported browser (*https://oreil.ly/shZdR*) and click on your new Function App as shown in Figure 7-2.

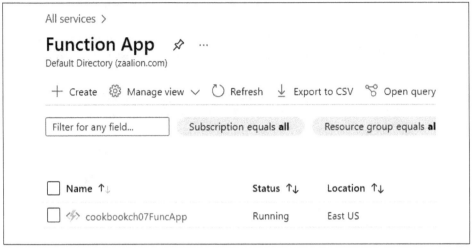

*Figure 7-2. Clicking on your new Function App*

5. Now you can create your new HTTP web API in the Azure portal. Under Functions, click on Functions and then click the Create button as shown in Figure 7-3.

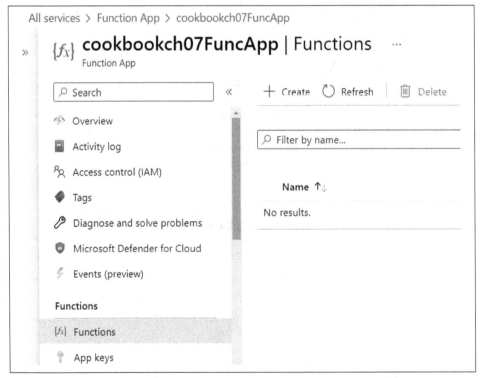

*Figure 7-3. Creating a new function*

6. Choose the HTTP trigger template and click on the Create button as shown in Figure 7-4.

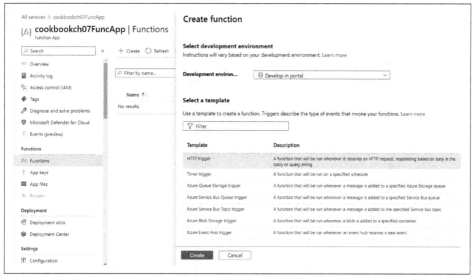

Figure 7-4. Creating a new HTTP-triggered function

7. Now you can write your function code in the Azure portal. Under Developer, click on Code + Test as shown in Figure 7-5.

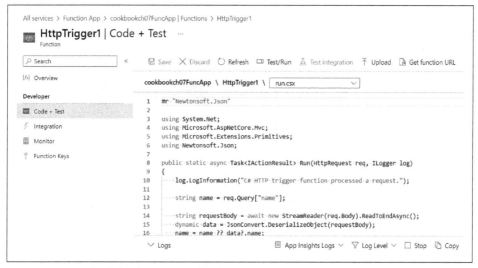

Figure 7-5. Loading the function code editor

8. Replace the body of the `public static async Task<IActionResult> Run(HttpRequest req, ILogger log)` function with the following code and then click Save. This code takes two numbers from the request query string and returns the sum as the response, as shown in Figure 7-6:

```
{
    log.LogInformation("C# HTTP trigger function processed a request.");

    int num01 = int.Parse(req.Query["num01"]);
    int num02 = int.Parse(req.Query["num02"]);

    int addition = num01 + num02;

    return new OkObjectResult(addition);
}
```

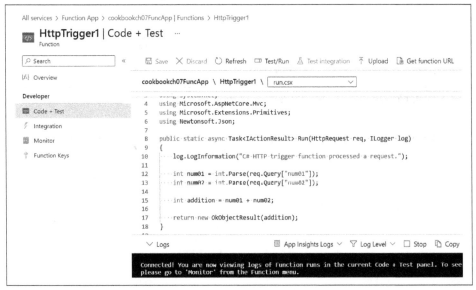

*Figure 7-6. Updating the function code*

9. Now it's time to test your new function. This is an HTTP-triggered function, so you need the function's URL to call it. Click on the "Get function URL" button and copy the URL to the clipboard as shown in Figure 7-7.

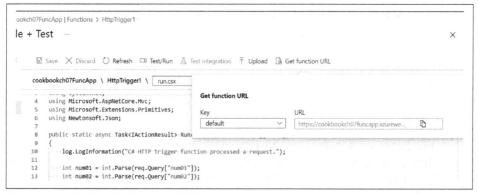

*Figure 7-7. Getting the function URL*

10. Simply pass two numbers to the URL by adding &num01=10&num02=15 at the end of your URL. A completed URL will be similar to the following:

```
# Replace the below URL with your version from the previous step

https://cookbookch07funcapp.azurewebsites.net/api/HttpTrigger1
    ?code=HYq0YHsrbSdWQV_W5MUuJ2tCs8j9ER6I_O_R-G319dJKAzFuODgPog
    ==&num01=10&num02=15
```

> Make sure you leave the code query string parameter intact. This security code is required by the HTTP function to confirm the validity of the incoming request.

11. Copy the URL and call it using a browser. You should see the result "25" as a response, as shown in Figure 7-8.

*Figure 7-8. Calling your HTTP web API*

12. Run the following command to delete the resources you created in this recipe:

```
az group delete --name $rgName
```

You successfully implemented an HTTP web API using HTTP-triggered Azure functions.

## Discussion

An Azure Function App is a tool to implement microservices, services, and APIs. Azure functions support different trigger types (*https://oreil.ly/xtSsa*). This recipe used the HTTP trigger (*https://oreil.ly/19aL1*) because you needed to implement an HTTP web API.

When developing code for an Azure function, you must follow the Function App programming interface, as you saw in this recipe. This interface specifies the type of trigger used as well as the inputs and outputs of your function. You can develop the function app code directly in the Azure portal or deploy the code using ZIP deployment (*https://oreil.ly/IEDQh*) or from supported source control platforms such as GitHub (*https://oreil.ly/P1vKy*).

After the function app is deployed, you can call its functions using their triggers. In this recipe, you called an HTTP function by submitting an HTTP GET request right from your browser (other HTTP clients such as cURL can be used, too). To successfully call a function, you need to authenticate it. In this recipe, this was achieved by including the code query string (code=) in the request. See the Azure function security documentation (*https://oreil.ly/QKWY1*) for details.

In the following recipes, you will work with other Azure function triggers such as the blob trigger and timer trigger.

 A single Azure Function App can host one or more functions. In this recipe, you hosted a single function (HttpTrigger1) in your function app. In the next recipe, you will add new functions to this function app.

# 7.2 Invoking an Azure Function on a Schedule Using the Timer Trigger

## Problem

You need to invoke an Azure function on a schedule.

---

## Solution

Create an Azure Function App and then create your API as a *time-triggered* function.

### Steps

1. Complete steps 1 through 4 in Recipe 7.1 to create a new Azure Function App and navigate to it in the Azure portal.

    Multiple functions can be added to one Azure Function App, so you can continue using the Function App from Recipe 7.1 if you have not deleted it.

2. Now create a new timer-triggered function in the Azure portal. Under Functions, click on Functions, and then click the Create button as shown in Figure 7-9.

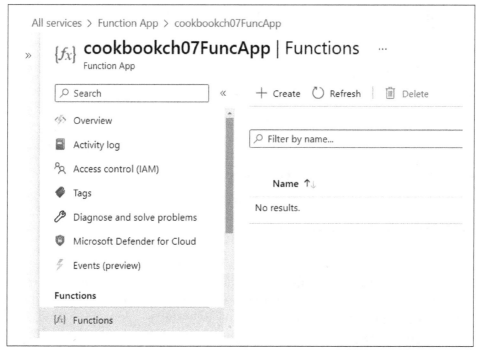

*Figure 7-9. Creating a new function*

3. Choose the Timer trigger template and click the Create button as shown in Figure 7-10.

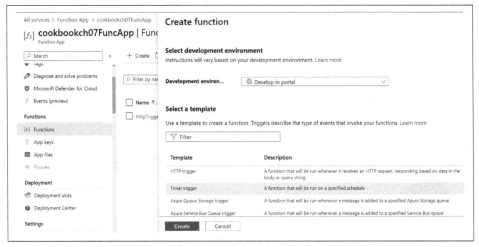

Figure 7-10. Creating a new timer-triggered function

4.  Under Developer, click on Code + Test as shown in Figure 7-11.

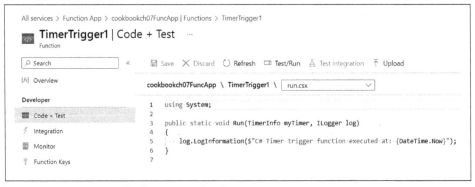

Figure 7-11. Opening the function code editor

5.  Make sure you are looking at the *run.csx* file. This file contains the logic you want to run on an interval. Confirm that the function prints a string into the function logs. The code should be similar to the following block. This will print the function execution datetime into the function log stream:

```
using System;

public static void Run(TimerInfo myTimer, ILogger log)
{
    log.LogInformation($"C# Timer trigger function executed at:
    {DateTime.Now}");
}
```

6. Now, let's define how often the function should run. From the file selector drop-down, choose *function.json* as shown in Figure 7-12.

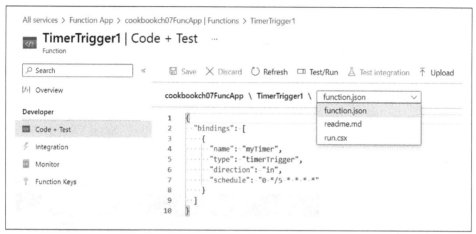

*Figure 7-12. Loading function.json into the file editor*

7. By default, the function will run every 5 minutes as defined in this line: `"schedule"`: `"0 */5 * * * *"`. See the Azure documentation for details on *CRON expressions* (*https://oreil.ly/oRr_k*). Set the function interval (schedule) to every 10 seconds by updating the *function.json* content to the following and clicking Save:

```
{
  "bindings": [
    {
      "name": "myTimer",
      "type": "timerTrigger",
      "direction": "in",
      "schedule": "*/10 * * * * *"
    }
  ]
}
```

8. Now it's time to test your new function. Make sure Filesystem Logs (*https://oreil.ly/6g2eK*) is selected and wait for 10 seconds, as shown in Figure 7-13.

*Figure 7-13. Selecting Filesystem Logs*

9. You should see new log entries showing up in the log stream window every 10 seconds, as shown in Figure 7-14.

*Figure 7-14. The function creates new logs every 10 seconds*

10. Run the following command to delete the resources you created in this recipe:

```
az group delete --name $rgName
```

You successfully invoked an Azure function using the timer trigger. You used a CRON expression to define the desired schedule for your function.

## Discussion

You can use the Azure Functions timer trigger (*https://oreil.ly/0IJ10*) to run a function on a schedule. For instance, you can use it to check the status of a service or to send scheduled messages.

The CRON expression (*https://oreil.ly/B-bJQ*) can be used to define a variety of function schedules. Here are a few examples:

```
0 30 * * * *
```
Once every hour of the day at minute 30

```
0 */5 * * * *
```
Every 5 minutes all day

```
20-25 * * * * *
```
5 times a minute, at seconds 20 through 25, during every minute of every hour of each day

```
20,45 * * * * *
```
Twice a minute, at seconds 20 and 45, during every minute of every hour of each day

 You can also use IDEs such as Microsoft Visual Studio and Microsoft Visual Studio Code to develop and deploy your Azure functions. These IDEs have templates for all function triggers, including the timer trigger.

# 7.3 Invoking an Azure Function on Blob Upload Using the Blob Trigger

## Problem

You need to process a blob file right after it is uploaded or created.

## Solution

Create a *blob-triggered* function in an Azure Function App that will run after a new blob is uploaded, as illustrated in Figure 7-15.

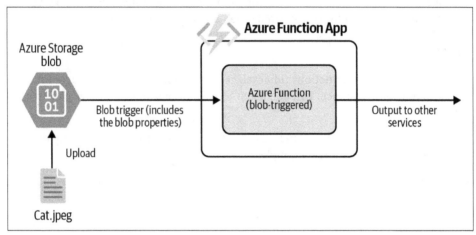

*Figure 7-15. Uploading a new blob file triggers the function execution*

### Steps

1. Log in to your Azure subscription in the Owner role and create a new resource group for this recipe. See "General Workstation Setup Instructions" on page xii for details.

2. Create a new Azure storage account and a child blob container using the following commands:

```
storageAccountName="<storage-account-name>"

az storage account create \
    --name $storageAccountName \
    --resource-group $rgName \
    --sku Standard_LRS

storageKey=$(az storage account keys list \
    --resource-group $rgName \
    --account-name $storageAccountName \
    --query [0].value \
    --output tsv)

az storage container create \
    --name "newblobs" \
    --account-name $storageAccountName \
    --account-key $storageKey
```

```
storageConnectionString=$(az storage account \
  show-connection-string \
  --resource-group $rgName \
  --name $storageAccountName \
  --output tsv)
```

3. Complete steps 2 and 3 in Recipe 7.1 to create a new Azure Function App.

4. Add new configuration app settings for the Function App. Name it *StorageTo Monitor*. For the value, specify the storage account connection string. You will use these settings later to configure the blob trigger:

```
az functionapp config appsettings set \
  --name $functionAppName \
  --resource-group $rgName \
  --settings "StorageToMonitor=$storageConnectionString"
```

5. Navigate to the Function App page (*https://oreil.ly/1cyay*) and click on your new Function App as shown in Figure 7-16.

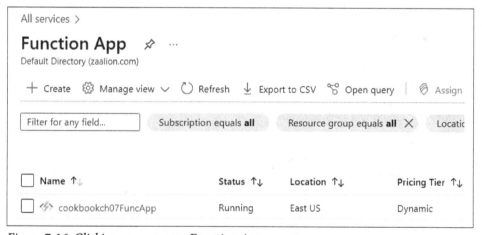

*Figure 7-16. Clicking on your new Function App*

6. Now let's create a new blob-triggered function in the Azure portal. Under Functions, click on Functions and then click the Create button as shown in Figure 7-17.

7. Choose the Azure Blob Storage trigger template. Enter *newblobs/{name}* for the Path and StorageToMonitor for Storage account connection. Click on the Create button as shown in Figure 7-18.

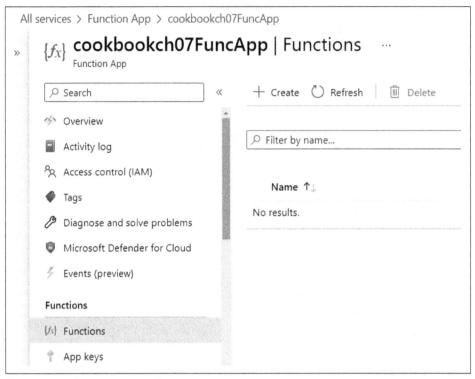

*Figure 7-17. Creating a new function*

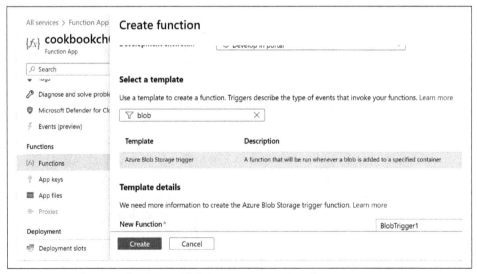

*Figure 7-18. Choosing the Azure Blob Storage trigger template*

8. Under Developer, click on Code + Test as shown in Figure 7-19.

*Figure 7-19. Opening the function code editor*

9. Confirm that you see the following code block. When a new blob is uploaded, this function will be triggered; log the blob filename and size in the function log stream. In the next step, you will define which storage account blob container to monitor:

```
public static void Run(Stream myBlob, string name, ILogger log)
{
    log.LogInformation($"Processed blob Name:{name},
    Size: {myBlob.Length} Bytes");
}
```

10. Select Filesystem Logs from the logs selector, as shown in Figure 7-20.

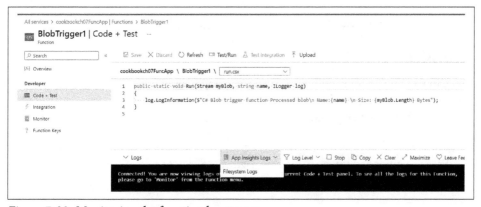

*Figure 7-20. Monitoring the function log stream*

11. Choose a file on your machine to upload to the `newblobs` container. This command assumes the file name is *myBlob01.txt*. Replace `<local-file-path>` with the path to your file:

```
az storage blob upload \
    --account-key $storageKey \
    --file <local-file-path>\myBlob01.txt \
    --account-name $storageAccountName \
    --container-name "newblobs" \
    --name "myBlob01.txt"
```

12. Confirm that you can see a new log entry created, as shown in Figure 7-21.

*Figure 7-21. The blob-triggered function is invoked*

13. Run the following command to delete the resources you created in this recipe:

```
az group delete --name $rgName
```

You successfully invoked an Azure function using the blob trigger.

## Discussion

You can use the Azure function blob trigger (*https://oreil.ly/DIEcs*) to react to new or updated blobs in a storage account container. The blob properties are also passed to the function, so further processing on the blob can be done. The following are a couple of use cases:

- Pass the uploaded image to Azure Cognitive Services image API
- Import the blob JSON content into an Azure Cosmos DB container

In the next recipe, you will enhance the Azure function created in this recipe to write the uploaded blob properties to a Cosmos DB container.

# 7.4 Inserting Function App Output into Azure Cosmos DB

## Problem

You want to insert data records into Azure Cosmos DB using Azure functions.

## Solution

Create a Cosmos DB *output binding* for your Azure function and use it to update Cosmos DB, as illustrated in Figure 7-22.

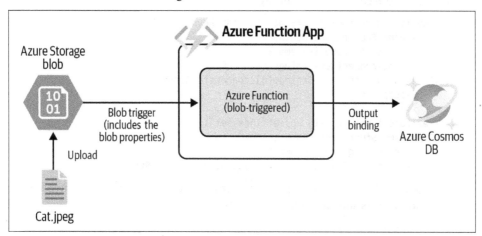

*Figure 7-22. Azure Function App output bindings*

### Steps

1. Follow Recipe 7.3 to create a blob-triggered function app. In this recipe, you will enhance your Azure function so that the uploaded blob properties are inserted into a Cosmos DB container.

2. Create a new Azure Cosmos DB NoSQL account, a database, and a container using the following commands. Replace *<cosmos-account-name>* with the desired unique name:

```
cosmosDBAccountName="<cosmos-account-name>"

az cosmosdb create \
  --name $cosmosDBAccountName \
  --resource-group $rgName

az cosmosdb sql database create \
  --account-name $cosmosDBAccountName \
  --name MyDB \
  --throughput 1000 \
```

```
      --resource-group $rgName

    MSYS_NO_PATHCONV=1 az cosmosdb sql container create \
      --name UploadedBlobs \
      --partition-key-path "/name" \
      --throughput 400 \
      --database-name MyDB \
      --account-name $cosmosDBAccountName \
      --resource-group $rgName
```

3. Use the following commands to add the Cosmos DB connection string to the Function App configuration settings:

```
    cosmosConnectionString=$(az cosmosdb keys list \
      --name $cosmosDBAccountName \
      --resource-group $rgName \
      --type connection-strings \
      --query connectionStrings[0].connectionString \
      --output tsv)

    az functionapp config appsettings set \
      --name $functionAppName \
      --resource-group $rgName \
      --settings "CosmosConnection=$cosmosConnectionString"
```

4. Navigate to the Function App page (*https://oreil.ly/DrLfi*) and click on your Function App as shown in Figure 7-23.

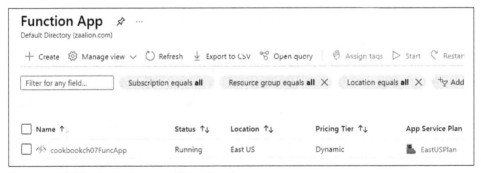

*Figure 7-23. Navigating to your Function App*

5. Click on your function, BlobTrigger1, as shown in Figure 7-24.

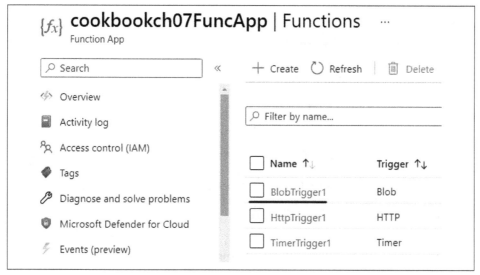

*Figure 7-24. Navigating to your function*

6. Click on Integration and "Add output" as shown in Figure 7-25.

*Figure 7-25. Integration*

7. Complete the Cosmos DB output settings as shown in Figure 7-26. Leave other default values/fields untouched and click OK.

*Figure 7-26. Creating the output binding*

8. Click on Code + Test. Update the *run.csx* content with the following, and then click Save:

```
public static void Run(Stream myBlob, string name
    , out object outputCosmos, ILogger log)
{

    log.LogInformation($"Processed blob Name:{name},
    Size: {myBlob.Length} Bytes");

    outputCosmos = new
    {
        name,
        myBlob.Length
    };
}
```

9. Upload a new text file (e.g., *myBlob02.txt*) to your storage account using this command:

```
az storage blob upload \
    --account-key $storageKey \
    --file <local-file-path>\myBlob02.txt
    --account-name $storageAccountName \
    --container-name "newblobs" \
    --name "myBlob02.txt"
```

10. Now you can confirm if the blob properties are inserted into Azure Cosmos DB. Navigate to the Azure Cosmos DB page (*https://oreil.ly/OT_57*) and click on your Cosmos DB account name as shown in Figure 7-27.

*Figure 7-27. Clicking on the Cosmos DB account name*

11. Click on Data Explorer and then select MyDB > UploadedBlobs > Items and confirm the JSON document with the name and Length properties is present, as shown in Figure 7-28.

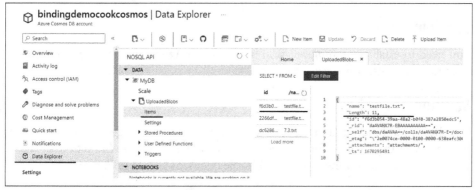

*Figure 7-28. Checking JSON documents in the UploadedBlobs Cosmos DB container*

---

12. Run the following command to delete the resources you created in this recipe:

```
az group delete --name $rgName
```

You successfully invoked an Azure function upon new blob uploads and inserted the blob properties into Azure Cosmos DB using an output binding.

### Discussion

You can use Azure function output bindings to easily define outputs for your Azure functions. Check the Azure functions documentation (*https://oreil.ly/r-Bqn*) for more details on bindings.

Azure function output bindings also support several services, including the following:

- Blob storage
- Event Grid
- Event Hubs
- Queue storage
- Service Bus
- Table storage

In this recipe, you configured a function output binding in the Azure portal. You can also create bindings in code IDEs, such as Microsoft Visual Studio or Visual Studio Code (*https://oreil.ly/8vmj7*).

# 7.5 Establishing Communication Between Azure Functions Using the Service Bus Queue Trigger

## Problem

You need to establish communication between two Azure functions so that a *sender* function can message a *receiver* function.

## Solution

Use the output binding in the sender function to put the messages into a Service Bus queue. Make the receiver function a *Service Bus Queue triggered* function so that it gets invoked upon new message arrival in the queue, as shown in Figure 7-29.

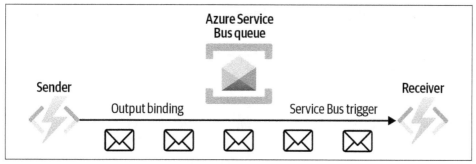

*Figure 7-29. Using queues for Azure function communication*

### Steps

1. Follow Recipe 5.4 to create a new Azure Service Bus queue.

2. Follow Recipe 7.1 (steps 2 and 3) to create an Azure Function App. In this recipe, you will deploy two Azure functions (named Sender and Receiver) to this app.

3. Use the following commands to add the Service Bus connection string to the Function App configuration settings. Your functions will use this queue for communication:

```
serviceBusConnectionString=$(az servicebus namespace \
  authorization-rule keys list \
  --resource-group $rgName \
  --namespace-name $namespaceName \
  --name RootManageSharedAccessKey \
  --query primaryConnectionString \
  --output tsv)

az functionapp config appsettings set \
  --name $functionAppName \
  --resource-group $rgName \
  --settings "ServiceBusConnection=$serviceBusConnectionString"
```

 Using role-based access controls (RBAC) is a more secure option to grant Service Bus access to functions because you don't need to worry about the Service Bus keys being exposed in the code. In this recipe, we use connection strings (with the key) for simplicity. See the Azure documentation (*https://oreil.ly/0L8ok*) for details.

4. In Recipe 7.4, you created your functions directly in the Azure portal. In this recipe, you will deploy the functions by uploading a ZIP file. This ZIP file is created from a Microsoft Visual Studio solution. Download the ZIP package from the recipe repository (*https://oreil.ly/5tKIW*) and save it on your local machine.

Run the following command to deploy the ZIP package to your Azure Function App:

```
az functionapp deployment source config-zip \
    --resource-group $rgName \
    --name $functionAppName \
    --src deploymentPackage.zip
```

 See the recipe repository (*https://oreil.ly/oz1Wb*) for instructions on how to create this ZIP file from the Visual Studio solution.

5. You deployed the `Sender` and `Receiver` functions. Before proceeding, let's get the Sender function code (*https://oreil.ly/VhJkW*) and examine it. Note that this function has an output binder that puts a message into the Service Bus queue, `ordersqueue`:

```
/*
https://github.com/zaalion/AzureCookbook/blob/main/Chapter07
    /7.5/CommunicationDemo/CommunicationDemo/Sender.cs
*/

[FunctionName("Sender")]
[return: ServiceBus("ordersqueue", Connection = "ServiceBusConnection")]
public static string Run(
    [HttpTrigger(AuthorizationLevel.Function,
    "get", Route = null)] HttpRequest req,
    ILogger log)
{
    log.LogInformation("C# HTTP trigger function processed a request.");

    var output = new
    {
        Kind=req.Query["kind"],
        Count = req.Query["count"]
    };

    string queueMessage = JsonConvert.SerializeObject(output);
    return queueMessage;
}
```

6. Also, get the Receiver function code (*https://oreil.ly/ySjXS*) and examine it. This function gets invoked by a Service Bus queue trigger, `ServiceBusTrigger`, and prints the received message into the function log stream:

```
/*
https://github.com/zaalion/AzureCookbook/blob/main/Chapter07
    /7.5/CommunicationDemo/CommunicationDemo/Receiver.cs
*/

[FunctionName("Receiver")]
public void Run([ServiceBusTrigger
    ("ordersqueue", Connection = "ServiceBusConnection")]
    string myQueueItem, ILogger log)
{
    log.LogInformation
        ($"Received from queue >>>> " +
        $"{myQueueItem}");
}
```

7. Now it's time to test your solution. Visit the Function App page (*https://oreil.ly/NyJuB*) and click on your Function App name as shown in Figure 7-30.

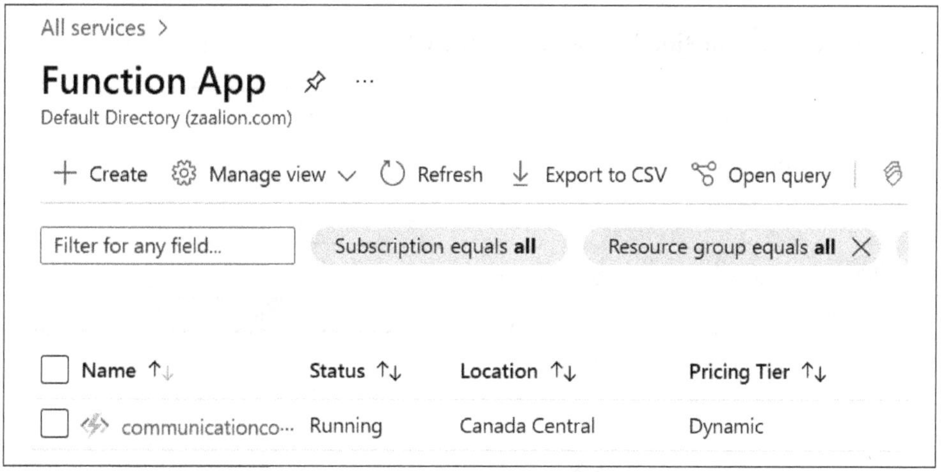

All services >

## Function App
Default Directory (zaalion.com)

+ Create    ⚙ Manage view ∨    ⟳ Refresh    ↓ Export to CSV    ⁰ᵒ Open query    ⌇

| Filter for any field... | Subscription equals **all** | Resource group equals **all** ✕ |

| Name ↑↓ | Status ↑↓ | Location ↑↓ | Pricing Tier ↑↓ |
|---|---|---|---|
| ⟨⁄⟩ communicationco··· | Running | Canada Central | Dynamic |

*Figure 7-30. Locating your Function App in the Azure portal*

8. Click on Functions and the Sender function, as shown in Figure 7-31.

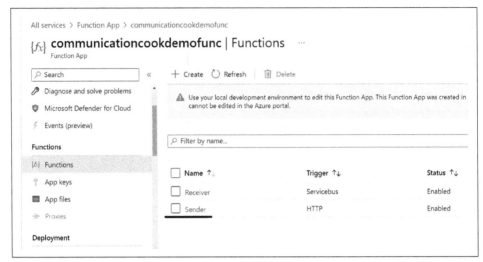

Figure 7-31. Clicking on the Sender function

9. Click on Get Function URL and copy the URL, as shown in Figure 7-32.

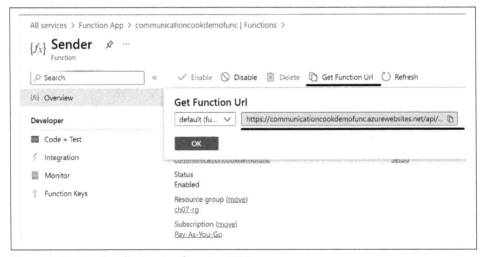

Figure 7-32. Getting the Sender function URL

10. In the Receiver function portal, open the Filesystem logs, as shown in Figure 7-33.

Figure 7-33. Getting the function log stream

11. In a separate browser window, call the Sender function and pass the kind and count query string parameters. A sample URL follows. (Replace *<sender-function-url>* with the URL you got in step 9):

    *<sender-function-url>*&kind=cheese&count=2

12. Confirm that the Receiver function got the message and prints the kind and count parameters, as shown in Figure 7-34.

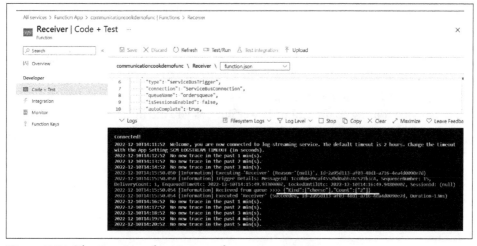

Figure 7-34. The Receiver function got the queue message

13. Run the following command to delete the resources you created in this recipe:

```
az group delete --name $rgName
```

You successfully deployed your functions using the ZIP deployment. Your Azure functions can now communicate using Azure Service Bus queues and function triggers. We created both Sender and Receiver functions in the same Function App, but they also could exist in different Function Apps if needed. In the next recipe, you will restrict network access to this Function App.

## Discussion

You can use Azure Function Apps to implement microservices, services, and APIs. Use the combination of Azure function output bindings (*https://oreil.ly/J10dJ*) and triggers to establish reliable communication between two or more functions.

In addition to Azure Service Bus queues, you can use the following services to enable functions to communicate with each other:

- Azure Service Bus topics
- Azure Queue Storage (Azure storage accounts)
- Azure Event Hubs
- Azure Event Grid

You have multiple options when it comes to deploying an Azure Function App. So far in this chapter, you created your functions directly in the Azure portal. This option is great for learning, but it is not scalable. You can deploy Azure Function Apps using the following methods as well:

- Direct deployment from IDEs such as Microsoft Visual Studio or Visual Studio Code (*https://oreil.ly/zUACW*)
- Packaging the Function App executable in a ZIP file (*https://oreil.ly/fNB1k*) and deploying it using Azure CLI or PowerShell, as you did in this recipe
- Using source control integration, so that each check-in to the code repository triggers (*https://oreil.ly/Z9f9Z*) a new Function App deployment

See the Azure Functions documentation for more details on deployment options (*https://oreil.ly/fb-PN*).

# 7.6 Restricting Network Access to Azure Function Apps

## Problem

You want to restrict Azure Function App access to desired clients only, based on their IP address.

## Solution

Configure network access restrictions for your Azure Function Apps, based on their IP address or Azure Virtual Network subnet.

### Steps

1. Log in to your Azure subscription in the Owner role and create a new resource group for this recipe. See "General Workstation Setup Instructions" on page xii for details.

2. Create a new Azure VNet, and a default subnet, using the following CLI command. Replace *<vnet-name>* with the desired value:

   ```
   vnetName="<vnet-name>"

   az network vnet create \
       --resource-group $rgName \
       --name $vnetName \
       --address-prefix 10.0.0.0/16 \
       --subnet-name Subnet01 \
       --subnet-prefix 10.0.0.0/26
   ```

3. Make sure you have a working function app with an HTTP-triggered function to start with. You can work with the function app created in Recipe 7.5. Use the following command to store the function app name in a variable. Replace *<function-app-name>* with the name of your function app:

   ```
   functionAppName="<function-app-name>"
   ```

4. By default, HTTP-triggered Azure Function Apps allow traffic from all networks. Let's create an access restriction rule to allow traffic only from your public IP address. Replace *<ip-address>* with your IP address.:

   ```
   az functionapp config access-restriction add \
       --resource-group $rgName \
       --name $functionAppName \
       --rule-name allowMyIP \
       --action Allow \
       --ip-address <ip-address> \
       --priority 100
   ```

You can visit ipaddress.com to find your public IP address.

5. You can also allow access based on a client's VNet subnet. Let's create another access restriction rule to allow clients from a subnet to call your function app:

```
az functionapp config access-restriction add \
    --resource-group $rgName \
    --name $functionAppName \
    --rule-name app_gateway \
    --action Allow \
    --vnet-name $vnetName \
    --subnet Subnet01 \
    --priority 200
```

 You can also define *deny* rules. The rules with a smaller `priority` value will be processed first. See the Azure CLI documentation (*https://oreil.ly/uC3Ll*) for details.

6. Now that you have the rules in place, try to access your Azure HTTP function from a different IP address (for instance by using a VPN), and you should receive the response "Error 403 - Forbidden," as shown in Figure 7-35.

*Figure 7-35. The HTTP function is not available from other IP addresses*

7. Run the following command to delete the resources you created in this recipe:

```
az group delete --name $rgName
```

You successfully restricted network access to your Azure Function App.

---

## Discussion

You can use access restriction rules to allow only the desired clients to access your HTTP functions. This adds another layer of defense against unauthorized access. In order to define access restrictions, you need to have the desired client's IP address, address range, or Azure VNet subnet.

 In some cases your functions are meant to be called from the internet (for example from a client's browser). Unless you know all the client IP addresses to allow, no IP restriction rules can be defined.

Azure Function Apps can be deployed behind other Azure services such as Azure Application Gateway or Azure API Management. You can add access restriction rules to your functions to only allow traffic from the preceding service subnets, preventing clients from bypassing these services and directly calling your functions.

## CHAPTER 8

# Azure App Service

Azure App Service is a managed service that enables you to host HTTP-based applications, including web applications, websites, HTTP APIs, and mobile app backends. At the time of writing this book, the following languages and frameworks are supported:

- .NET
- .NET Core
- Java
- Ruby
- Node.js
- PHP
- Python

The recipes in this chapter will show you how to do the following tasks in Azure App Services. You will:

- Deploy markup and code using multiple deployment options
- Configure autoscaling
- Restrict client network access
- Host static websites on Azure Storage

You can also host containerized web applications on Azure Container Instances or Azure Container Apps. See Chapter 9 for details on containers.

## Workstation Configuration

You will need to prepare your workstation before starting on the recipes in this chapter. Follow "What You Will Need" on page xi to set up your machine to run Azure CLI commands. You can clone the book's GitHub repository using the following command:

```
git clone https://github.com/zaalion/AzureCookbook.git
```

# 8.1 Deploying a Web Application to Azure App Services Using ZipDeploy

## Problem

You want to deploy your website to an Azure App Service using Kudu ZipDeploy (*https://oreil.ly/7d8Rj*).

## Solution

Compress your website files into a ZIP file and deploy it to your Azure App Service using the `az webapp deployment source config-zip` command, as shown in Figure 8-1.

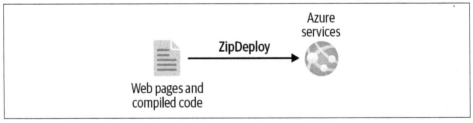

*Figure 8-1. Deploying files to an Azure App Service using Kudu ZipDeploy*

 We start this chapter by showing *ZipDeploy* and *FTP* deployment options because they are easy to configure and are best for quick deployment and testing.

## Steps

1. Log in to your Azure subscription in the Owner role and create a new resource group for this recipe. See "General Workstation Setup Instructions" on page xii for details.

2. Before creating an Azure App Service, you need to create an *App Service plan*. An App Service plan (*https://oreil.ly/fI4Mt*) defines the resources that are available to your App Service website, including memory and CPU cores. Use the following command to create an App Service plan in the *standard* SKU (S1, S2, or S3). Replace *<appservice-plan-name>* with the desired name:

```
planName="<appservice-plan-name>"

az appservice plan create \
  --resource-group $rgName \
  --name $planName \
  --number-of-workers 2 \
  --sku S1
```

3. Now, you can create an Azure App Service website using the following CLI command. You will deploy a .NET Core application, so dotnet:6 is passed as the App Service runtime. Replace *<appservice-name>* with a unique name:

```
appServiceName="<appservice-name>"

az webapp create \
  --resource-group $rgName \
  --plan $planName \
  --name $appServiceName \
  --runtime "dotnet:6"
```

 You can run the az webapp list-runtimes command to get a list of available runtimes.

4. Now you are ready to deploy your code. Download the ZIP package (*https://oreil.ly/cwRYP*) we provided and save it on your local machine. This is a simple ASP.NET Core website complied and packaged into a ZIP file. The Visual Studio project is available in the recipe GitHub repository (*https://oreil.ly/oao2c*).

5. Use the following command to deploy the ZIP package to your Azure App Service. Replace *<path-to-downloaded-wwwroot.zip>* with the local path to the ZIP file:

```
az webapp deployment source config-zip \
    --resource-group $rgName \
    --name $appServiceName \
    --src "<path-to-downloaded-wwwroot.zip>"
```

6. Use the following command to get the public URL for your App Service web app. Then navigate to it using a browser. Confirm that you can see the website, as shown in Figure 8-2:

```
url="https://"$(az webapp show \
    --resource-group $rgName \
    --name $appServiceName \
    --query defaultHostName \
    --output tsv)

echo $url
```

ZipDeployDemo    Home    Privacy

# Welcome

Learn about Azure Cookbook: Zipdeploy demo!.

© 2022 - ZipDeployDemo - Privacy

*Figure 8-2. The deployed App Service*

7. Run the following command to delete the resources you created in this recipe:

```
az group delete --name $rgName
```

You successfully deployed your web application code to Azure App Service using ZipDeploy.

ZipDeploy erases any old files from the Azure App Service upon deployment.

## Discussion

In this recipe, you directly deployed a ZIP file to your Azure App Service. This ZIP file contains your website's markup, JavaScript, CSS, and .NET Core executables.

---

Deploying from a ZIP file is a convenient method to quickly get your web application up and running.

You can also use the following options (*https://oreil.ly/Y1UyH*) to manually deploy your code to Azure App Service:

- FTP
- SSH
- Dropbox or OneDrive
- Git repository on local machine (local Git)

In most projects, you need to set up *continuous deployment* so that every change to the code repository triggers an automatic deployment. This can be achieved by using features such as GitHub Actions (*https://oreil.ly/sZHwo*) or Azure Pipelines (*https://oreil.ly/-qrYU*).

Later in this chapter, you will deploy code to Azure App Services using the FTP and local Git options, as these options are commonly used. For details on the Dropbox and OneDrive options, take a look at the Azure App Services documentation (*https://oreil.ly/OW-1A*).

# 8.2 Deploying a Web Application to Azure App Service Using FTP

## Problem

You want to deploy your website to an Azure App Service using FTP (*https://oreil.ly/W1OeU*).

## Solution

Deploy your files to your Azure App Service using FTP, as shown in Figure 8-3.

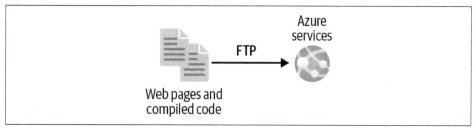

*Figure 8-3. Deploying files to an Azure App Service using FTP*

## Steps

1. Log in to your Azure subscription in the Owner role and create a new resource group for this recipe. See "General Workstation Setup Instructions" on page xii for details.

2. Use the following command to create a Linux App Service plan in the standard SKU. Replace *<appservice-plan-name>* with the desired name:

```
planName="<appservice-plan-name>"

az appservice plan create \
   --resource-group $rgName \
   --name $planName \
   --is-linux \
   --number-of-workers 2 \
   --sku S1
```

3. Create a PHP website using the following CLI command. Replace *<appservice-name>* with a unique name:

```
appServiceName="<appservice-name>"

az webapp create \
   --resource-group $rgName \
   --plan $planName \
   --name $appServiceName \
   --runtime "PHP:8.0"
```

 You can run the `az webapp list-runtimes` command to get a list of available runtimes.

4. Create a PHP file on your local machine with the following content and save it in your current working directory as *index.php*:

```
<html>
<body>
  <h1>
    <?php echo "Trying FTP Deployment..." ?>
  <h1>
</body>
</html>
```

5. To use FTP deployment, you need the *FTP publish profile* details. Use the following command to store the FTP public URL, username, and password in a variable:

```
ftpDetails=($(az webapp deployment list-publishing-profiles \
  --name $appServiceName \
  --resource-group $rgName \
  --query "[?contains(publishMethod, 'FTP')].
  [publishUrl,userName,userPWD]" \
  --output tsv))
```

6. At this point, you can use any FTP client to upload your files to the Azure App Service. Let's use cURL to upload *index.php*:

```
curl -T index.php -u ${ftpDetails[1]}:${ftpDetails[2]} ${ftpDetails[0]}/
```

7. Use the following command to get the public URL for your App Service web app. Then navigate to it using a browser. Confirm that you can see the deployed PHP page as shown in Figure 8-4:

```
url="https://"$(az webapp show \
  --resource-group $rgName \
  --name $appServiceName \
  --query defaultHostName \
  --output tsv)"/index.php"

echo $url
```

*Figure 8-4. The deployed App Service*

8. Run the following command to delete the resources you created in this recipe:

```
az group delete --name $rgName
```

You successfully deployed your files to Azure App Service using FTP.

## Discussion

In this recipe, you uploaded a single PHP file to your Azure App Service using FTP (*https://oreil.ly/nmdOr*). This is a quick and simple method to deploy websites and APIs to Azure App Services and Function Apps. Any FTP client works in this scenario. All you need is the FTP publish endpoint (URL), username, and password.

In the next scenario, you will deploy a public Git repository to Azure App Services using Azure CLI.

# 8.3 Deploying a Web Application from a Public GitHub Repository to Azure App Service

## Problem

You want to deploy your website from a Git repository to an Azure App Service.

## Solution

Associate your Git repository with the desired Azure App Service and trigger a deployment as needed, as shown in Figure 8-5.

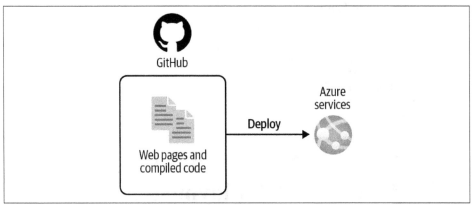

*Figure 8-5. Deploying files to an Azure App Service from a Git repository*

### Steps

1. Follow steps 1 through 3 in Recipe 8.2 to create a PHP Azure App Service resource.

2. In this recipe, you will deploy a single PHP file from a public GitHub repository (*https://oreil.ly/y9bp3*) to your Azure App Service. Use the following command to associate your App Service with the repository and deploy the repository content, including the PHP file, to the App Service:

```
az webapp deployment source config \
  --branch master \
  --manual-integration \
  --name $appServiceName \
  --repo-url https://github.com/Azure-Samples/php-docs-hello-world \
  --resource-group $rgName
```

The previous command associates a Git repository with your App Service and initializes the first code deployment. For later deployments, you need to manually run the `az webapp deployment source sync` command to synchronize the repository changes to the App Service. Alternatively, you can set up continuous deployment as described in the Azure documentation (*https://oreil.ly/8wzdU*).

3. Use the following command to get the public URL for your App Service web app. Then navigate to it using a browser. Confirm that you can see the deployed PHP file, as shown in Figure 8-6:

```
url="https://"$(az webapp show \
    --resource-group $rgName \
    --name $appServiceName \
    --query defaultHostName \
    --output tsv)"/index.php"

echo $url
```

---

← → C    🔒 ch08cookgit-app.azurewebsites.net

# Hello World!

---

*Figure 8-6. The deployed App Service*

4. Run the following command to delete the resources you created in this recipe:

```
az group delete --name $rgName
```

You successfully deployed your web application from a public GitHub repository to an Azure App Service.

## Discussion

The FTP and ZipDeploy methods are great for development, experimental, and testing scenarios. However, it is a better practice to deploy your applications from a source control repository. This makes deployments more reliable and easy to roll back. This also enables organizations to continuously deploy and deliver new features to the testing team and the end users.

In this recipe, you manually deployed a PHP application to your Azure App Service from a public GitHub repository.

In this recipe, you did not need to authenticate to GitHub because you were deploying from a public repository. In most cases, authentication is required by providing a security token or other credentials. See the Azure documentation (*https://oreil.ly/v3sj0*) for details.

At the time of writing this book, the following repositories are supported for App Service continuous deployment projects. See the Azure App Service documentation (*https://oreil.ly/Bggfz*) for details:

- Azure Repos (*https://oreil.ly/5MI1z*)
- GitHub
- External Git (*https://oreil.ly/TB1le*)
- Local Git (*https://oreil.ly/hvI98*)
- Mercurial (*https://oreil.ly/_4kC7*)

In this recipe, you had to manually trigger the deployment upon new repository updates. Automatic deployment (continuous deployment) can be set up using the following options:

- GitHub Actions (*https://oreil.ly/17pC3*)
- Azure DevOps Pipelines (*https://oreil.ly/zHEwO*)
- Continuous deployment using CLI (*https://oreil.ly/YHhW5*)

# 8.4 Configuring Autoscaling for Your Azure App Service Plan

## Problem

You need to configure your Azure App Service plan so that it automatically accommodates increased traffic.

## Solution

Configure autoscaling for your App Service plan so new workers (VMs) are automatically added upon increased demand, as shown in Figure 8-7.

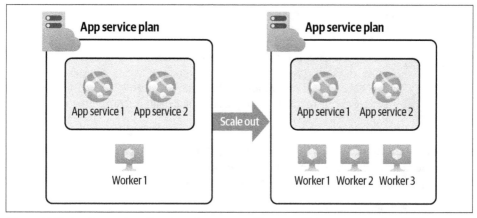

*Figure 8-7. An Azure App Service plan autoscaling to add two new worker VMs*

## Steps

1. Follow steps 1 through 3 in Recipe 8.3 to create an Azure App Service.

2. Use the following command to store the App Service plan ID in a variable:

```
appPlanId=$(az appservice plan show \
  --name $planName \
  --resource-group $rgName \
  --query id --output tsv)
```

3. Let's create a new *autoscale setting* resource. This command also sets the minimum (`--min-count`) and maximum (`--max-count`) number of workers as well as the default number of workers (`--count`). This ensures that your App Service plan does not get more than the desired number of workers:

```
az monitor autoscale create \
  --resource-group $rgName \
  --name MyAutoScale \
  --resource $appPlanId \
  --min-count 1 \
  --max-count 4 \
  --count 2
```

4. You need to create two rules, one for scaling out (adding workers) and another one for scaling in (removing workers). First, let's create the *scale out* rule. This rule will add a new worker instance to your App Service plan if the average CPU usage is above 60% over the past ten minutes:

```
az monitor autoscale rule create \
  --resource-group $rgName \
  --autoscale-name MyAutoScale \
  --scale out 1 \
```

```
--condition "CpuPercentage > 60 avg 10m" \
--cooldown 7
```

 The `--cooldown` parameter determines the number of minutes that must elapse (*https://oreil.ly/btSQ_*) before the next scaling event can happen. This is important because you don't want multiple scaling events to happen too quickly. The default is five minutes.

5. You also need to create a *scale in* rule so that the extra workers are removed when traffic is low. This rule removes a worker instance from your App Service plan if the average CPU usage over the past five minutes is below 30%:

```
az monitor autoscale rule create \
    --resource-group $rgName \
    --autoscale-name MyAutoScale \
    --scale in 1 \
    --condition "CpuPercentage < 30 avg 5m"
```

6. You can check the autoscaling settings by running the following command. A sample output can be found in the recipe repository (*https://oreil.ly/ErQ-x*):

```
az monitor autoscale rule list \
    --resource-group $rgName \
    --autoscale-name MyAutoScale
```

7. To check the autoscaling settings in the Azure portal, visit the App Service plan page (*https://oreil.ly/rB488*) and click on your plan name, as shown in Figure 8-8.

*Figure 8-8. App Service plans*

8. Under Settings, click on "Scale out (App Service plan)". You should see the auto-scale settings as shown in Figure 8-9.

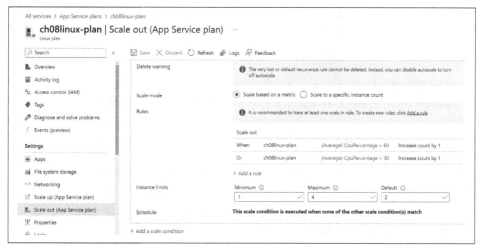

**ch08linux-plan | Scale out (App Service plan)** ···
Linux plan

| Search | « | ⊟ Save ✕ Discard ⟳ Refresh ⊡ Logs ⊠ Feedback |
|---|---|---|

■ Overview

▦ Activity log

ℛ Access control (IAM)

♦ Tags

🖉 Diagnose and solve problems

🕻 Events (preview)

**Settings**

⊞ Apps

🗄 File system storage

↷ Networking

☑ Scale up (App Service plan)

■ Scale out (App Service plan)

▥ Properties

🔒 ▏

Delete warning
     ⓘ The very last or default recurrence rule cannot be deleted. Instead, you can disable autoscale to turn off autoscale.

Scale mode
     ⦿ Scale based on a metric ○ Scale to a specific instance count

Rules
     ⓘ It is recommended to have at least one scale in rule. To create new rules, click Add a rule

Scale out

| When | ch08linux-plan | (Average) CpuPercentage > 60 | Increase count by 1 |
|---|---|---|---|
| Or | ch08linux-plan | (Average) CpuPercentage < 30 | Increase count by 1 |

+ Add a rule

Instance limits

| Minimum ⓘ | Maximum ⓘ | Default ⓘ |
|---|---|---|
| 1 | 4 | 2 |

Schedule
**This scale condition is executed when none of the other scale condition(s) match**

+ Add a scale condition

*Figure 8-9. App Service plan autoscale settings*

9. Run the following command to delete the resources you created in this recipe:

```
az group delete --name $rgName
```

You successfully configured autoscaling for your App Service plan. This autoscale setting affects all the child App Services under the App Service plan.

## Discussion

Azure App Services always run in an Azure App Service plan. Azure Functions can also optionally run in an App Service plan. The App Service plan defines a set of compute resources, such as memory and CPU, for all the child App Services. Under the hood, this memory and CPU are allocated to a set of worker virtual machines, which are assigned to your App Service plan.

When your App Services (such as web apps) receive more traffic, the parent App Service plan needs more resources, so it can keep up with the demand. There are two options to scale an App Service plan (*https://oreil.ly/L5XiS*):

*Scale up*

Manually dedicate bigger workers (virtual machines with more memory, CPU, etc.) to the App Service plan while keeping the number of workers the same. You will *scale down* your App Service plan when the resources are no longer required.

*Scale out*

Increase the number of worker virtual machines assigned to the App Service plan while keeping each worker size unchanged. This can be done manually or automatically (using autoscale settings). You will *scale in* the App Service plan when the extra resources are no longer required.

In this recipe, you created an autoscale setting with two rules:

- The first rule *scales out* your App Service plan by adding a new worker machine if the average CPU percentage is above 60% for the past ten minutes.

- The second rule *scales in* your App Service plan by removing a worker machine if the average CPU percentage is below 30% for the last five minutes.

You can also scale out/in your App Service plan by manually adding/removing workers. See the Azure CLI documentation (*https://oreil.ly/ZFINb*) for details.

Autoscale settings can be created for other Azure resources such as *Azure Virtual Machine Scale Sets* (*https://oreil.ly/JcJvP*).

# 8.5 Restricting Network Access to an Azure App Service

## Problem

You want to control network access to your Azure App Service web app based on the client IP address or Azure Virtual Network subnet.

## Solution

Configure network access restrictions for your App Service, as shown in Figure 8-10.

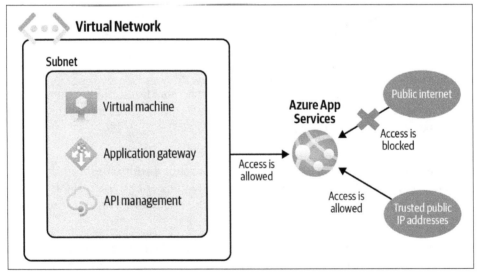

*Figure 8-10. Azure App Service network access restrictions*

## Steps

1. Follow steps 1 and 2 in Recipe 8.3 to create an Azure App Service. You don't need to deploy any content to this web app.

2. Get your App Service web app public URL and navigate to it using a browser. You should see the App Service default homepage, as shown in Figure 8-11, because we did not deploy any content to this web app. Any client can access this website at this point:

```
url="https://"$(az webapp show \
    --resource-group $rgName \
    --name $appServiceName \
    --query defaultHostName \
    --output tsv)

echo $url
```

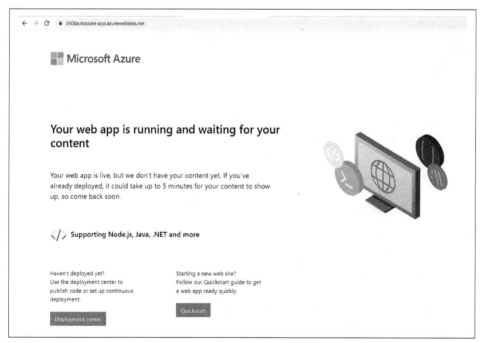

*Figure 8-11. Azure App Service default homepage*

3. Create an Azure VNet with a single subnet using the following command. Replace *<vnet-name>* with the desired value:

```
vnetName="<vnet-name>"

az network vnet create \
```

```
    --resource-group $rgName \
    --name $vnetName \
    --address-prefix 10.0.0.0/16 \
    --subnet-name Subnet01 \
    --subnet-prefix 10.0.0.0/26
```

4. Create a new access restriction rule using the following command. This rule restricts website access to clients within your VNet subnet:

```
az webapp config access-restriction add \
    --resource-group $rgName \
    --name $appServiceName \
    --rule-name vNetClients \
    --action Allow \
    --vnet-name $vnetName \
    --subnet Subnet01 \
    --priority 100
```

Adding the first access restriction rule will also add a default *deny all* rule, which blocks all requests except those that are explicitly allowed by your access restriction rules.

5. Try to access the website again using the URL from step 2. You should get the response "Error 403 - Forbidden," as shown in Figure 8-12.

*Figure 8-12. Azure App Service access is blocked to public clients*

6. At this point, only virtual machines (or other resources) in Subnet01 can access the web site. Let's create a new access restriction rule to unblock your public IP address. Note that the --priority parameter is set to 110 because the priority 100 is already taken by the first rule you created. Replace <my-public-ip> with your public IP address:

```
myPublicIPv4="<my-public-ip>"

az webapp config access-restriction add \
  --resource-group $rgName \
  --name $appServiceName \
  --rule-name myself \
  --action Allow \
  --ip-address $myPublicIPv4 \
  --priority 110
```

 You can visit ipaddress.com or similar websites to find your public IP address.

7. Wait for a few seconds and try to visit the App Service homepage using the URL from step 2. You should see the page shown in Figure 8-11.

8. You can check the existing network access restriction for an App Service using the following command. A sample command output can be found in the book's repository (*https://oreil.ly/NjuFt*):

```
az webapp config access-restriction show \
  --resource-group $rgName \
  --name $appServiceName
```

9. You can view the access restriction settings in the Azure portal, too. Visit the App Services page (*https://oreil.ly/KItRm*) and click on your App Service as shown in Figure 8-13.

*Figure 8-13. The App Services page*

10. Under Settings, click on Networking and "Access restriction" as shown in Figure 8-14.

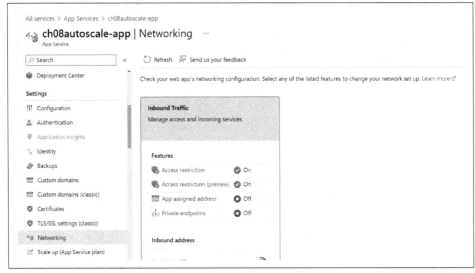

*Figure 8-14. App Services networking settings*

11. You should see three rules. The first two were added by you, and the last one is the default deny all rule, which blocks any request that does not match rules 100 and 110, as shown in Figure 8-15.

*Figure 8-15. App Services access restrictions*

12. Run the following command to delete the resources you created in this recipe:

```
az group delete --name $rgName
```

You successfully configured network access restrictions for your Azure App Service web app.

## Discussion

By default, Azure App Service websites can be accessed from any network including the public internet. However, in some scenarios, you need to control traffic to your App Services by only allowing requests from specific IP addresses or virtual network subnets. Here are a few examples:

- Your App Service hosts an internal or corporate website that should only be accessed internally.
- You need to develop and test a live App Service while keeping it hidden from the public.
- You need to ensure a web app is reachable only from an Azure API Management or Azure Application Gateway subnet.

In this recipe, you created two network access restriction rules, one to allow requests from your public IP address (*https://oreil.ly/YUzI7*) and one to allow requests from an Azure VNet subnet. All other traffic is denied due to the deny all rule that is automatically added. An access restriction rule (*https://oreil.ly/ZmsrG*) has the following properties:

- An action, which will *allow* or *deny* traffic.
- A priority, which indicates the order in which rules will be processed; rules with lower priority numbers will be processed first.

 You can create network access restrictions for Azure Function Apps as well. See the Azure Function App documentation (*https://oreil.ly/r7JwL*) for details.

# 8.6 Hosting Static Websites in Azure Storage

## Problem

You need to host your static website (HTML, CSS, JavaScript, image, and other media files) in Azure. However, you don't want to use Azure App Services and need to consider other low-cost options.

## Solution

Provision a new *general-purpose v2* or *BlockBlobStorage* Azure storage account and upload your static website in a blob container, as shown in Figure 8-16.

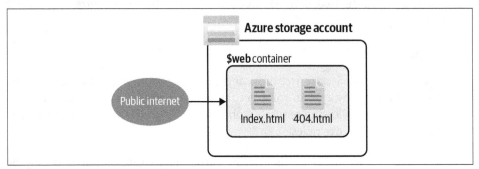

*Figure 8-16. Hosting static websites in Azure Storage*

### Steps

1. Log in to your Azure subscription in the Owner role and create a new resource group for this recipe. See "General Workstation Setup Instructions" on page xii for details.

2. Create a new Azure storage account using the following commands:

```
storageName="<storage-account-name>"

az storage account create \
    --name $storageName \
    --resource-group $rgName \
    --sku Standard_LRS \
    --default-action Allow

storageKey01=$(az storage account keys list \
    --resource-group $rgName \
    --account-name $storageName \
    --query [0].value \
    --output tsv)
```

3. Use the following command to enable the *static-website* feature in your storage account, in order to host your static websites:

```
az storage blob service-properties update \
    --account-name $storageName \
    --account-key $storageKey01 \
    --static-website \
    --404-document notfound.html \
    --index-document index.html
```

4. Now you are ready to upload your static website to the storage account. You can upload your files, or optionally download sample files from the recipe repository (*https://oreil.ly/qyx_m*). Store the downloaded files in a local folder named *staticwebsite*.

5. Use the following command to upload the content of your local folder to the $web container in your storage account. Replace `<path-to-local-folder>` with the path to the *staticwebsite* folder:

```
az storage blob upload-batch \
   --account-name $storageName \
   --destination $web \
   --source <path-to-local-folder>
```

6. Finally, find the website URL using the following command and navigate to it using a web browser. You should see the static *index.html* page, as shown in Figure 8-17:

```
webURL=$(az storage account show \
   --name $storageName \
   --resource-group $rgName \
   --query "primaryEndpoints.web" \
   --output tsv)

echo $webURL
```

*Figure 8-17. Static website hosted in an Azure Storage blob container*

7. Run the following command to delete the resources you created in this recipe:

```
az group delete --name $rgName
```

You successfully hosted a static website in an Azure Storage blob container.

## Discussion

Azure App Services can host any web application, including static websites. However, if you don't need a web server to render content (for example, when serving only HTML, CSS, JavaScript, and media files), you can host your website in an Azure Storage blob container. You will benefit from the serverless scalability and pricing options that Azure Storage offers.

Azure Storage static websites (*https://oreil.ly/PZfsz*) have a few limitations. For example, you can't directly configure headers for your storage account static website unless you use *Azure Content Delivery Network (Azure CDN)*.

Azure App Service remains a good choice if you need to render content on the backend (such as PHP, .NET, or Node.js applications).

 *Azure Static Web Apps (https://oreil.ly/jy-ch)* is a good alternative to storage account static websites. It supports setting headers as well as AuthN/AuthZ authentication. See the Azure documentation (*https://oreil.ly/zMiQh*) for details.

## CHAPTER 9

# Containers

Many dependencies must be in place so that an application properly works. Configuration files, environment variables, code binaries, libraries, markup, media files, Windows registry settings, databases, and web servers are just a few examples. You must properly configure these dependencies when deploying an application to a new environment. Companies used to (and still do) maintain lengthy deployment documents to make sure that solution dependencies are configured as expected. *Containers* are here to streamline the application deployment process.

Containers enable you to bundle (contain) your application code and dependencies into a single package called a *container image*. You will *push* this image into a *container registry* service, such as *Docker Hub*, so that it can later be pulled and run. Containers make application deployment to different environments more consistent. You can create a container image and deploy it to as many environments as you need and be certain that a tested container will continue to work in the next environment.

Microsoft Azure offers services to both host container images and run them. *Azure Container Registry (ACR)* is a container registry service (similar to Docker Hub) that hosts your container images. You can then *pull* these container images from ACR and run them in one of the following services (*https://oreil.ly/3FO03*):

*Azure Container Instances (https://oreil.ly/YvXp7)*
  This easy-to-configure solution runs isolated containers for simple applications.

*Azure Kubernetes Service (AKS) (https://oreil.ly/mbMVm)*
  This is a container orchestrator service, which can run multiple dependent containers. It automatically handles tasks such as container health monitoring and communications.

*Azure Container Apps (https://oreil.ly/A7CIA)*
Use this service if you are planning to run multiple containers but don't want to get involved with managing a Kubernetes cluster. Under the hood, this service is powered by Kubernetes.

*Azure Functions and Azure App Services*
Both of these services enable you to host Linux and Windows containers.

*Other services such as Azure Spring Apps and Azure Red Hat OpenShift*
See the Azure documentation (*https://oreil.ly/GU85h*) for details.

In this chapter, you will:

- Create a container image and push it to an Azure Container Registry.
- Run a container in Azure Container Instances and Azure App Services.
- Configure network security for these services.

## Workstation Configuration

You will need to prepare your workstation before starting on the recipes in this chapter. Follow "What You Will Need" on page xi to set up your machine to run Azure CLI commands. You can clone the book's GitHub repository using the following command:

```
git clone https://github.com/zaalion/AzureCookbook.git
```

## Chapter Prerequisites

To create container images, you need to install a container engine on your workstation. Follow the instructions for your OS:

### Windows

1. Install Docker Desktop (*https://oreil.ly/Ou2xM*).
2. Run Docker Desktop after the installation is complete.

### macOS

1. Install Docker Desktop (*https://oreil.ly/oe7B4*).
2. Run Docker Desktop after the installation is complete.

### Linux

1. Install Docker Desktop (*https://oreil.ly/QLcP0*).

2. Start the *Docker daemon*.

### Validating the Docker installation

Run the following command to confirm Docker is installed on your machine:

```
docker --version
```

You should see an output similar to the following:

```
Docker version 20.10.17, build 100c701
```

In Recipe 9.1, you will create a new container image on your workstation and push it to ACR. You can run the following command to get a list of container images on your local machine, as shown in Figure 9-1:

```
docker image
```

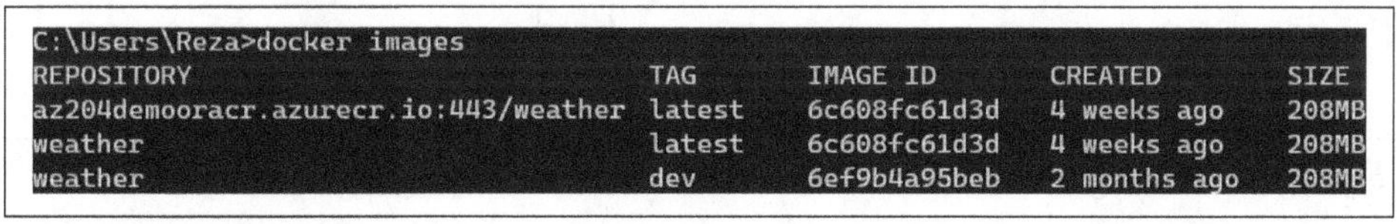

```
C:\Users\Reza>docker images
REPOSITORY                              TAG       IMAGE ID        CREATED        SIZE
az204demooracr.azurecr.io:443/weather   latest    6c608fc61d3d    4 weeks ago    208MB
weather                                 latest    6c608fc61d3d    4 weeks ago    208MB
weather                                 dev       6ef9b4a95beb    2 months ago   208MB
```

*Figure 9-1. Container images on a local workstation*

You will get the following error if the Docker process/daemon is not running. In this case, run Docker Desktop and execute the command again:

```
error during connect: This error may indicate that the docker daemon is
not running.:
Get "http://%2F%2F.%2Fpipe%2Fdocker_engine/v1.24/images/json":
open //./pipe/docker_engine: The system cannot find the file specified.
```

# 9.1 Building and Pushing a Container Image to Azure Container Registry

## Problem

You need to push your container image to Azure Container Registry.

## Solution

Build and tag your application into a Docker container image and push it to your ACR instance as a new repository, as shown in Figure 9-2.

---

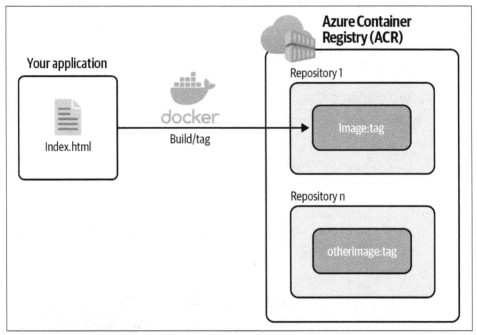

*Figure 9-2. Pushing a Docker container to Azure Container Registry*

## Steps

1. Log in to your Azure subscription in the Owner role and create a new resource group for this recipe. See "General Workstation Setup Instructions" on page xii for details.

2. Make sure Docker Desktop is running. See "Chapter Prerequisites" on page 240 for details.

3. First, create a new folder named *static* and put an HTML file with the following content in it. Name the file *index.html* (*https://oreil.ly/NgBBQ*):

   ```
   <html>
   <body>
   <h1>
   This page is served from a Docker container!
   </h1>
   </body>
   </html>
   ```

4. The goal is to package this simple website into a Docker image. Create a file in the *static* folder with the following content and name it *Dockerfile* (*https://oreil.ly/6CnY5*) (without an extension). Docker uses this file to create the image for you:

```
FROM nginx:alpine
COPY . /usr/share/nginx/html
```

 The command FROM nginx:alpine tells Docker to use the *NGINX* image as the base for your image. NGINX (*https://oreil.ly/zetuJ*) is a web server and reverse proxy (*https://oreil.ly/86dnP*). The second line, COPY . /usr/share/nginx/html, adds a new *layer* to the base layer by copying all root files in the *static folder* to the */usr/share/ nginx/html* folder in the container image.

5. Using the command line, set *static* as the working directory and run the following command to build your container image:

```
docker build -t static-html-image -f Dockerfile .
```

6. Run the docker images command to confirm a new container image named *static-html-image* was created. Make a note of its IMAGE ID, for instance dc89cef9b48b, as shown in Figure 9-3.

```
PS C:\Data\Repo\AzureCookbook\Chapter09\Static> docker images
REPOSITORY                              TAG         IMAGE ID        CREATED              SIZE
static-html-image                       latest      dc89cef9b48b    About a minute ago   40.7MB
cookbookacr.azurecr.io/static-html      version1.0  0d71ad6e1349    14 hours ago         40.7MB
```

*Figure 9-3. Confirming that your image is built*

7. Now use this command to provision your ACR resource. Replace *<registry- name>* with the desired name. Setting the --admin-enabled parameter to true ensures that the ACR administrator account is enabled. You will need this account later in this recipe:

```
registryName="<registry-name>"

az acr create \
  --resource-group $rgName \
  --name $registryName \
  --sku Basic \
  --admin-enabled true
```

8. Use the following command to find the ACR login URL, admin user, and admin password values:

```
acrLoginServer=$(az acr show \
  --resource-group $rgName \
  --name $registryName \
  --query loginServer \
  --output tsv)
```

```
acrAdminUser=$(az acr credential show \
  --name $registryName \
  --query username \
  --output tsv)

acrAdminPass=$(az acr credential show \
  --name $registryName \
  --query passwords[0].value \
  --output tsv)
```

9. Before pushing your container image, you need to *tag* (*https://oreil.ly/ZmYYE*) it. Tagging enables you to create multiple versions of a container image. Use the following command to tag your image. Replace *<IMAGE-ID>* with the ID from step 6:

```
docker tag <IMAGE-ID> $acrLoginServer/static-html-image:ver1.0
```

10. Log in to the ACR using the following command and confirm that you see a "Login Succeeded" message:

```
docker login $acrLoginServer \
  --username $acrAdminUser \
  --password $acrAdminPass
```

11. Use the following command to push your tagged image to ACR. Wait for the command to push the image to ACR; this might take up to several minutes based on your connection speed:

```
docker push $acrLoginServer/static-html-image:ver1.0
```

The command might retry a few times before completely pushing your image. This is OK. If the command fails due to connection issues, simply re-run it.

12. Use the following command to confirm that a new *repository* was created in ACR. You should see static-html-image in the command output:

```
az acr repository list \
  --resource-group $rgName \
  --name $registryName
```

You successfully packaged a website into a Docker image, tagged it, and then pushed it to an Azure Container Registry repository. In the remaining recipes in this chapter, you will pull this image and host it in several Azure services, including Azure Container Instances and Azure Container Apps.

# Discussion

In this recipe, you built a Docker image from a simple HTML website. Web and console applications, databases, and other services such as cache servers can also run from a container. A container should "contain" all of your application's dependencies. This explains why the NGINX base image was included in the image *Dockerfile*. These dependencies vary for each application. For instance, a .NET Core 6.0 application requires that the *mcr.microsoft.com/dotnet/sdk:6.0* base image be included (*https://oreil.ly/_JpTv*).

After the container is built, it should be tagged. Tagging allows you to create multiple versions of your container image and push them to ACR (or other registries) as individual images. This enables you to deploy a new version of your application and quickly roll back if needed.

The following services support pulling and running Docker images from ACR:

- Azure Function Apps
- Azure App Services
- Azure Container Instances
- Azure Kubernetes Service
- Azure Container Apps

To pull container images, these services need to successfully authenticate to ACR. At the time of writing this book, the following authentication types (*https://oreil.ly/GCbdL*) are supported:

- Individual AD identity
- AD service principal
- Managed identity for Azure resources
- AKS cluster managed identity
- AKS cluster service principal
- Admin user
- ACR repository-scoped access token

In this recipe, you used the admin user method to authenticate to ACR and push your sample image.

# 9.2 Pulling and Running a Docker Image in Azure Container Instances

## Problem

You want to pull and run a Docker container image in a simple and easy-to-configure Azure service.

## Solution

Provision a new Azure Container Instances service that pulls and runs your image from Azure ACR, as shown in Figure 9-4.

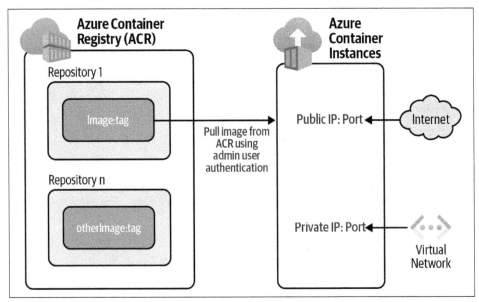

*Figure 9-4. Pulling and running a Docker image in Azure Container Instances*

### Steps

1. Complete Recipe 9.1 so that you have a container image in ACR to start with. Make sure the $acrLoginServer, $acrAdminUser, and $acrAdminPass variables still have a valid value.

2. Use the following command to create an Azure Container Instances resource with a public IP address. It will also pull the desired container image from ACR. This image contains a website, so let's open ports 80 and 443 as well. Replace *<aci-name>* with the desired name for your Azure Container Instances resource:

```
aciName="<aci-name>"

az container create \
  --resource-group $rgName \
  --name $aciName \
  --image $acrLoginServer/static-html-image:ver1.0 \
  --cpu 2 \
  --memory 2 \
  --registry-username $acrAdminUser \
  --registry-password $acrAdminPass \
  --ip-address Public \
  --ports 80 443
```

 This command assigns two CPU vCores and two GiB memory to the new Azure Container Instances resource. You can adjust these numbers according to your application needs.

3. You need the Azure Container Instances URL to reach your web application. Use the following command to get the service's public IP address:

```
aciIP=$(az container show \
  --name $aciName \
  --resource-group $rgName \
  --query ipAddress.ip \
  --output tsv)

aciURL="http://"$aciIP"/index.html"

echo $aciURL
```

4. Using a web browser, navigate to the $aciURL address. Confirm that you can see the website homepage, as shown in Figure 9-5.

```
←  →  C   🔒 Not secure | 20.246.163.100/index.html
```
# This page is served from a Docker container!

*Figure 9-5. Website running from a Docker container*

 It can take several minutes for Azure Container Instances to pull your image from ACR and run it. You might get a "404 Not Found" error. If this happens, wait a few minutes and try again.

You successfully ran a containerized website in Azure Container Instances. This website is accessible on a public IP address.

## Discussion

Azure Container Instances (*https://oreil.ly/OfAhc*) is an easy-to-configure service that enables you to pull and run isolated container images. Use this service to run independent microservices, websites, and other applications. When provisioning this service, you can choose to assign a private or public IP address to your application. One or multiple ports can also be opened/allowed based on your application needs.

> You can host and run multiple containers in a single Azure Container Instances resource using *container groups* (*https://oreil.ly/Gy7EY*).

Azure Container Instances needs to authenticate to Azure Container Registry (ACR) to pull and run the desired Docker image. As you saw in this recipe, this authentication is done using the ACR's admin user account.

Azure Container Instances is not the recommended service (*https://oreil.ly/EJXDk*) for every scenario. Use Azure Kubernetes Service (AKS) (*https://oreil.ly/84uru*) or Azure Container Apps (*https://oreil.ly/pm_aE*) if you plan to host multiple interconnected containers, complex applications, or if you need container orchestration services.

You also have other options, such as Azure App Services and Azure Function Apps to pull and run images from ACR. In Recipe 9.3, you will run the same simple website from an Azure App Service.

# 9.3 Pulling and Running a Containerized Website in Azure App Services

## Problem

You want to pull and run a containerized web application in Azure App Services.

## Solution

Provision a new Azure App Services instance, which pulls and runs your image from Azure ACR, as shown in Figure 9-6.

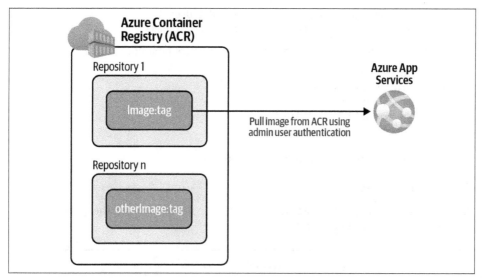

*Figure 9-6. Pulling and running a Docker image in Azure App Services*

### Steps

1. Complete Recipe 9.1 so that you have a containerized website image in ACR. Make sure the `$acrLoginServer`, `$acrAdminUser`, and `$acrAdminPass` variables still have a valid value.

2. Use the following command to create a new Linux App Service plan. Windows App Service plans are also OK. Replace *<plan-name>* with the desired name:

```
planName="<plan-name>"
```

```
az appservice plan create \
  --name $planName \
  --resource-group $rgName \
  --is-linux
```

3. Use the following command to create an Azure App Service resource. This command uses ACR admin user credentials to authenticate to Azure Container Registry and pull the desired container image. The image then runs in the App Service plan. Replace *<app-name>* with a globally unique name:

```
appName="<app-name>"
```

```
az webapp create \
  --resource-group $rgName \
  --plan $planName \
  --name $appName \
  --deployment-container-image-name
    $acrLoginServer/static-html-image:ver1.0 \
```

```
--docker-registry-server-user $acrAdminUser \
--docker-registry-server-password $acrAdminPass
```

4. Use the following command to get the App Service host name (URL):

```
appHost=$(az webapp show \
  --resource-group $rgName \
  --name $appName \
  --query defaultHostName \
  --output tsv)

appURL="https://"$appHost"/index.html"

echo $appURL
```

5. Navigate to the $appURL address. Confirm that you can see the website homepage, as shown in Figure 9-7.

← → C   🔒 mydockcook2551erapp.azurewebsites.net/index.html

## This page is served from a Docker container!

*Figure 9-7. Website running from an Azure App Service*

You successfully pulled a containerized website image into an Azure App Service.

 Make sure you delete the new App Service plan and App Services after you are done with this recipe.

## Discussion

Both Azure App Services and Azure Function Apps can pull container images from container registries (such as Azure ACR, Docker Hub, etc.) and run them. In this recipe, you configured a new Azure App Service to authenticate to ACR and pull the desired image.

You conveniently used the ACR admin user for this authentication. This is not the most secure method because you need to handle a username and password string. Anyone having these credentials can access the images stored in your ACR instance. To eliminate this threat, it is recommended that you use other ACR authentication methods (*https://oreil.ly/Fl6os*) if possible. For instance, you can assign the *AcrPull* RBAC role to the managed identity of your Azure App Service, enabling it to pull images from ACR without providing admin user credentials. See the Azure App Services documentation (*https://oreil.ly/3f1CY*) for details.

You can also enable CI/CD (continuous delivery/continuous integration) for your App Services so that a new image push to Azure ACR automatically triggers a deployment to your App Services. See the Azure App Services documentation (*https://oreil.ly/D5wQW*) for more details.

# 9.4 Pulling and Running a Containerized Website in Azure Container Apps

## Problem

You want to pull and run one or more containerized applications on a serverless platform (*https://oreil.ly/Os6Dw*).

## Solution

Provision a new *Azure Container Apps Environment* and one (or multiple) Azure Container Apps that pull and run your container image, as shown in Figure 9-8.

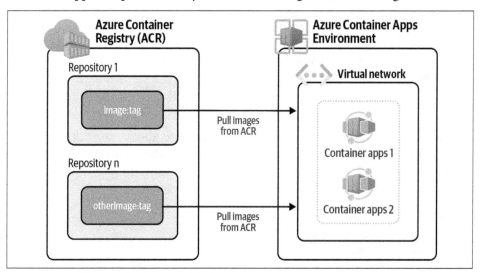

*Figure 9-8. Pulling and running a Docker image in Azure Container Apps Environment*

### Steps

1. Complete Recipe 9.1 so that you have a container image in your ACR. Make sure the $acrLoginServer, $acrAdminUser, and $acrAdminPass variables still have valid values.

2. Use the following command to install the `containerapp` CLI extension in your environment:

```
az extension add --name containerapp --upgrade
```

3. To provision Azure Container Apps, you need to have the following provider registered in your Azure subscription. Use the following command to do so:

```
az provider register --namespace Microsoft.App
```

4. *Azure Monitor Log Analytics workspace* is a mandatory dependency for the Azure Container Apps resource. You might need to register the following provider as well:

```
az provider register --namespace Microsoft.OperationalInsights
```

5. Now the stage is set to start provisioning your resources. First let's create a parent Azure Container Apps Environment. You can create multiple Azure Container Apps in the same environment. These apps share the same Azure Virtual Network and can securely communicate with one another:

```
envName="cookbook-env"

az containerapp env create \
  --name $envName \
  --resource-group $rgName
```

 This command will take several minutes to complete. Wait for the command to succeed before proceeding to the next step.

6. Now you are ready to create an Azure Container Apps resource in your new environment. Use the following command to create the app by pulling your simple image from ACR. The ACR admin user is used for authentication:

```
registryName="<acr-name>"
appName="cookbook-container-app01"

az containerapp create \
  --name $appName \
  --resource-group $rgName \
  --image $acrLoginServer"/static-html-image:ver1.0" \
  --environment $envName \
  --ingress external \
  --target-port 80 \
  --registry-server $acrLoginServer \
  --registry-username $acrAdminUser \
  --registry-password $acrAdminPass
```

By default, external clients can't access the container apps. By setting `--ingress external` you allow external clients from other networks, including the internet, to access the container app over the designated port(s). The preceding command opens port 80 by setting the `--target-port 80` parameter.

7. Wait for the command to succeed. Now, use the following command to get the public URL of your Azure Container App:

```
appHost=$(az containerapp show \
  --name $appName \
  --resource-group $rgName \
  --query properties.configuration.ingress.fqdn \
  --output tsv)

appURL="http://"$appHost

echo $appURL
```

8. Navigate to the `$appURL` address and confirm that you can see the website homepage.

9. Make sure to delete the resources you created in this recipe to avoid extra charges. First, use the following command to delete your child Azure Container Apps instance:

```
az containerapp delete \
  --resource-group $rgName \
  --name $appName
```

10. Now delete the Container Apps Environment:

```
az containerapp env delete \
  --name $envName \
  --resource-group $rgName
```

 This command will take several minutes to complete.

You successfully pulled and ran a containerized website on an Azure Container Apps instance.

## Discussion

In this recipe, you deployed a single container to an Azure Container Apps instance. However, this service is designed to host more complex applications consisting of multiple containers and microservices. Azure Container Apps are deployed inside a parent *Azure Container Apps Environment*. An environment creates a secure boundary around the child container apps. Container Apps in the same environment share the same Azure VNet and write resource logs to a single Azure Log Analytics workspace.

Azure Container Apps is a serverless service. This means the service can dynamically scale based on metrics such as HTTP traffic volume or CPU and memory usage. This service is ideal for (*https://oreil.ly/LU5kc*):

- Running multiple containers or container revisions
- Running multiple microservices
- Autoscaling (serverless)
- Splitting traffic among application revisions for scenarios such as A/B testing
- Building microservices with *Dapr*

Azure Container Apps is built on top of a Kubernetes cluster (*https://oreil.ly/eGhQB*). This enables you to use Kubernetes-style apps with features such as service discovery and traffic splitting without getting involved with Kubernetes management tasks. On the other hand, if you need to access Kubernetes APIs and its control plane, you should look into Azure Kubernetes Service (AKS) (*https://oreil.ly/MT5q6*).

So far in this chapter, you worked with several services capable of running containers in Azure. For single containers, choose Azure Container Instances, Azure App Services, or Azure Function Apps, depending on your scenario. For more complex applications, you can choose between Azure Container Apps and Azure Kubernetes Service. Take a look at the Azure container options documentation (*https://oreil.ly/a126U*) for more details.

# 9.5 Limiting Azure Container Registry Public Network Access

## Problem

You need to limit Azure Container Registry (ACR) public network access to protect your images from unauthorized access.

## Solution

Disable public network access on your ACR and configure your Azure Container Instances to use a trusted managed identity to pull images from ACR, as shown in Figure 9-9.

---

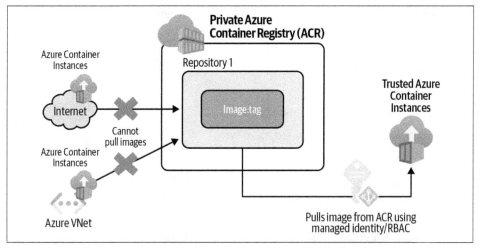

*Figure 9-9. Pulling a Docker image from ACR using managed identities*

### Steps

1. Complete Recipe 9.1 to push a container image to your public ACR. Make sure the $acrLoginServer variable has a valid value. You don't need $acrAdminUser and $acrAdminPass for this recipe.

2. ACR instances in the Basic and Standard tiers (SKUs) don't support (*https://oreil.ly/lrReq*) limiting network access. Use the following command to upgrade your ACR SKU to Premium:

   ```
   registryName="<acr-name>"

   az acr update \
     --name $registryName \
     --resource-group $rgName \
     --sku Premium
   ```

    Make sure to delete your ACR or downgrade it to the Basic tier after completing this recipe.

3. Store the ACR resource ID in a variable:

   ```
   acrId=$(az acr show \
     --name $registryName \
     --resource-group $rgName \
     --query id \
     --output tsv)
   ```

4. Now let's update the ACR public network access settings (firewall) so incoming traffic from public networks is denied. This will dramatically improve your ACR security:

```
az acr update \
  --name $registryName \
  --resource-group $rgName \
  --public-network-enabled false
```

5. Create a user-assigned managed identity:

```
aciIdentityName="<identity-name>"

az identity create \
  --resource-group $rgName \
  --name $aciIdentityName
```

6. Get the new identity ID and service principal ID and store them in two variables. You will use these values in the next step:

```
identityId=$(az identity show \
  --resource-group $rgName \
  --name $aciIdentityName \
  --query id \
  --output tsv)

identitySpId=$(az identity show \
  --resource-group $rgName \
  --name $aciIdentityName \
  --query principalId \
  --output tsv)
```

7. Your goal is to enable the new identity to pull container images from your ACR registry. Let's assign the AcrPull RBAC role to this identity over your ACR scope:

```
acrId=$(az acr show \
  --name $registryName \
  --resource-group $rgName \
  --query id \
  --output tsv)

az role assignment create \
  --assignee $identitySpId \
  --scope $acrId \
  --role acrpull
```

 Previously in this chapter, you used the ACR admin user for authentication. Using an identity-based authentication is more secure because you do not need to handle the admin user's credentials.

8. The new identity can now perform the image pull (AcrPull) operation on your ACR registry. In other words, the ACR registry *trusts* this identity. However, your ACR is now a private container registry, and its firewall will block any incoming requests. Configure your ACR firewall to exempt *trusted resources*:

```
az acr update \
  --name $registryName \
  --resource-group $rgName \
  --allow-trusted-services true
```

9. You are ready to create a new Azure Container Instances resource by pulling your image from the private ACR. Note that you don't need to use the ACR admin user credentials to pull your image. The user-assigned managed identity $identityId is used instead:

```
aciName="<container-instance-name>"
```

```
az container create \
  --name $aciName \
  --resource-group $rgName \
  --image $acrLoginServer/static-html-image:ver1.0 \
  --cpu 2 \
  --memory 2 \
  --assign-identity $identityId \
  --acr-identity $identityId \
  --ip-address Public \
  --ports 80 443
```

 This command also assigns the user-assigned managed identity to the new Azure Container Instances resource (--assign-identity $identityId). The identity is used to authenticate your Container Instance to ACR and pull the container image.

10. Obtain the public URL for the new Azure Container Instance and access it in a browser. Confirm that the container is running:

```
aciIP=$(az container show \
  --name $aciName \
  --resource-group $rgName \
  --query ipAddress.ip \
  --output tsv)

aciURL="http://"$aciIP"/index.html"

echo $aciURL
```

The new Azure Container Instance might take up to 15 minutes to pull and run your container image. In the meantime, you will get the "404 Not Found" response.

11. Run the following command to delete the resources you created in this recipe:

```
az group delete --name $rgName
```

You successfully pulled a container image from a private Azure Container Registry using trusted Azure services (Azure Container Instances).

## Discussion

In the previous recipes in this chapter, you pulled container images from a public Azure Container Registry. All clients, including clients connecting from the public internet, could authenticate to this ACR instance and pull container images. This leaves the doors open to attacks from unknown networks. It is recommended that you limit public network access to Azure Container Registry using firewall network rules. Only the ACR Premium pricing tier supports configuring network access rules (*https://oreil.ly/W4iTm*).

In this recipe, you upgraded your ACR pricing tier to Premium and disabled all network access (including public internet). Trusted Azure services are exempt from ACR firewall rules, so you used a trusted Azure Container Instances service to successfully pull the desired image from ACR. At the time of writing this book, only the following trusted services (*https://oreil.ly/XgfMH*) can bypass the ACR networking rules. More Azure services might be added in the future:

- Azure Container Instances
- Microsoft Defender for Cloud
- ACR Tasks
- Azure Machine Learning
- Azure Container Registry

ACR public network access can be set to one of the following values. If you need to pull ACR images from services other than items mentioned previously (such as Azure App Services, Function Apps, or AKS), you can use options 2 through 4:

1. Disabled (was used in this recipe)
2. All networks (not recommended)

3. Selected networks (allowing specific Azure VNets to see and use ACR)

4. Private endpoints (using Azure Private Link)

Public network access should be limited not only for the ACR registry but also for other container services such as Azure Container Instances, Azure App Services, Azure Function Apps, Azure Kubernetes Service, and Azure Container Apps. This adds a powerful defense against unauthorized access and data loss.

## CHAPTER 10

# Azure Cognitive Services

Machine learning (ML) (*https://oreil.ly/mZHSG*) is a subset of artificial intelligence (AI). It's the process of developing and training mathematical models that use data to help computers learn without direct instructions. The ML model is used to improve the performance and accuracy of a task.

Microsoft Azure employs AI/ML to enrich its service capabilities. AI-driven adaptive protection (*https://oreil.ly/8zr5o*) enables Microsoft Defender to adapt to new types of attacks and further protect your services. Azure Firewall threat intelligence-based filtering (*https://oreil.ly/Uv1St*) denies traffic from malicious IP addresses and URLs. Azure SQL *Advanced Threat Protection* uses AI/ML (and other sources) to detect anomalies indicating possible attempts to exploit databases. Microsoft leverages AI/ML not only to enhance Azure services but also to enable Azure clients to use AL/ML to solve their own business problems.

Creating a trained model can be time consuming, needs big training datasets, and is generally performed by field experts. Data scientists can use services such as Azure Machine Learning (*https://oreil.ly/2COgP*) or Azure Databricks (*https://oreil.ly/Y2tbj*) to build, deploy, and manage ML models. These services are recommended for AI/ML specialists who need to train their own new models. They generally take the following steps to create, optimize, and employ machine learning models for a given problem/scenario:

1. Choose the right *machine learning algorithm* based on the problem at hand.

2. Prepare *training datasets* by processing raw data.

3. Use the training datasets with the ML algorithm to train an *ML model*.

4. Repeat steps 2 and 3 until the desired model accuracy is achieved.

5. Deploy the trained model to a host machine, so that it can be used.

6. Pass real data to the trained model and receive the outcome.

Many companies, on the other hand, are not interested (or don't have the resources) to go through this process. They need to use common AI/ML capabilities to quickly develop smart applications. Microsoft answered this need by creating several pre-trained ML models under the Azure Cognitive Services (*https://oreil.ly/he8Ra*) umbrella. These models address a wide variety of common AI/ML scenarios and can easily be used by any application capable of making HTTP API calls. At the time of writing this book, Azure Cognitive Services is categorized into five groups:

*Speech*
: Offering speech-to-text, text-to-speech, speech translation, and speaker recognition APIs

*Language*
: Offering entity recognition, sentiment analysis, question answering, conversational language understanding (CLU) (*https://oreil.ly/wkc61*), and translator APIs

*Vision*
: Including computer vision, face API, and custom vision APIs

*Decision*
: Offering anomaly detector, content moderator, and personalizer APIs

*Azure OpenAI Service*
: Offering OpenAI service

Using Azure Cognitive Services, you can bring the power of AI/ML into your applications without any AI/ML knowledge. Here are a few capabilities that you can add to your applications using these services:

- Create transcripts from audio and video files
- Translate to/from supported languages
- Process live video surveyance footage
- Perform facial recognition
- Convert text to speech using customizable voice profiles
- Detect anomaly in time series data (live streams)
- Moderate text, image, and video content

Azure Cognitive Services offers a wide variety of APIs to address common AI/ML scenarios. If these APIs don't meet your project requirements, you can train your own models using Azure Machine Learning or similar services. See the Azure Machine Learning documentation (*https://oreil.ly/ZbAZv*) for details.

In this chapter, you will work with a few common Azure Cognitive Services APIs to:

- Provision a new multi-service Azure Cognitive Services account
- Convert text to speech
- Translate a sentence from English to Spanish
- Analyze a picture for insights
- Analyze facial expressions using the Face API
- Identify personally identifiable information (PII) in text
- Perform sentiment analysis using the language APIs

## Workstation Configuration

You will need to prepare your workstation before starting on the recipes in this chapter. Follow "What You Will Need" on page xi to set up your machine to run Azure CLI commands. You can clone the book's GitHub repository using the following command:

```
git clone https://github.com/zaalion/AzureCookbook.git
```

## Postman Collection

In this chapter, we will use cURL (*https://curl.se*) to call Cognitive Services HTTP APIs. If you prefer to use Postman (*https://www.postman.com*), you can download (*https://oreil.ly/w4pJO*) the corresponding Postman collection file from the chapter repository.

# 10.1 Provisioning a Multi-Service Azure Cognitive Services Resource

## Problem

You want to provision the required resources so that you can start using multiple Azure Cognitive Services APIs such as *ComputerVision*, *AnomalyDetector*, or *SpeechServices*.

## Solution

Provision a new multi-service Azure Cognitive Services resource and obtain the service endpoint and key.

### Steps

1. Log in to your Azure subscription in the Owner role and create a new resource group for this recipe. See "General Workstation Setup Instructions" on page xii for details.

2. Use the following command to get a list of the kinds of Azure Cognitive Services available:

   ```
   az cognitiveservices account list-kinds
   ```

3. Confirm the command output. At the time of writing this book, the following services are available:

   ```
   [
       "AnomalyDetector",
       "CognitiveServices",
       "ComputerVision",
       "ContentModerator",
       "ConversationalLanguageUnderstanding",
       "CustomVision.Prediction",
       "CustomVision.Training",
       "Face",
       "FormRecognizer",
       "ImmersiveReader",
       "Internal.AllInOne",
       "LUIS",
       "LUIS.Authoring",
       "LanguageAuthoring",
       "MetricsAdvisor",
       "Personalizer",
       "QnAMaker.v2",
       "SpeechServices",
       "TextAnalytics",
       "TextTranslation"
   ]
   ```

4. You plan to use multiple Cognitive Services APIs (vision, speech, etc.) using a single endpoint and key. To achieve this, you need to create a multi-service Azure Cognitive Services resource. The following command achieves this by passing CognitiveServices to the --kind parameter. Replace <cog-service-name> with the desired value. If prompted, answer Y to the statement "I certify that use of this service is not by or for a police department in the United States":

```
serviceName="<cog-service-name>"

az cognitiveservices account create \
    --name $serviceName \
    --resource-group $rgName \
    --sku S0 \
    --kind CognitiveServices \
    --location $region
```

 The multi-service Azure Cognitive Services only offers paid SKUs (such as S0). Most single-use Azure Cognitive Services also offer a free tier, such as F0, enabling you to try the services for free. See the Cognitive Services documentation (*https://oreil.ly/9nSLC*) for details.

5. Wait for the command to succeed. To start using Cognitive Services, you need a service key. Use the following command to get one:

```
key1=$(key1=$(az cognitiveservices account keys list \
    --name $serviceName \
    --resource-group $rgName \
    --query key1 \
    --output tsv))

echo $key1
```

You successfully provisioned a multi-service Azure Cognitive Services resource. In the other recipes in this chapter, you will use the service key to call multiple Azure Cognitive Services APIs.

## Discussion

You can provision two types of Azure Cognitive Services instances:

*Multi-service resource*
    Enables you to use multiple Azure Cognitive Services APIs (in vision, speech, language, decision categories) using a single key.

*Single-service resource*
    The service key can only be used to call one service type. At the time of writing this book, the following single-service types are available:

    - ComputerVision

    - Face

    - CustomVision

    - LUIS (*https://www.luis.ai*)

---

- ConversationalLanguageUnderstanding
- TextTranslation
- TextAnalytics
- QnAMaker
- ImmersiveReader
- SpeechServices
- FormRecognizer
- LanguageAuthoring
- MetricsAdvisor
- Personalizer
- AnomalyDetector
- ContentModerator

You can create a multi-service resource if you plan to use multiple Cognitive Services kinds with the same endpoint and key. You will get billed against the single multi-service resource.

You can use the single-service type if you plan to use a *single* cognitive API such as ComputerVision or SpeechServices. The single-service resources offer a free tier that you can use to evaluate the service before deciding to move to the paid tier. The multi-service resource only offers paid SKUs.

Azure Cognitive Services is a serverless service (*https://oreil.ly/Ep51A*). Even in the paid tier, you will only get billed when you call a Cognitive Services API (*https://oreil.ly/PUhZO*).

# 10.2 Converting Text to Speech

## Problem

You want to convert text to speech using Azure Cognitive Services.

## Solution

Use the text-to-speech endpoint and the Cognitive Services key to convert a text block to speech.

### Steps

1. Follow Recipe 10.1 to create a multi-service Cognitive Services resource. Make sure the service key is correctly stored in the $key1 variable.

2. Get the text-to-speech endpoint by running the following command. Note that the `$region` variable holds your preferred Azure region name, for example eastus:

```
endpoint=
    "https://"$region".tts.speech.microsoft.com/cognitiveservices/v1"
```

> Check the Azure documentation (*https://oreil.ly/ee3xe*) to find service endpoints for your region.

3. You can use any HTTP client to make a call to Azure Cognitive Services HTTP APIs. In this recipe, you will use the cURL command line tool (*https://curl.se*). Run the following commands to pass a text block to the text-to-speech API and save the speech voice file to your local machine. Replace *<file-path>* with the desired path on your local machine, for example *c://data/*:

```
text="You successfully converted a sample \
    text to speech using Azure Cognitive Services."

outputPath="<file-path>/speech.wav"

curl -X POST $endpoint \
    -H "Ocp-Apim-Subscription-Key: $key1" \
    -H X-Microsoft-OutputFormat: riff-24khz-16bit-mono-pcm \
    -H Content-Type: application/ssml+xml \
    -d "<speak version=1.0 xml:lang=en-US><voice xml:lang=en-US \
xml:gender=Male name=en-CA-LiamNeural>$text</voice></speak>" \
    >> $outputPath
```

> Note that the request `Content-Type` is set to `application/ssml` `+xml`. Speech Synthesis Markup Language (SSML) (*https://oreil.ly/ PwUsD*) is an XML-based markup language used to control output voice attributes such as pitch, pronunciation, speaking rate, volume, and more. The request body (`-d` parameter) is an SSML document.

4. Go to the filepath you specified in the preceding code and play the *speech.wav* file. Confirm that the generated voice matches your text input.

You successfully converted a text block to a speech voice file using Azure Cognitive Services.

## Discussion

You can use Azure Cognitive Services to easily bring text-to-speech functionality to your applications. This is useful especially for improving the accessibility of your applications.

You need to authenticate with Azure Cognitive Services to successfully call its APIs. The following two authentication methods (*https://oreil.ly/pAEZ1*) can be used:

*Ocp-Apim-Subscription-Key*
Uses the Cognitive Services key. This method is used in this scenario.

*Authorization Bearer*
Uses a security token. This token is valid for 10 minutes. You can obtain a token using your service key. See the Cognitive Services documentation (*https://oreil.ly/QPJ5U*) for details on obtaining this token.

You can control the following properties of the generated voice:

- The audio output format. Multiple *streaming* and *nonstreaming* formats are supported. You need to pass the desired format as the `X-Microsoft-OutputFormat` HTTP request header.

- The voice gender.

- The voice name (profile), such as `en-CA-LiamNeural`. You have a wide variety of voices to choose from. Each voice profile has a unique accent (for example English, Canadian, Japanese, Indian, Arabic, Chinese, German, French, etc.). You can get a list of available voice profiles by calling an API. See the documentation (*https://oreil.ly/cGeOf*) for details.

Customizable text-talker voices can be generated for a more realistic experience. Check the service documentation (*https://oreil.ly/29FEo*) for details. Visit the official text to speech page (*https://oreil.ly/JneK4*) for more details on this service.

 You can also use Azure Cognitive Services to convert speech to text (*https://oreil.ly/uVhEC*).

# 10.3 Translating Text

## Problem

You want to translate your text content to another language.

---

## Solution

Use the Azure Cognitive Services Translator API to translate your content to a supported language.

### Steps

1. Complete Recipe 10.1 to create a multi-service Cognitive Services resource. Make sure the service key is correctly stored in the `$key1` variable.

2. First let's find out which languages are supported by the Translator API. Run the following command to call the Languages API (*https://oreil.ly/T0qAV*) (Get). This API does not need an authentication header:

   ```
   endpoint="https://api.cognitive.microsofttranslator.com"

   curl --request GET $endpoint"/languages?api-version=3.0"
   ```

3. The API returns a JSON array of the supported Translator languages. You will find the following records in the output. You can see a sample output in the book's repository (*https://oreil.ly/1zIiP*):

   ```
   {
       "name": "Spanish",
       "nativeName": "Español",
       "dir": "ltr",
       "code": "es"
   }

   {
       "name": "English",
       "nativeName": "English",
       "dir": "ltr",
       "code": "en"
   }
   ```

4. In this recipe, you will translate text from English to Spanish. Use the following command to autodetect the source language:

   ```
   detectionEndpoint=$endpoint"/detect?api-version=3.0"

   curl -X POST $detectionEndpoint \
       -H "Ocp-Apim-Subscription-Key: $key1" \
       -H "Ocp-Apim-Subscription-Region: $region" \
       -H 'Content-Type: application/json' \
       -d '[{ "Text": "Cognitive Services brings
           AI within reach of every developer." }]'
   ```

The service region (location) should be passed as the value for Ocp-Apim-Subscription-Region header to authenticate with Translator APIs.

5. Confirm that the command returns the following response. The content language is successfully detected as English with the code en:

```
[
    {
        "language": "en",
        "score": 1.0,
        "isTranslationSupported": true,
        "isTransliterationSupported": false
    }
]
```

6. Finally, use this command to translate your content to Spanish:

```
translationEndpoint=$endpoint"/translate?api-version=3.0&from=en&to=es"

curl -X POST $translationEndpoint \
    -H "Ocp-Apim-Subscription-Key: $key1" \
    -H "Ocp-Apim-Subscription-Region: $region" \
    -H 'Content-Type: application/json' \
    -d '[{ "Text": "Cognitive Services brings AI
        within reach of every developer." }]'
```

7. Confirm that the following translation is returned:

```
[{"translations": [{
    "text": "Cognitive Services pone la IA al alcance de todos los
        desarrolladores.",
    "to": "es"
}]}]
```

You successfully translated your content from English to Spanish using the Azure Cognitive Services Translator API.

## Discussion

At the time of writing this book, over 100 languages (*https://oreil.ly/IBYIN*) are supported by the translator service. In this recipe, you worked with three Translator APIs to get the list of currently supported languages, autodetect the content source language, and translate the content from English to Spanish.

Both the Detect and Translate APIs accept the source text as a JSON array, enabling you to pass your content as multiple paragraphs and get the corresponding

---

translation back. At the time of writing this book, the following APIs (*https://oreil.ly/ NmkbG*) are offered by the Translator service:

*Languages*
Returns the languages currently supported by the translation, transliteration, and dictionary APIs

*Detect*
Identifies the source language

*Translate*
Translates the specified source text into the destination language

*Transliterate*
Maps the source language script or alphabet to the target language script or alphabet

*BreakSentence*
Returns an array of integers representing the length of sentences in a source text

*Dictionary/lookup*
Gives alternatives for single-word translations

*Dictionary/examples*
Shows how a term is used in context

In this recipe, you used the multi-service resource key created in Recipe 10.1. If you plan to use only the Translator API, you can alternatively create a single-service resource. You will get a different key, but the API endpoint and signature will be identical. See the Translator documentation (*https://oreil.ly/mUi3_*) for more details.

# 10.4 Performing Sentiment Analysis on Text

## Problem

You need to perform sentiment analysis on your text content.

## Solution

Use the Azure Cognitive Services Sentiment API to get a sentiment prediction score for your text content.

## Steps

1. Complete Recipe 10.1 to create a multi-service Cognitive Services resource. Make sure the service key is correctly stored in the $key1 variable.

2. Run the following command to pass your text content to the Sentiment API:

```
endpoint="https://"$region".api.cognitive.microsoft.com/"
sentimentEndpoint=$endpoint"/text/analytics/v3.0/sentiment"

curl -X POST $sentimentEndpoint \
    -H "Ocp-Apim-Subscription-Key: $key1" \
    -H 'Content-Type: application/json' \
    -d '{"documents":[{"language":"en","id":"1",
        "text":"I love sunny days!"}]}'
```

 You can pass multiple text blocks using the documents array and get the corresponding sentiment analysis score back for each of them.

3. Confirm that the preceding command returns a response similar to the following document. As you can see, the sentiment is positive with a confidence score of 1:

```
{
    "documents": [
        {
            "id": "1",
            "sentiment": "positive",
            "confidenceScores": {
                "positive": 1.0,
                "neutral": 0.0,
                "negative": 0.0
            },
            "sentences": [
                {
                    "sentiment": "positive",
                    "confidenceScores": {
                        "positive": 1.0,
                        "neutral": 0.0,
                        "negative": 0.0
                    },
                    "offset": 0,
                    "length": 18,
                    "text": "I love sunny days!"
                }
            ],
            "warnings": []
        }
```

```
    ],
    "errors": [],
    "modelVersion": "2022-11-01"
}
```

4. Run the following command to get another sentiment score:

```
curl -X POST $sentimentEndpoint \
    -H "Ocp-Apim-Subscription-Key: $key1" \
    -H 'Content-Type: application/json' \
    -d '{"documents":[{"language":"en","id":"1",
        "text":"I am not feeling too well!"}]}'
```

5. Confirm that the preceding command contains the following. As you can see, the sentiment is negative with a confidence score of 0.99:

```
"id": "1",
"sentiment": "negative",
"confidenceScores": {
    "positive": 0.0,
    "neutral": 0.01,
    "negative": 0.99
}
```

You successfully performed sentiment analysis on your text content.

## Discussion

Azure Cognitive Services Sentiment API enables you to easily get the sentiment analysis of your text content. A sentiment score has the following properties:

*id*

> The ID of the corresponding text element. This enables you to obtain sentiment scores for multiple text blocks in one API call.

*sentiment*

> The overall sentiment prediction for your content. Possible values are negative, positive, and neutral.

*confidenceScores*

> Individual confidence scores for negative, positive, and neutral sentiments. Each value is between 0.00 and 1.00, and the total sums up to 1.00, as the following sample demonstrates:

```
"confidenceScores":
{
    "positive": 0.75,
    "neutral": 0.05,
    "negative": 0.20
}
```

You can use Azure Cognitive Services Sentiment API to automate sentiment analysis for scenarios such as analyzing product reviews or call-center transcripts. See the Sentiment API documentation (*https://oreil.ly/Cb44s*) for more details.

# 10.5 Detecting Objects in Images

## Problem

You want to add image-analysis capabilities to your application so that it detects objects in images.

## Solution

Use the Azure Cognitive Services Vision API to detect objects in the desired images.

### Steps

1. Complete Recipe 10.1 to create a multi-service Cognitive Services resource. Store the service key in the $key1 variable.

2. Your goal is to detect objects in an image, so you need an image. You can use your own image or download (*https://oreil.ly/UGxFa*) the test image for this recipe, as shown in Figure 10-1.

*Figure 10-1. Detecting objects in an image*

The Computer Vision APIs accept images in JPEG, PNG, GIF, and BMP formats. The image size should be less than 4 MB. See the Vision API documentation (*https://oreil.ly/AD5tt*) for details.

3. Run the following command to upload your test image (as a form data) to the Vision Detect API. Note that *city.jpg* should exist in your working directory. Note that the `$region` variable holds the region of your Cognitive Services resource created in Recipe 10.1, for example `eastus`:

```
endpoint="https://"$region".api.cognitive.microsoft.com/"
imageDetectionEndpoint=$endpoint"/vision/v3.1/detect"
```

```
curl -X POST $imageDetectionEndpoint \
    -H "Ocp-Apim-Subscription-Key: $key1" \
    -F 'image=@city.jpg'
```

 In addition to uploading your own images, you can also analyze publicly available images by passing their URL to the Vision API. See the Vision API documentation (*https://oreil.ly/CzGGL*) for details.

4. Confirm that the preceding command returns the following response. As you can see, three buildings with their corresponding bounding box dimensions are returned. The `confidence` field (from 0.0 to 1.0) can be used to assess the accuracy of the detection:

```
{
    "objects": [
        {
            "rectangle": {
                "x": 139,
                "y": 42,
                "w": 179,
                "h": 509
            },
            "object": "tower",
            "confidence": 0.515,
            "parent": {
                "object": "building",
                "confidence": 0.849
            }
        },
        {
            "rectangle": {
                "x": 743,
```

```
            "y": 345,
            "w": 189,
            "h": 182
        },
        "object": "building",
        "confidence": 0.717
    },
    {
        "rectangle": {
            "x": 374,
            "y": 250,
            "w": 360,
            "h": 293
        },
        "object": "building",
        "confidence": 0.612
    }
],
"requestId": "4760d0f9-f507-4a70-9e9c-124df985d209",
"metadata": {
    "height": 658,
    "width": 935,
    "format": "Jpeg"
}
}
```

You successfully detected objects in a picture using Azure Cognitive Services Vision
API.

## Discussion

Azure Cognitive Services Computer Vision enables you to detect objects in an image.
You can pass the image to the API by providing its public URL (if applicable) or sim‐
ply uploading it as a binary object (as done in this recipe).

At the time of writing this book, the Computer Vision service provides the following
functionalities (*https://oreil.ly/wPUvC*):

*Image Analysis (https://oreil.ly/uMkGK)*
    Detects objects or describes images

*Face (https://oreil.ly/3lyeK)*
    Detects, recognizes, and analyzes human faces in images

*OCR (Optical Character Recognition) (https://oreil.ly/MN528)*
    Extracts printed or handwritten text from images

*Spatial Analysis (https://oreil.ly/UDVok)*
> Analyzes the presence and movement of humans on a video feed and produces events that other systems can respond to

Later in this chapter you will work with the Describe image and OCR APIs.

# 10.6 Creating Captions for Images

## Problem

You want to automatically create accurate captions for your images.

## Solution

Use the Azure Cognitive Services Computer Vision Describe Images API to create captions for your images.

### Steps

1. Complete Recipe 10.1 to create a multi-service Cognitive Services resource. Store the service key in the $key1 variable.

2. You can use your own image or download (*https://oreil.ly/9GnWi*) the test image for this recipe, as is shown in Figure 10-2.

*Figure 10-2. Describing an image*

3. The following command uploads your image to the Describe Image API. The *trees.jpg* file should exist in your working director:

```
endpoint="https://"$region".api.cognitive.microsoft.com/"
imageDescribeEndpoint=$endpoint"/vision/v3.1/describe"

curl -X POST $imageDescribeEndpoint \
    -H "Ocp-Apim-Subscription-Key: $key1" \
    -F 'image=@trees.jpg'
```

4. The preceding command returns the following response. As you can see, the caption "a sidewalk with trees and buildings" is returned:

```
{
    "description": {
        "tags": [
            "tree",
            "outdoor",
            "way",
            "stone",
            "old",
            "sidewalk",
            "surrounded"
        ],
        "captions": [
            {
                "text": "a sidewalk with trees and buildings",
                "confidence": 0.2869868874549866
            }
        ]
    },
    "requestId": "6404c4d2-3874-4cb3-bcfe-f4b73d7790c1",
    "metadata": {
        "height": 998,
        "width": 1331,
        "format": "Jpeg"
    }
}
```

You successfully created a caption for your image using Azure Cognitive Services Describe Image API.

## Discussion

The Describe Image API (*https://oreil.ly/a9j0H*) can be used to create captions for your image library. An array of keywords will also be returned, which can be used to tag your images. As you saw in this recipe, the following tags are returned for your test image:

```
"tree",
"outdoor",
"way",
"stone",
"old",
"sidewalk",
"surrounded"
```

# 10.7 Extracting Text from Images Using OCR

## Problem

You need to extract printed or handwritten text from images.

## Solution

Use the Azure Cognitive Services Computer Vision OCR API (Optical Character Recognition) (*https://oreil.ly/T2vfd*) to extract text from images.

### Steps

1. Complete Recipe 10.1 to create a multi-service Cognitive Services resource. Store the service key in the $key1 variable.

2. As with the other Computer Vision APIs, you can use your own image or download (*https://oreil.ly/IK2pb*) the test image, as shown in Figure 10-3. Save this image to your working directory.

*Figure 10-3. Extracting text from an image*

```
endpoint="https://"$region".api.cognitive.microsoft.com/"
imageOCREndpoint=$endpoint"/vision/v3.1/ocr?detectOrientation=true"

curl -X POST $imageOCREndpoint \
    -H "Ocp-Apim-Subscription-Key: $key1" \
    -F 'image=@Yosemite.jpg'
```

4. The preceding command should return the following JSON response. You can see the extracted words with their coordinates. These coordinates can be used to place the words into the right sentences. The picture quality greatly contributes to the accuracy of the OCR result:

```
{
"language": "en",
"textAngle": 0.0,
"orientation": "Up",
"regions": [
    {
        "boundingBox": "80,165,407,117",
        "lines": [
            {
                "boundingBox": "80,165,53,11",
                "words": [
                    {
                        "boundingBox": "80,165,53,11",
                        "text": "*UNITED."
                    }
                ]
            },
            {
                "boundingBox": "90,181,79,11",
                "words": [
                    {
                        "boundingBox": "90,181,79,11",
                        "text": "DEPARTMENT"
                    }
                ]
            },
            {
                "boundingBox": "86,196,152,13",
                "words": [
                    {
                        "boundingBox": "86,197,65,10",
                        "text": "NATIONAL."
                    },
                    {
                        "boundingBox": "153,198,31,9",
                        "text": "PARK"
```

```json
                },
                {
                    "boundingBox": "189,196,49,13",
                    "text": "SÉQVice"
                }
            ]
        },
        {
            "boundingBox": "88,235,399,47",
            "words": [
                {
                    "boundingBox": "88,235,399,47",
                    "text": "YOSEMITE"
                }
            ]
        }
    ]
},
{
    "boundingBox": "509,236,152,43",
    "lines": [
        {
            "boundingBox": "512,236,149,17",
            "words": [
                {
                    "boundingBox": "512,236,149,17",
                    "text": "NATIONAL"
                }
            ]
        },
        {
            "boundingBox": "509,262,74,17",
            "words": [
                {
                    "boundingBox": "509,262,74,17",
                    "text": "PARK"
                }
            ]
        }
    ]
}
]}
```

You successfully extracted text from your image using Azure Cognitive Services Computer Vision OCR API.

## Discussion

The OCR API (*https://oreil.ly/86thk*) can be used to extract printed and handwritten text from images or scanned documents.

Multiple languages are supported by the OCR API. New languages might be added to this list in the future. See the OCR documentation (*https://oreil.ly/zths6*) for the current list of the supported languages.

> You can also use the Form Recognizer service if you need to extract content from PDF, Office, HTML, and image documents. Check the Form Recognizer documentation (*https://oreil.ly/jw6Vt*) for details.

# 10.8 Detecting PII in Text

## Problem

You want to automatically detect personally identifiable information (PII) in your text content.

## Solution

Use Azure Cognitive Services Content Moderator API to find and flag PII in your text content.

### Steps

1. Complete Recipe 10.1 to create a multi-service Cognitive Services resource. Store the service key in the $key1 variable.

2. You can use the following command to pass your text content to the Content Moderator API. This content has several instances of PII that need to be detected. By passing PII=true, you instruct the API to find and flag any PII in the content:

```
endpoint="https://"$region".api.cognitive.microsoft.com/"
textModerationEndpoint=\
    $endpoint"contentmoderator/moderate/v1.0/ProcessText/Screen?PII=true"

curl -X POST $textModerationEndpoint \
    -H "Ocp-Apim-Subscription-Key: $key1" \
    -H "Content-Type: text/plain" \
    -d "My email address is reza@abcd.com, \
    phone: 9957789887, IP: 255.255.255.255, \
    1005 Gravenstein Highway North Sebastopol, CA 95472"
```

3. The preceding command will return the following response. As you can see, an IP address, email address, phone number, and mailing address are flagged as PII:

```
{
    "OriginalText": "My email is reza@abcd.com, phone: 9957789887,\
        IP: 255.255.255.255, 1005 Gravenstein Highway
        North Sebastopol, CA 95472",
    "NormalizedText": " email  reza@abcd.com, phone: 9957789887,\
        IP: 255.255.255.255, 1005 Gravenstein Highway
        North Sebastopol, CA 95472",
    "Misrepresentation": null,
    "PII": {
        "Email": [
            {
                "Detected": "reza@abcd.com",
                "SubType": "Regular",
                "Text": "reza@abcd.com",
                "Index": 12
            }
        ],
        "IPA": [
            {
                "SubType": "IPV4",
                "Text": "255.255.255.255",
                "Index": 50
            }
        ],
        "Phone": [
            {
                "CountryCode": "US",
                "Text": "9957789887",
                "Index": 34
            }
        ],
        "Address": [
            {
                "Text": "1005 Gravenstein Highway
                North Sebastopol, CA 95472",
                "Index": 67
            }
        ],
        "SSN": []
    },
    "Language": "eng",
    "Terms": null,
    "Status": {
        "Code": 3000,
        "Description": "OK",
        "Exception": null
    },
```

```
    "TrackingId": "33e82de8-aa5d-453e-bedf-46997abf37f9"
}
```

4. Run the following command to delete the resources you created in this recipe:

```
az group delete --name $rgName
```

You can use the returned information to flag content as a sensitive/classified data or even remove the PII from it as your business requirements indicate.

## Discussion

The Content Moderator (*https://oreil.ly/FFyLK*) service is categorized under the Azure Cognitive Services Decision family. Content moderation refers to the process of scanning content for inappropriate or forbidden text, images, or videos. At the time of writing this book, the following APIs are offered under the Content Moderator (*https://oreil.ly/vNymA*) service:

- Image Moderation API
- Text Moderation API (also supports detecting PII)
- Video Moderation API

You can use the responses from the moderator APIs to flag, block, or classify content as your business scenario or policy dictates.

 PII refers to any information that enables someone to identify an individual. Name, phone number, mailing address, email address, Social Security number, and IP address are considered PII. Data privacy policies enforce strict regulations for storing and handling PII.

---

## CHAPTER 11

# Management and Monitoring

So far in this book you have provisioned and configured several Azure services that enable you to implement business solutions in the Azure cloud. You created these services in your Azure subscription, which exists under your Azure account. In this chapter, we discuss the services and tools that enable you to manage and monitor the resources under your Azure account.

Almost all Azure resources (*https://oreil.ly/Z-Qkb*) support *tags*. Azure tags (*https://oreil.ly/4OciO*) are metadata elements that you can apply to Azure resources. For example, you can track which department should pay for the provisioned resources by adding *department=finance* or *department=IT* tags. Tagging also enables you to easily find resources belonging to the same project and generate reports for them. In this chapter, you will add tags to resources, manage the tags, and list the resources with the same tag values.

Managing costs is critical for the success of any project. Microsoft helps you estimating the cost of resources before provisioning them using the Azure pricing calculator (*https://oreil.ly/OUKi_*). This gives the cloud architects and infrastructure professionals the information they need to choose the best resources for their budgets. After the resources are provisioned, you can see the billing history and current cost reports using the Microsoft Cost Management and Billing suite of tools (*https://oreil.ly/-OdVv*) in the Azure portal. In this chapter, you will work with both the Azure pricing calculator and Microsoft Cost Management and Billing tools.

You should monitor your provisioned Azure resources to detect performance issues, find and resolve bugs, and detect/respond to security incidents. Azure Monitor (*https://oreil.ly/uO36F*) is a group of services for collecting, analyzing, and acting on telemetry/platform logs. Azure Monitor collects several platform log types from resources including:

- Activity logs (*https://oreil.ly/KB07i*)
- Metrics (*https://oreil.ly/cRX4c*)
- Resource logs (*https://oreil.ly/mML1G*)

You will conclude this chapter by configuring an Azure resource to send its platform logs to an Azure Log Analytics workspace. Then you will use KQL (*https://oreil.ly/UrzHs*) to query these logs.

## Workstation Configuration

You will need to prepare your workstation before starting on the recipes in this chapter. Follow "What You Will Need" on page xi to set up your machine to run Azure CLI commands. Clone the book's GitHub repository using the following command:

```
git clone https://github.com/zaalion/AzureCookbook.git
```

# 11.1 Managing Azure Resource Tags

## Problem

You want to assign metadata to your Azure resources so that you can identify and track resources relevant to your projects.

## Solution

Assign tags (*https://oreil.ly/feFsM*) to your Azure resources and use them to generate reports for relevant resources with the same tag value.

### Steps

1. Log in to your Azure Subscription in the Owner role and create a new resource group for this recipe. See "General Workstation Setup Instructions" on page xii for details.

2. Let's create a few test resources. Use the following commands to create a new Azure VNet and an Azure storage account:

```
vnetName="<vnet-name>"
az network vnet create \
    --location $region \
    --resource-group $rgName \
    --name $vnetName \
    --address-prefix 10.0.0.0/16 \
    --subnet-name Subnet01 \
    --subnet-prefix 10.0.0.0/26
```

```
storageName="<storage-account-name>"
az storage account create \
    --name $storageName \
    --resource-group $rgName \
    --location $region \
    --sku Standard_LRS
```

You can assign tags to resources at the time of provisioning. See the
Azure CLI documentation (*https://oreil.ly/QCV-A*) for details.

3. To tag your resources, you need to grab their resource IDs. Run the following
   commands to find the storage account and VNet IDs. Confirm that both IDs are
   valid:

```
storageId=$(az storage account show \
    --resource-group $rgName \
    --name $storageName \
    --query "id" \
    --output tsv)

vnetId=$(az network vnet show \
    --resource-group $rgName \
    --name $vnetName \
    --query "id" \
    --output tsv)

echo $storageId

echo $vnetId
```

4. Let's imagine that the preceding resources belong to a project called TravelPortal
   and the finance department is responsible for paying for this resource. The following command assigns two new tags to your Azure VNet:

```
az tag create \
    --resource-id $vnetId \
    --tags Department=Finance Project=TravelPortal
```

5. The following command assigns the same tags to the storage account:

```
az tag create \
    --resource-id $storageId \
    --tags Department=Finance Project=TravelPortal
```

If your tag names (or values) include spaces, enclose them in quotation marks; for example, `--tags "Project Name"=TravelPortal Department="Information technology"`. See the CLI documentation (*https://oreil.ly/K93R3*) for details.

6. You can create, see, and manage resource tags in the Azure portal or programmatically. The following command lists all the tags for a specific resource:

```
az tag list \
    --resource-id $vnetId
```

7. Confirm that the command returns an output similar to the following JSON:

```
{
  "id": ".../providers/Microsoft.Resources/tags/default",
  ...
  "properties": {
    "tags": {
      "Department": "Finance",
      "Project": "TravelPortal"
    }
  },
  "type": "Microsoft.Resources/tags"
  ...
}
```

8. So far you have tagged a few Azure resources related to the TravelPortal project. You can now list these resources based on their tag values. Run the following command and confirm that you can see the storage account and VNet names in the command output:

```
az resource list \
    --tag Project=TravelPortal \
    --query [].name
```

9. You can remove tags if you don't need them anymore. For example, this command removes the `Project` tag from the VNet:

```
az tag update --resource-id $vnetId \
    --operation Delete \
    --tags Project=TravelPortal
```

10. Confirm that the tag is removed by running the following command:

```
az tag list \
    --resource-id $vnetId
```

11. Run the following command to delete the resources you created in this recipe:

```
az group delete --name $rgName
```

You successfully added tags (also called *taxonomy tags*) to a few Azure resources, listed resources based on their tag value, and removed a tag from a resource.

## Discussion

Resource tags enable you to add metadata to your Azure resources. Later, you can use tags to list resources with the same tag name or value, generate cost reports per tag (*https://oreil.ly/_Gurj*), or define legal holds (*https://oreil.ly/FWraY*) for immutable blob data.

Although adding resource tags is not mandatory, it is a good practice and we strongly recommend it. Many organizations require tags as part of their regulatory and compliance standards. You can use Azure Policy (*https://oreil.ly/e7vrd*) to enforce adding tags to resources, resource groups, or subscriptions. Here are a few useful policies (*https://oreil.ly/8_KYy*) in relation to tags:

- Require a tag and its value on resource groups
- Require a tag and its value on resources
- Require a tag on resource groups
- Require a tag on resources

> Child resources do not inherit resource group tags by default. You can use the "Inherit a tag from the resource group" (*https://oreil.ly/uvgcq*) Azure policy to automatically add resource group tags to child resources.

At the time of writing this book, the following limits (*https://oreil.ly/iLaPi*) apply to resource tags:

- Up to 50 tags can be assigned to a resource, resource group, or subscription.
- Maximum tag name (key) length is 512 characters.
- Maximum tag value length is 256 characters.

# 11.2 Estimating Costs for Azure Resources

## Problem

You want to estimate the total cost of Azure resources before provisioning them.

## Solution

Use the Azure pricing calculator (*https://oreil.ly/QS3od*) to estimate the total hourly or monthly cost of desired Azure resources before creating them.

### Steps

1. Using a web browser, visit the pricing calculator portal (*https://oreil.ly/QS3od*).

2. You can optionally log in to the portal using a Microsoft account. This allows you to save or share your estimation session. To log in, click on the "Sign in" link on the top right corner, as shown in Figure 11-1.

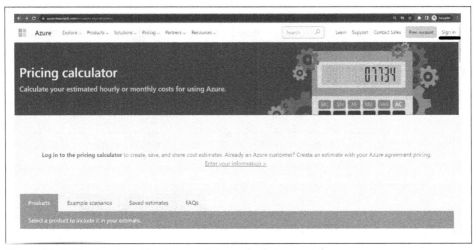

*Figure 11-1. Signing in to the Azure pricing calculator portal*

3. Let's estimate costs for a simple solution consisting of a single storage account and an Azure Key Vault. Type key vault in the Search Product field, and choose the Key Vault resource as shown in Figure 11-2.

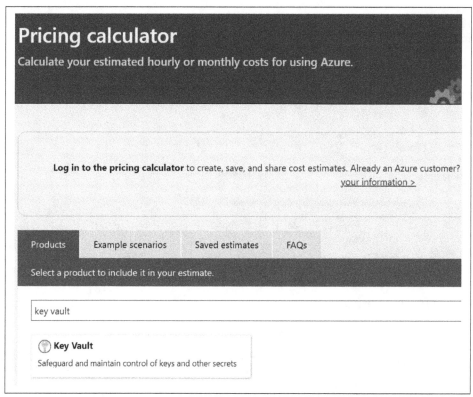

*Figure 11-2. Adding a Key Vault resource to the estimation session*

4. Scroll down until you see the Key Vault section. You can change your Key Vault properties as desired. For example, you can change the region or specify the number of Key Vault operations per month, as shown in Figure 11-3. These options will differ for each Azure resource type.

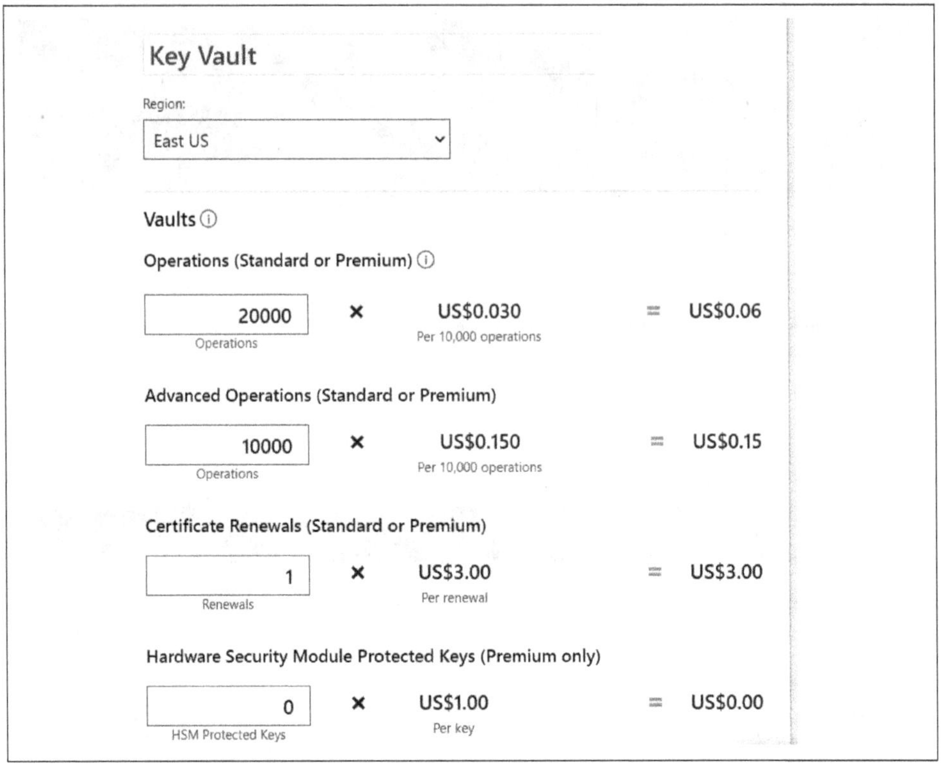

## Key Vault

Region:

East US

Vaults ⓘ

**Operations (Standard or Premium)** ⓘ

| 20000 | × | US$0.030 | = | US$0.06 |
| Operations | | Per 10,000 operations | | |

**Advanced Operations (Standard or Premium)**

| 10000 | × | US$0.150 | = | US$0.15 |
| Operations | | Per 10,000 operations | | |

**Certificate Renewals (Standard or Premium)**

| 1 | × | US$3.00 | = | US$3.00 |
| Renewals | | Per renewal | | |

**Hardware Security Module Protected Keys (Premium only)**

| 0 | × | US$1.00 | = | US$0.00 |
| HSM Protected Keys | | Per key | | |

*Figure 11-3. Updating the Key Vault properties to get accurate estimation*

5. Scroll up and add a new storage account, as shown in Figure 11-4.

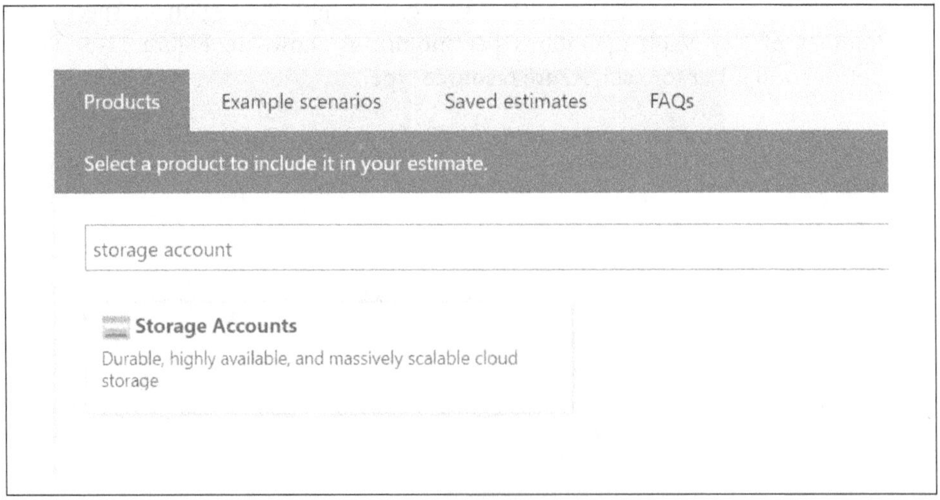

| Products | Example scenarios | Saved estimates | FAQs |

Select a product to include it in your estimate.

storage account

**Storage Accounts**
Durable, highly available, and massively scalable cloud storage

*Figure 11-4. Adding a storage account to the Estimation Session*

6. Confirm that the storage account is added, as shown in Figure 11-5.

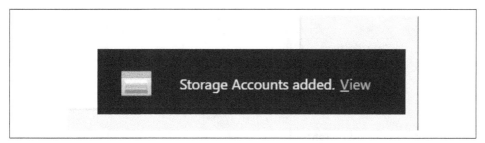

*Figure 11-5. Verifying the storage account is added*

7. Scroll down until you get to the Storage Accounts section. Update the properties such as region, tier, and redundancy, as shown in Figure 11-6.

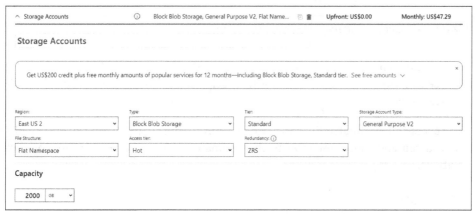

*Figure 11-6. Updating the desired storage account properties*

8. At the bottom of the page, look for Estimated monthly cost. Here you can see the monthly cost for your resources. The default currency is USD and can be changed from the CURRENCY dropdown, as shown in Figure 11-7.

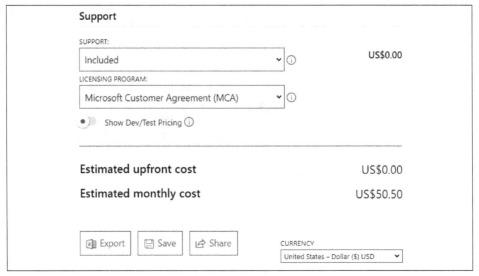

Figure 11-7. Getting the monthly cost estimation

9. You can export the estimation details to a CSV file and share it with the team if needed. The exported CSV file for this recipe can be found in this *https://oreil.ly/ xcSM-* repository].

You successfully estimated the cost for two Azure resources using the pricing calculator. You can add more resources to this estimation session to cover more complex solutions.

## Discussion

Azure pricing calculator (*https://oreil.ly/ADyE3*) is a great tool to help obtain accurate cost estimations for Azure projects before the actual resources are provisioned. This enables managers, cloud architects, and infrastructure professionals to choose the resources matching the company need and budget.

You can export the estimation to a CSV file, share the estimation session through a URL, and even save the session for later use.

 Azure pricing calculator should not be confused with the Total Cost of Ownership (TCO) Calculator (*https://oreil.ly/5JQMX*). You can use TCO to estimate the cost savings you can achieve by migrating your on-premises workloads to Azure. You enter your on-premises workload properties into TCO, and it returns the potential savings.

# 11.3 Monitoring Costs of Provisioned Azure Resources

## Problem

You need to monitor the cost of the provisioned Azure resources in your subscription.

## Solution

Use the Microsoft Cost Management and Billing suite of tools (*https://oreil.ly/bndZ-*) to monitor and analyze the cost of provisioned Azure resources.

### Steps

1. Log in to your Azure subscription in the Owner role and create a new resource group for this recipe. See "General Workstation Setup Instructions" on page xii for details.

2. Using a web browser, visit the Cost Management + Billing (*https://oreil.ly/ThyC1*) page in the Azure portal. You should land on the page shown in Figure 11-8.

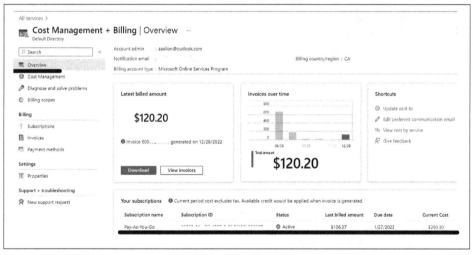

*Figure 11-8. Cost Management + Billing Overview page*

3. In this dashboard, you can see an overview of cost and billing reports for all your subscriptions, including the latest billed amount and a history of invoices over time. At the bottom of the page you will see a list of all your subscriptions. Click on the subscription name that you want to analyze the costs for. You should land

on the billing page for your subscription as shown in Figure 11-9. On this page you can see the billing and invoicing history for your subscription.

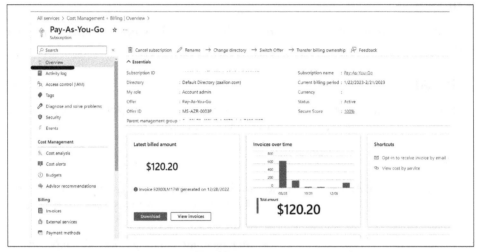

*Figure 11-9. Cost Management + Billing for a Pay-As-You-Go subscription*

4. From the left-hand menu, under Cost Management, click on "Cost analysis". You should land on the Cost analysis dashboard as shown in Figure 11-10. On this page you will see the current actual cost of subscription resources, as well as the forecasted cost for the rest of the month. You can also find how much an individual resource costs you. These reports can be saved or downloaded if needed.

*Figure 11-10. Cost Analysis dashboard for a subscription*

You successfully used the Microsoft Cost Management and Billing tools (*https://oreil.ly/ATvRw*) to analyze the cost for provisioned Azure resources.

## Discussion

You can use the Microsoft Cost Management suite of tools to monitor, analyze, and optimize the cost of your Azure workloads. Use the Billing tool to manage your invoices and payment methods, and make a payment. You can also set up automatic payments for your monthly subscription bills.

Use Cost Management and Billing to:

- Create reports and analyze costs in the Azure portal (*https://oreil.ly/vfmBK*).
- Monitor costs proactively by creating budget limits (*https://oreil.ly/EY3_C*).
- Create alert rules (*https://oreil.ly/pMXu2*) so that you get notified if your spending exceeds a percentage of your allowed budget.
- Split shared costs with cost allocation rules (*https://oreil.ly/WPyK4*).
- Configure payment options and pay invoices (*https://oreil.ly/gtwyC*) manually or automatically.

You have several options to save costs (*https://oreil.ly/RkO1P*) on your Azure resources, including using the free services (*https://oreil.ly/1k874*) for nonproduction, testing, and development workloads whenever possible.

# 11.4 Collecting Platform Logs for an Azure Resource

## Problem

You want to collect platform logs (including metrics, activity, audit, and resource logs) in a workspace for later analysis.

## Solution

Configure diagnostic settings (*https://oreil.ly/NJ6Wm*) for your Azure resources so that resource platform logs are sent to the desired destination (*https://oreil.ly/5xUe0*) as shown in Figure 11-11.

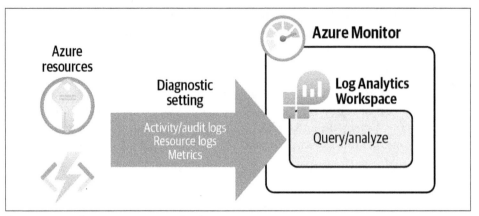

*Figure 11-11. Diagnostic settings for Azure resources*

### Steps

1. Log in to your Azure subscription in the Owner role and create a new resource group for this recipe. See "General Workstation Setup Instructions" on page xii for details.

2. In this recipe, you will configure diagnostic settings for an Azure Key Vault so that its platform logs are sent to an Azure Log Analytics workspace. First, use the following command to create a new Azure Key Vault and store the Key Vault resource ID in a variable:

```
kvName="<key-vault-name>"

az keyvault create \
  --name $kvName \
  --resource-group $rgName \
  --location $region \
  --enabled-for-disk-encryption

vaultID=$(az keyvault show \
    --resource-group $rgName \
    --name $kvName \
    --query "id" \
    --output tsv)
```

3. Platform logs can be sent to several destinations (*https://oreil.ly/pMr0Z*), including the Log Analytics workspace, Event Hubs, or even storage accounts. In this recipe, you will send your resource logs to an Azure Log Analytics workspace. Use the following command to provision a new Log Analytics workspace. Replace *<log-analytics-ws-name>* with the desired name:

```
workspaceName="<log-analytics-ws-name>"

az monitor log-analytics workspace create \
    --resource-group $rgName \
    --name $workspaceName \
    --retention-time 31

workspaceID=$(az monitor log-analytics workspace show \
    --resource-group $rgName \
    --workspace-name $workspaceName \
    --query "id" \
    --output tsv)
```

> You can configure the retention period (*https://oreil.ly/7Lcgt*) for the logs by passing the --retention-time parameter. For instance, the logs sent to this workspace will be automatically deleted after 31 days. You should set the retention time based on your business and regulatory needs.

4. Now the stage is set to configure diagnostic settings for your Key Vault resource. Let's send Key Vault audit and metrics logs to the new Log Analytics workspace:

```
az monitor diagnostic-settings create \
    --resource $vaultID  \
    --name myKeyVault-logs \
    --workspace $workspaceID \
    --logs '[{"category": "AuditEvent","enabled": true}]' \
    --metrics '[{"category": "AllMetrics","enabled": true}]'
```

> You can control which metrics and log categories to send using the --logs and --metrics parameters. The settings are in JSON format and can be passed inline (as we did here) or from an external JSON file. See the command documentation (*https://oreil.ly/KZzgu*) for details.

5. Now, let's create a new secret in your Key Vault using the following command to generate some logs:

```
az keyvault secret set \
   --name "MySecret" \
   --vault-name $kvName \
   --value "MySecretValue"
```

6. You can check and configure diagnostic settings in the Azure portal as well. Let's check the setting you created. Using a supported browser (*https://oreil.ly/iYt2y*), visit the Key vaults page in the Azure portal (*https://oreil.ly/mK3rC*) and select your Key Vault as shown in Figure 11-12.

*Figure 11-12. Selecting your Azure Key Vault*

7. Under Monitoring, click on "Diagnostic settings." You should see the myKeyVault-logs setting. Click on "Edit setting" as shown in Figure 11-13.

*Figure 11-13. Editing diagnostic settings in the Azure portal*

8. Confirm that the Audit Logs and AllMetrics options are checked and sent to your Log Analytics workspace, as shown in Figure 11-14.

9. Run the following command to delete the resources you created in this recipe:

```
az group delete --name $rgName
```

In this recipe, you successfully configured diagnostic settings for an Azure Key Vault. In the next recipe you will query your Log Analytics workspace to find the corresponding audit logs and metrics for your Key Vault.

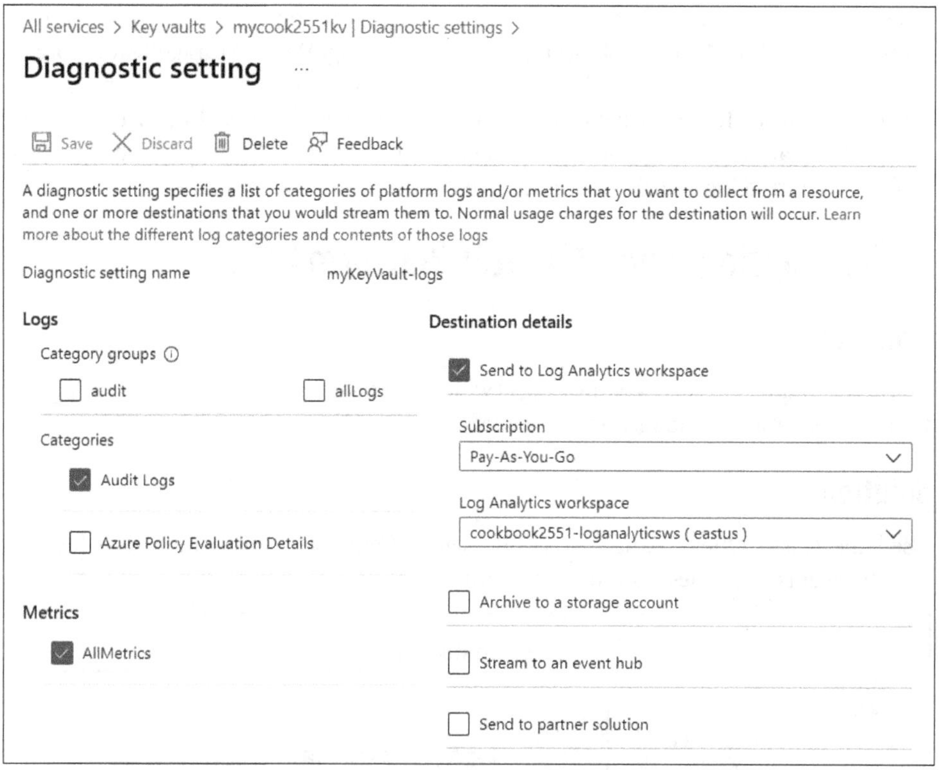

## Diagnostic setting ...

💾 Save    ✕ Discard    🗑 Delete    🗨 Feedback

A diagnostic setting specifies a list of categories of platform logs and/or metrics that you want to collect from a resource, and one or more destinations that you would stream them to. Normal usage charges for the destination will occur. Learn more about the different log categories and contents of those logs

Diagnostic setting name         myKeyVault-logs

**Logs**

  Category groups ⓘ

    ☐ audit             ☐ allLogs

  Categories

    ☑ Audit Logs

    ☐ Azure Policy Evaluation Details

**Metrics**

  ☑ AllMetrics

**Destination details**

  ☑ Send to Log Analytics workspace

  Subscription

  [ Pay-As-You-Go        ⌄ ]

  Log Analytics workspace

  [ cookbook2551-loganalyticsws ( eastus )    ⌄ ]

  ☐ Archive to a storage account

  ☐ Stream to an event hub

  ☐ Send to partner solution

*Figure 11-14. Checking diagnostic settings for Key Vault*

# Discussion

Diagnostic settings (*https://oreil.ly/PYXiW*) enable you to send Azure Monitor (*https://oreil.ly/r4Jfi*) resource metrics and logs to supported destinations for further analysis or storage. Set the following properties for your diagnostic setting:

- The setting name (for example, myKeyVault-logs).
- The log categories to include/send (for example, Audit logs).
- The metrics to include/send (for example, AllMetrics).
- Log destinations. The following destinations (*https://oreil.ly/iahni*) are supported:
  - Azure Log Analytics workspace, to query/analyze the logs using Kusto (KQL) (*https://oreil.ly/hoivs*)
  - Azure Storage, to store the logs for long periods or indefinitely
  - Azure Event Hubs (*https://oreil.ly/nWw7k*)
  - Third-party solutions

Each Azure resource type supports a relevant set of log and metrics categories. For example, while Azure Blob Storage supports StorageWrite, StorageRead, StorageDelete, and Transactions, the Azure Key Vault offers AuditEvent. You can see supported categories for each resource when creating diagnostic settings in the Azure portal. You can also check the Azure Monitor documentation (*https://oreil.ly/Ghjfx*) to find supported log categories for your resource.

# 11.5 Analyzing Azure Monitor Platform Logs

## Problem

You want to query Azure Monitor logs (which were sent to Log Analytics workspace) to find logs for a specific resource or event.

## Solution

Used the Kusto Query Language (KQL) (*https://oreil.ly/H_EEB*) to search logs for specific events or entries, as shown in Figure 11-15.

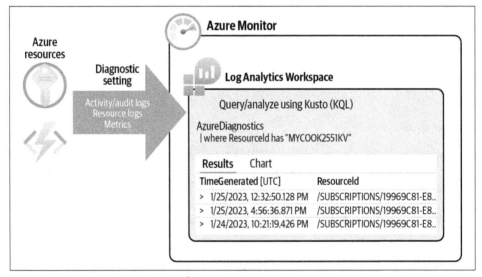

*Figure 11-15. Diagnostic settings for Azure resources*

## Steps

1. Log in to your Azure subscription in the Owner role and create a new resource group for this recipe. See "General Workstation Setup Instructions" on page xii for details.

2. Complete Recipe 11.4 to configure diagnostic settings for an Azure Key Vault.

3. Depending on which logs are sent to your Log Analytics workspace, you need to query a different table. Run the following command to get a list of available tables in your Log Analytics workspace. Replace *<log-analytics-ws-name>* with the name of your workspace created in Recipe 11.4:

```
workspaceName="<log-analytics-ws-name>"

az monitor log-analytics workspace table list \
    --resource-group $rgName \
    --workspace-name $workspaceName \
    --query "[].name"
```

For a complete list of Azure Monitor Log tables, visit the Azure Monitor Logs table reference page (*https://oreil.ly/BgSiq*). The output for the preceding command can be found in the chapter repository (*https://oreil.ly/FuLBt*).

4. First, obtain the GUID identifier of your Log Analytics workspace:

```
wsGUID=$(az monitor log-analytics workspace show \
    --resource-group $rgName \
    --name $workspaceName \
    --query customerId \
    --output tsv)
```

5. In Recipe 11.4, you configured Azure Key Vault diagnostic settings so that resource metrics and audit logs are sent to a Log Analytics workspace. Use the following command to query all available metrics for your Key Vault. Replace *<key-vault-resource-name>* with your Key Vault name:

```
kvName="<key-vault-resource-name>"

az monitor log-analytics query \
    --workspace $wsGUID \
    --analytics-query \
    "AzureMetrics | where ResourceId has \"$kvName\""
```

If you're prompted to install the Log Analytics extension, answer Y. You must have an internet connection to install this extension.

6. The following is a sample record from the preceding command output. As you can see, the metric name, ServiceApiLatency, and its value are returned:

```
{
    "Average": "15",
    "Count": "2",
    "DurationMs": "None",
    "Maximum": "16",
    "MetricName": "ServiceApiLatency",
    "Minimum": "14",
    "RemoteIPLatitude": "None",
    "RemoteIPLongitude": "None",
    "Resource": "MYCOOK2551KV",
    "ResourceGroup": "CH11",
    "ResourceId": ".../MYCOOK2551KV",
    "ResourceProvider": "MICROSOFT.KEYVAULT",
    "Severity": "None",
    "SourceSystem": "Azure",
    "TableName": "PrimaryResult",
    "TenantId": "00000000-0000-0000-0000-000000000000",
    "TimeGenerated": "2023-01-25T16:14:00Z",
    "TimeGrain": "PT1M",
    "Total": "30",
    "Type": "AzureMetrics",
    "UnitName": "Milliseconds",
    "_ResourceId": ".../microsoft.keyvault/vaults/mycook2551kv"
}
```

If the preceding command does not return any results, confirm that the diagnostic settings are properly configured.

7. Now, let's query audit logs for your Key Vault. To do this, you have to query a different table, called AzureDiagnostics, as you see in the following command:

```
--workspace $wsGUID \
--analytics-query \
"AzureDiagnostics | where ResourceId has \"$kvName\""
```

8. The following is a sample audit entry returned by the preceding command. The OperationName is VaultGet and the identity live.com#zaalion@outlook.com performed this operation. The CallerIPAddress is also logged:

```
{
    "CallerIPAddress": "<xx.xx.xx.xx>",
    "Category": "AuditEvent",
    "DurationMs": "16",
    "OperationName": "VaultGet",
    "OperationVersion": "2021-10-01",
    "Resource": "MYCOOK2551KV",
    "ResourceGroup": "CH11",
```

```
    "ResourceId": ".../VAULTS/MYCOOK2551KV",
    "ResourceProvider": "MICROSOFT.KEYVAULT",
    "ResourceType": "VAULTS",
    "ResultSignature": "OK",
    "ResultType": "Success",
    "SubscriptionId": "00000000-0000-0000-0000-000000000000",
    "TableName": "PrimaryResult",
    "TenantId": "d61fb72d-c32d-4ea9-b242-9b0a3c99a153",
    "TimeGenerated": "2023-01-25T12:32:50.1285329Z",
    "Type": "AzureDiagnostics",
    "_ResourceId": ".../vaults/mycook2551kv",
    "clientPort_d": "None",
    "httpStatusCode_d": "200",
    "id_s": "https://mycook2551kv.vault.azure.net/",
    "identity_claim_appid_g": "00000000-0000-0000-0000-000000000000",
    "identity_claim": "live.com#zaalion@outlook.com",
    "properties_enableSoftDelete_b": "True",
    "properties_enabledForDeployment_b": "False",
    "properties_enabledForDiskEncryption_b": "True",
    "properties_enabledForTemplateDeployment_b": "None",
    "properties_sku_Family_s": "A",
    "properties_sku_Name_s": "standard",
    "properties_softDeleteRetentionInDays_d": "90"
}
```

 If the command does not return any results, confirm that the diagnostic settings are properly configured and that the Key Vault is used after diagnostic settings were configured (e.g., adding a secret, getting a secret, etc.).

9. You can also query resource logs in the Azure portal. To see Key Vault logs, visit the Key vaults page in the Azure portal (*https://oreil.ly/ra1AN*) and select your Key Vault, as shown in Figure 11-16.

*Figure 11-16. Selecting your Azure Key Vault*

10. Under Monitoring, select Logs, and then close the Queries window, as shown in Figure 11-17.

*Figure 11-17. Selecting your Azure Key Vault logs*

11. Enter your KQL query and click Run, as shown in Figure 11-18.

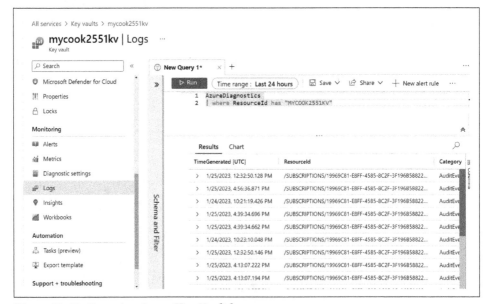

*Figure 11-18. Querying Azure Key Vault logs*

12. Run the following command to delete the resources you created in this recipe:

```
az group delete --name $rgName
```

In this recipe, you successfully queried your Log Analytics workspace to find metrics and audit logs for your Azure Key Vault.

## Discussion

You can use KQL to query and analyze resource platform logs sent to a Log Analytics workspace. Azure Monitor logs are saved into different Log Analytics tables depending on their categories (*https://oreil.ly/DeHFk*); therefore, you need to find the correct table in your query. Check Azure Monitor logs table reference (*https://oreil.ly/jxhBI*) for a complete list of tables and their corresponding categories.

In this recipe, you queried the following tables:

*AzureMetrics (https://oreil.ly/a6qyh)*
This table stores resource metric data that measures the health and performance of resources.

*AzureDiagnostics (https://oreil.ly/4hNFz)*
This table stores logs for Azure services that use Azure Diagnostics mode (*https://oreil.ly/JLp_U*). These logs give insights into the internal operation of Azure resources. In this recipe, you queried this table because Azure Key Vault used the Azure Diagnostics mode for logging.

Not all Azure resources use the Azure Diagnostics mode for logging. Some use the resource-specific logging mode (*https://oreil.ly/3oTLh*) instead. These services store their logs in their own specific tables and do not use the AzureDiagnostics table. At the time of writing this book, the following resources use the resource-specific logging mode:

- API Management services (*https://oreil.ly/Bgu3k*)
- Azure Cosmos DB (*https://oreil.ly/1ntd0*)
- Azure Data Factory v2 (*https://oreil.ly/nHMj1*)
- Azure IoT Hub (*https://oreil.ly/lI-1g*)
- Recovery Services vaults (*https://oreil.ly/XC1YO*)

Check the Azure Monitor logs table reference (*https://oreil.ly/B2KbQ*) and supported categories for Azure Monitor resource logs (*https://oreil.ly/phtlR*) to find the corresponding Log Analytics table names for these resources.

# Index

and Azure VM, 12
  managing subnets based on, 32-33, 40-42,
    213-215, 230-235
  network peering, 43-45
Azure, account setup instructions, xi-xii

# B

backing up Azure SQL single databases,
    113-115
batch data (historical data), 139
big data, 139-181
  cost saving on idle Azure Synapse serverless
    pools, 155-158
  ETL/ELT operations using ADF, 172-181
  live data stream processing, 140-147
  processing datafiles, 158-171
  querying CSV file content, 147-155
BitLocker (Windows VM), 17
blob container, static website hosting in, 237
blob files and objects, 49
  (see also Azure Storage)
  access tiers for blob objects, 70
  Azure VM disks as blob objects, 18
  creating and accessing new file versions,
    65-67
  snapshots, 62-65
blob-triggered function for blob upload,
    195-200
blocking anonymous access to blobs, 19-20
BreakSentence API, Translator Service, 271
built-in user roles, 7

# C

CanNotDelete lock, 79
captioning of images, 277-278
Cassandra API, 85
CDN (content delivery network), 238
cells, Azure Databricks notebook, 166-169
certificates, storing and retrieving, 23-25
CI/CD (continuous delivery/continuous inte-
    gration), 251
CIDR range, 31
clusters for processing datafiles, 171
CMK (customer-managed keys), 50, 53
collections (see containers)
Computer Vision service, 274-277
confidenceScores property, sentiment score,
    273

connection monitor, Azure Network Watcher,
    46-48
connectivity verification, Azure VNet, 46-48
container groups, 248
container image, 239, 240-248, 250
container registry service, 239
containers, 84, 239-258
  Azure App Service, 248-251
  Azure Container Apps, 251-254
  Docker image in Azure Container Instan-
    ces, 246-248
  enabling soft delete for, 78
  limiting ACR public network access,
    254-258
content delivery network (CDN), 238
Content Moderator API, 282-284
continuous delivery/continuous integration
    (CI/CD), 251
continuous software deployment, 226
Contributor user role, 2, 5
cool access tier for blob objects, 70
copying blobs or files to or from storage, 71-75
cost estimation and monitoring for resources,
    289-297
CRON expression, 193
CSV file content, querying with Azure Synapse
    Analytics, 147-155
cURL command line tool, 121, 263
custom Azure role, creating, 5-7
customer-managed keys (CMK), 50, 53

# D

data pipeline, in ADF, 173-181
data plane, RBAC access to, 97
data redundancy, 49
  (see also Azure Storage)
data residency laws, 11
data store (see Azure Storage)
data streams, Azure Stream Analytics, 140-147
databases, 81
  (see also Azure Cosmos DB; Azure SQL)
DataFrame, Spark, 158, 171
datasink container, 172, 175-178
datasource container, 172, 173-175
dead-letter queue, 128, 130
decision group, Azure Cognitive Services, 262,
    284
dedicated SQL pool, Azure Synapse, 154-156,
    158

delete lock, storage account, 78

deletion, protecting blobs from accidental, 76-78

deny rules, network access, 214, 232

deploying web apps to Azure App Service
with FTP, 221-223
from GitHub repository, 224-226
with ZipDeploy, 218-221

Describe Image API, 277-278

Detect API, Translator Service, 271

diagnostic settings for resource metrics and logs, 301

Dictionary/examples API, Translator Service, 271

Dictionary/lookup API, Translator Service, 271

dm-crypt (Linux VM), 17

DNAT rules, Azure Firewall, 40

Docker container, 240-248

Docker Hub, 239

## E

elastic pool, Azure SQL Database, 103-106

encryption
Azure Key Vault keys, 23-25
Azure Storage data, 50-53
VM disks, 17-19

ETL/ELT operations, processing on big data with ADF, 172-181

event handlers, Azure Event Grid, 136

event sources, Azure Event Grid, 136

events (see messaging and events)

## F

face recognition, Computer Vision service, 276

file shares, AzCopy to upload to Azure Storage, 73-75

firewall
Azure Cosmos DB, 88-91
Azure SQL IP rules, 108-111
Azure SQL VNet rules, 111-112
Azure Synapse Analytics, 155
WAF with Azure Application Gateway, 25-28
with ACR, 257

fixed throughput, assigning to database, 84

forward slash (/) issue, storage account key, 115

FTP, deploying web apps to Azure App Service, 221-223

## G

General Data Protection Regulation (GDPR), 11

geo-redundant storage (GRS), 115

geo-zone-redundant storage (GZRS), 115

geospatial applications and products, 88

GitHub repository, deploying web apps to Azure App Service, 224-226

global distribution, Azure Cosmos DB, 85

graph databases, 86-88

Gremlin (Graph) API, 85, 86-88

## H

hosting static websites in Azure Storage, 235-238

hot access tier for blob objects, 70

## I

IaaS (infrastructure as a service), 81

id property, sentiment score, 273

images
captioning of, 277-278
container image, 240-248
extracting text from, 279-282
formats accepted by Vision API, 275
object detection in, 274-277

infrastructure as a service (IaaS), 81

inheriting tags from resource group, setting up, 289

Internet of Things (IoT), 87, 122-125, 146

IP addresses, managing subnets, 33, 213-215, 232-235

IP filter rules, 89, 108-111

isolated private network, Azure VNet, 30-31

## J

JSON documents, storing in Azure Cosmos DB, 82-85

jump server/box/host, 16

## K

Kubernetes cluster, Azure Container Apps, 254

Kudu ZipDeploy, 218-221

Kusto Query Language (KQL), 302-307

## L

language group, Azure Cognitive Services, 262

serverless compute tier for Azure SQL single databases, 106-108
storing tabular data in Azure storage tables, 98-100
VNet rules configuration, 111-112
personally identifiable information (PII), detecting in text, 282-284
platform as a service (PaaS), 81
policy assignment, defining, 8
pool servers, Azure Synapse, 150, 154, 155-158
Postman, 263
pricing calculator, 285, 289-294
principle of least privilege, 5, 58
private access endpoints, 56, 91-93, 155
private VM, Azure Bastion, 11-17
provisioned throughput, assigning to database, 84
provisioned versus compute tier, Azure SQL single database, 108
publish-subscribe pattern, Azure Service Bus topics, 131-133
purge protection in Key Vault, 53

## Q

querying CSV file content, Azure Synapse Analytics, 147-155

## R

RBAC (role-based access control), 2, 3-7
    Azure Function Apps to Azure Storage access, 59-62
    Azure Function Apps to Cosmos DB access, 95-98
    Azure Service Bus access, 207
    security advantage of, 250
ReadOnly lock, 80
recommendation engines, 88
rehydration of archived blobs, 70
resources
    allowed location assignments, 10-11
    assigning types in subscription, 7-10
    collecting platform logs for, 297-302
    cost estimation for, 289-294
    cost monitoring of provisioned, 295-297
    provisioning in Azure Cognitive Services, 263-266
    tag management, 285, 286-289
    tools to get started with Azure, xi
retention period, platform logs, 299

role-based access control (see RBAC)
route tables, 34-39
RowKey property, storage table, 99

## S

SAS (shared access signature) tokens, 22, 56-59
scale in rule for autoscaling App Service plan, 228
scale out option, App Service plan, 229
scale up option, App Service plan, 229
scheduling with timer trigger to invoke Azure function, 190-195
scope of user role, defining, 6
secrets, storing and retrieving in Azure Key Vault, 23-25
security, 1-28
    allowed locations, assigning for resources, 10-11
    authentication (see authentication)
    authorization bearer method, 268
    Azure AD authorization configuration, 21-22
    Azure Function Apps access to Cosmos DB, 94-98
    Azure Key Vault, 18, 23-25, 50-53
    blocking anonymous access to blobs, 20
    and connectivity, 29
    custom role for user, 5-7
    firewall (see firewall)
    network security groups, 40-42
    private VM, with Azure Bastion, 11-17
    resource types, assigning in subscription, 7-10
    user in Azure account, 2-5
    virtual network integration, 31
    VM disk encryption, 17-19
    WAF with Azure Application Gateway, 25-28
Sentiment API, 271
sentiment property, sentiment score, 273
Server Message Block (SMB) protocol, 50
serverless compute tier, 106-108
serverless services, 183-215
    Azure Cognitive Services, 266
    Azure Container Apps, 254
    Azure Cosmos DB, 103, 201-206
    Azure Function Apps, implementing web APIs, 184-190

Azure Function Apps, restricting network access, 213-215
Azure Service Bus Queue trigger for Azure function, 206-212
Azure Synapse pools, 147-158
blob trigger to invoke Azure function, 195-200
invoking function on schedule with timer trigger, 190-195
service level agreements (SLAs), 100, 102
shared access signature (SAS) tokens, 22, 56-59
single database type, Azure SQL, 103-108, 113-115
single-service resources, Azure Cognitive Services APIs, 266
SMB (Server Message Block) protocol, 50
snapshots of blob objects, 62-65
social networks, graph databases for, 87
soft-delete option in Azure Key Vault, 53, 76
Spark, 155-158, 171
spatial analysis, Computer Vision service, 276
speech group, Azure Cognitive Services, 262
Speech Synthesis Markup Language (SSML), 267
SQL (see Azure SQL Database)
SQL (Core) API, 85
SQL pools, Azure Synapse, 154
SQL queries of CSV file content, 147-155
SSH keys for Linux VMs, 13
SSML (Speech Synthesis Markup Language), 267
storage (see Azure Storage)
storage account keys, 22, 57, 59
streaming data, 139
subnets, managing with Azure VNet, 32-33, 40-42, 213-215, 230-235

## T

Table API, 85, 100
tabular data, storing in Azure Storage tables, 98-100
tag metadata, Azure management, 285
tagging container image, 245
tags, metadata, Azure management, 286-289
taxonomy tags, 289
TCO (Total Cost of Ownership) Calculator, 294
text
    detecting PII in, 282-284
    extracting from image with OCR, 279-282

sentiment analysis on, 271-274
text-to-speech conversion, 266-268
translating, 268-271
threat intelligence-based filtering, 40, 261
timer trigger to invoke Azure function, 190-195
Total Cost of Ownership (TCO) Calculator, 294
training datasets, 261
Translate API, Translator Service, 271
translating text, 268-271
Translator API, Azure Cognitive Services, 268-271
Transliterate API, Translator Service, 271
trigger types, Azure Function App, 190
    Azure Service Bus queue, 206-212
    blob-triggered function for blob upload, 195-200
    timer trigger to invoke Azure function, 190-195
trusted services and sources, exempting for ACR firewall, 257

## U

user-assigned identities, Azure Function App, 60-61
user-defined routes, routing network traffic, 34-36
users, creating and setting roles/permissions, 2-7

## V

versioning, blob, 65-67
virtual appliance, 36
virtual network peering, 43-45
Vision API, 274-277
vision group, Azure Cognitive Services, 262
VM disks, 17-19, 49

## W

web application firewall (WAF), 25-28
websites, Azure Storage hosting for static, 235-238
Windows, 240

## Z

ZipDeploy, 218-221
zone redundancy, Azure Cosmos DB, 85
zone redundant storage (ZRS), 115

## About the Author

**Reza Salehi** has great passion for science and technology. He's been active in the professional technology field for the past 25 years and has helped organizations move to the cloud as a Software Developer, Cloud Architect, and Site Availability Engineer. He has trained thousands of students in person, and online in the O'Reilly Online Learning platform, as well as through other major players in the IT training industry. He has been a member of the Microsoft Certified Trainer (MCT) community since 2008.

## Colophon

The animal on the cover of *Azure Cookbook* is a blue grosbeak (*Passerina caerulea*), a medium-size bird native to North America. The birds have a range from the southern United States to northern Mexico and migrate to Central America in winter.

Grosbeaks get their name from their large, thick beaks. The male birds are blue, with two brown bars on the wings. The female is mostly brown with some blue feathers, and she also has two brown bars on the wings.

The blue grosbeak usually nests low in small trees or shrubs. The female builds the nest from twigs, bark, and found objects. She will lay a clutch of 3 to 5 pale blue eggs and incubate them for 12 to 13 days. Grosbeaks are thought to be monogamous, and each pair will raise up to two broods per breeding season. The young leave the nest about 10 days after hatching.

The IUCN conservation status of the blue grosbeak is Least Concern. Many of the animals on O'Reilly covers are endangered; all of them are important to the world.

The cover illustration is by Karen Montgomery, based on an antique line engraving from *Shaw's Zoology*. The cover fonts are Gilroy Semibold and Guardian Sans. The text font is Adobe Minion Pro; the heading font is Adobe Myriad Condensed; and the code font is Dalton Maag's Ubuntu Mono.

Printed in the USA
CPSIA information can be obtained
at www.ICGtesting.com
JSHW051057270424
61991JS00005B/74

9 781098 135799